Literary Culture in Early New England.

LITERARY CULTURE

IN

EARLY NEW ENGLAND

1620-1730

By Thomas Goddard Wright,
Late Instructor in English in Yale University.

EDITED BY HIS WIFE

NEW HAVEN:
YALE UNIVERSITY PRESS.
London: Humphrey Milford: Oxford University Press.
MDCCCCXX.

Contents.

6 Contents.

PART III

THE NEW CENTURY

APPENDIX

Memorial Note.

THOMAS GODDARD WRIGHT, the author of this book, was born at Fort Ann, New York, the seventeenth of August, 1885. He was the son of the Reverend William Russell Wright and Alma (Boardman) Wright. He was graduated from the Hartford Public High School in 1903, and then entered Yale University, where he received the degree of B.A. in 1907, M.A. in 1908, and Doctor of Philosophy in 1917. On the seventh of June, 1913, he was married to Mabel Hyde Kingsbury, daughter of Dr. and Mrs. Edward N. Kingsbury, of Woonsocket, Rhode Island. From the year 1908 he had served first as Assistant, and later as Instructor in English in the Sheffield Scientific School of Yale University.

This book is in his favourite field of study, and is in part representative of his special research therein covering a period of five or six years. While primarily intended for the use of scholars in history and literature, it is by no means without interest for the general reader.

In the death of Dr. Wright, Yale University suffers a severe loss from the ranks of its scholars and teachers. He was intensely beloved both by his colleagues and by his pupils. His character and personality had an extraordinary charm; he was modest, generous, unselfish, faithful and pure in heart. I never knew a man more free from the meaner vices of self-interest and self-importance. The advancement of his rivals pleased him more than his own achievements. No one could know him without feeling a sense of elevation. His high-minded and unassuming devotion to his work was an example to us all, and his influence will be permanently fruitful.

WILLIAM LYON PHELPS.

Yale University, Tuesday, 3 June, 1919.

Preface.

THE subject of the study which follows was suggested to me by Professor Henry A. Beers, to whom I owe more than I can express for his wise guidance and sympathetic encouragement throughout the preparation of this work. I wish to acknowledge also the assistance of Professor William Lyon Phelps, under whose supervision the work was carried on after the retirement of Professor Beers from active teaching.

I owe much to Professor Keogh and Messrs. Gruener and Ginter of the Yale University Library, and Mr. Sanborn, formerly of the Library, all of whom I have found invariably responsive to any demands which I have made upon them for help in finding material for this work. I wish to acknowledge also the kindness of Mr. Julius H. Tuttle of the Massachusetts Historical Society, Mr. Clarence S. Brigham of the American Antiquarian Society, and Messrs. William C. Lane and Walter B. Briggs of the Harvard University Library, who assisted me in my search for material. To Mr. Albert Matthews of the Colonial Society of Massachusetts and Professor Charles M. Andrews of Yale, who kindly read my manuscript, I am indebted for many valuable suggestions.

Finally to those who, in connection with the various historical and antiquarian societies of New England, have gathered and made accessible a wealth of valuable material I owe an inestimable debt; without the fruits of their labor my task would have been an impossible one.

T. G. W.

Introduction.

MOST students of our colonial literature devote themselves primarily to the appraisal of its value as literature. The pages which follow will not attempt to weigh colonial literature, either to condemn or defend it (although at times they may endeavor to correct impressions which, to the writer, seem erroneous), but rather will attempt to determine that which lies back of any literature, the culture of the people themselves, and to study the relation between their culture and the literature which they produced. In the attempt to determine the culture of the people of New England the writer has made a study of their education, their libraries, their ability to obtain books, their use and appreciation of books, their relations with political and literary life in England, and their literature. In the course of the study certain generally accepted notions of the low estate of colonial culture will be shown to be incorrect or exaggerated. There were in New England as in Old England many people who were without culture and even illiterate; but the general state of culture in the colonies will be shown to be higher than it has usually been rated.

This study has been limited approximately to the first one hundred years of colonial life, and to the New England colonies with Boston as their center. These colonies form a distinct unit, akin to each other, and differing from any other colony, or group of colonies, in both antecedents and interests. That much more is said of those who settled on Massachusetts Bay than of those elsewhere in New England is due partly to the greater comprehensiveness and accessibility of the extant records of that region, and partly to the fact that Boston was the literary and cultural center as well as the chief city of these colonies. It must have a predominant place in this discussion, just as London would in a similar study of the literary culture of England.

It is not easy to divide the first century of colonial life into cultural periods which have definite limits. To attempt to discuss conditions according to generations, first, second, third, is impossible, because of the range of age of the first settlers, and their varying longevity. Brewster, Hooker, and Winthrop all died in the forties; John Norton and John Wilson lived into the sixties, the latter almost outliving the Reverend John Eliot, Jr., who had been born in New England. For convenience the one hundred years will be discussed as if divided into three periods, the first of fifty years, the second of thirty, and the last of twenty. The first, ending about 1670, covers the years during which those who came to America as settlers, men born and educated in England, were in control of the affairs of the colony, and determined its culture. By 1670 practically all of these men had died, and government, education, and culture were in the hands of men reared and trained in the New World. The second period ends with the seventeenth century, partly because the century mark makes a convenient terminal, and partly because there are certain differences in the life of the colonists before and after the opening of the century. The third period covers the rest of the one hundred years. It must be remembered, however, that the limits of the periods are approximate, *not* exact; the last period, for example, instead of stopping absolutely at 1720, includes a discussion of certain events in the half-dozen years immediately following that date.

The writer recognizes that his study is incomplete. It never can be complete because too many of the records have perished. Certain records which are preserved but which have been inaccessible might throw more light upon the subject; but presumably these would merely add detail and in no way affect the main conclusions.

Part I:
The Early Settlers.
1620-1670.

Chapter I: Education.

WITH the exception of the group which settled Plymouth, the founders of New England included in their ranks a remarkably high proportion of university men. The settlers of Plymouth, mostly village and country folk of no particular education,[1] lost rather than gained educationally during the years of their hardships in Holland (which was one reason for their desire to leave), so that when the *Mayflower* crossed the seas it carried but one man of university training, and even he did not have a degree. William Brewster had entered St. Peter's, or Peterhouse, Cambridge, December 3, 1580,[2] and had there spent a year or two before leaving for active life as a private secretary or confidential servant to William Davison, later Secretary of State, and then busy helping to carry out Queen Elizabeth's designs in Scotland and Holland. Until Ralph Smith, the first settled minister of Plymouth, arrived in 1629, Brewster was the only university man in the colony.[3] In the thirty years that followed less than a score of university men came to the colony, and of these only three remained and followed their calling. "Able men, like Norton, Chauncy, Hooke, and Williams, tarried but a short time and went to wider fields."[4] "Prior to 1650 Harvard College neither received from Plymouth nor contributed to that place more than one or two persons."[5] The other settlements presented a striking contrast to Plymouth. Even before Winthrop

[1] "In the main they were plain farmers." H. M. Dexter, The England and Holland of the Pilgrims, p. 379.

[2] *Ibid.*, p. 256.

[3] F. B. Dexter, Massachusetts Historical Society, Proceedings, 1st Series, xvii. 344.

[4] William Bradford, History of Plymouth Plantation, i. 134 note.

[5] *Ibid.*, i. 134 note.

came in 1630, university men had settled on the shores of Massachusetts Bay,[6] and with Winthrop, or following him in the next ten or fifteen years, were Oxford and Cambridge men to the number of nearly one hundred[7] out of a total population of not more than 25,000.[8] Of these at least fifty were the possessors of advanced degrees, and half a dozen had been appointed Fellows. Nearly every college of each university was represented here, and among the colonists were men who had been in Cambridge when Milton was studying there, although no one who was in Christ's College with him. Thomas Shepard, John Norton, Abraham Pierson, John Harvard, Henry Dunster, and Roger Williams may be mentioned among the contemporaries of Milton and Jeremy Taylor, and of these Williams was, at a later period at least, a personal friend of Milton's.[9] The friendship may well have dated back to college days.

Such an unusual proportion of university men gave to the young colony a cultural tone unique in the history of colonization. And if it must be acknowledged that a dozen of the men included in the figures given above left the universities without qualifying for degrees, among them John Winthrop, Harry Vane, Richard Saltonstall, and Giles Firmin, the list may be supplemented by such names as Nathaniel Eaton, who studied at Franeker, Hol-

[6] William Blackstone settled in Boston Bay in 1623 and on the site of Boston in 1625. The Rev. William Morell, author of the Latin and English poem on New England (Nova Anglia), with whom Blackstone may have come to these shores, had lived at Weymouth a year and a half (1623 to 1625), then returning to England. In 1629 Francis Higginson, Samuel Skelton, Francis Bright, and Ralph Smith were among the settlers of Salem. Bright soon returned to England; Smith went to Plymouth the same year.

[7] F. B. Dexter, Massachusetts Historical Society, Proceedings, 1st Series, xvii. 340.

[8] Dexter, ibid., p. 344, and Estimates of Population in the American Colonies.

[9] Williams wrote to John Winthrop, Jr., July 12, 1654, "It pleased the Lord to call me for some time and with some persons to practice the Hebrew, the Greeke, Latine, French and Dutch: The Secretarie of the Councell, (Mr Milton) for my Dutch I read him, read me many more Languages." (Massachusetts Historical Society, Collections, 3rd Series, x. 3.)

land;[10] John Winthrop, Jr., who studied at Dublin, was admitted to the Inner Temple as lawyer in 1625,[11] and later
spent fourteen months touring the Continent, spending
three months in Constantinople, and visiting practically all
the countries of Europe on the way;[12] Henry Whitfield, who
studied "at the university, and then at the Inns of Court;"[13]
Thomas Parker, who, withdrawing from Oxford on the exile
of his father, studied at Dublin under Dr. Usher, and at
Leyden under Dr. Ames, and "proceeded master" before the
age of twenty-two with "the special esteem of Maccovius,
a man renowned in the Belgick universities;"[14] and Dr.
Robert Child of Corpus Christi, Cambridge, "a gentleman
that hath travelled other parts before hee came to us,
namely Italy . . . . he tooke the degree of Doctor in
Physick at Padua."[15]

Many of these men were recognized by their contempora-
ries in England and on the Continent as scholars of ability.
That several were elected Fellows at the universities has
already been noted.   Charles Chauncy, later president of
Harvard, was elected professor of Hebrew, and served as
professor of Greek, in Trinity College, Cambridge.[16] Thomas
Fuller classed Thomas Shepard, Thomas Hooker, Nathaniel
Ward, and John Cotton among "the learned writers of
Emmanuel College,"[17] and of John Norton's answer to Apollonius he wrote, " . . . . of all the *Authors* I have perused
concerning the *opinions* of these *Dissenting Brethren*, none
to me was more *informative*, then Mr *John Norton*, (One of
no less *learning* then *modesty*) . . . . in his answer to

[10] F. B. Dexter,   Massachusetts Historical Society, Proceedings, 1st Series, xvii.
344.
[11] R. C. Winthrop, Life and Letters of John Winthrop, i. 203.
[12] *Ibid*, i. 263.
[13] Cotton Mather, Magnalia Christi Americana, i. 592.
[14] *Ibid.*, i. 481.
[15] Edward Winslow,   New England's Salamander Discovered, Massachusetts
Historical Society, Collections, 3rd Series, ii. 117.
[16] Magnalia, i. 465.
[17] Fuller, History of Cambridge University, p. 147.

Apollonius."[18] Henry Dunster was an Oriental scholar of
reputation, as is shown by his correspondence with Ravius.[19]
The esteem in which many of the colonists were held is
further shown by the fact that three New England ministers, John Davenport, John Cotton, and Thomas Hooker,
were invited to sit in the Westminster Assembly,[20] and that
several were recalled to high positions in England, as was
Hugh Peter, who became Cromwell's chaplain. Of this more
will be said later.[21]

It is not surprising that a colony comprising so many
educated men should take an active interest in the problem
of the training of the young men whom they brought with
them. Some were trained, as was Thomas Thacher, by
residing with and studying under some minister of scholarly
repute. Thacher, the son of a minister of Salisbury, England, had been offered his choice of either university, but
had preferred the more congenial atmosphere of New England, where he came in 1635. He "was now cast into the
family and under the tuition of that reverend man, Mr.
Charles Chancey; . . . . Under the conduct of that eminent scholar, he became such an one himself."[22] But such
methods did not satisfy the colony, and in 1636 the General
Court voted £400 for the establishing of a college. When
John Harvard, the first minister in the colony to die without
leaving dependents, bequeathed to the college in 1638 his

[18] Magnalia, i. 290. Fuller, Church-History of Britain, xvii Century, xi Book,
p. 213.
[19] Chaplin, Life of Henry Dunster, p. 86. Ravius (Christian Rau) after travel
and study in the Orient was professor of Oriental languages successively at
Gresham College and the Universities of Utrecht, Oxford, and Upsala.
[20] Winthrop's Journal, i. 223 note; ii. 71.
[21] See Chapter III, below.
[22] Magnalia, i. 490. Mather mentions thirteen others who were educated in
this manner: Samuel Arnold of Marshfield, John Bishop of Stamford, Edward
Bulkly of Concord, Thomas Carter of Woburn, Francis Dean of Andover, James
Fitch of Norwich, Thomas Hunford of Norwalk, John Higginson of Salem, Samuel
Hough of Reading, Thomas James of Easthampton, Roger Newton of Milford,
John Sherman of Watertown, and John Woodbridge of Newberry. (Magnalia, i.
237.)

library and one half of his estate,[23] the beginning of college education in America was made possible. The first teacher appointed, Nathaniel Eaton, had been educated in Holland, at Franeker. When he proved unsatisfactory for reasons other than scholastic,[24] Henry Dunster was appointed in his place, and under him the first class of nine completed its course in 1642. For a colony only twelve years old this was no small achievement.

The course of studies was similar to that of the English universities, including Logic, Physics, Ethics, Politics, Arithmetic, Geometry, Astronomy, Greek, Hebrew, Chaldee, and Syriac, with especial emphasis on Rhetoric, it being required that "every scholler . . . . declaime once a moneth."[25] Much Latin and some Greek were required for admission,[26] and the college rules stipulated the use of Latin for all conversation in the college. Under such scholars as Dunster and Chauncy the standards were undoubtedly as high here as in England.[27] On both sides of the water the chief purpose of the universities was to train men in divinity, and

[23] The college received by this bequest £779.17.02. College Record Book III. 1.

[24] Nathaniel Eaton went from Massachusetts to Virginia and thence, after some years, to Italy, where he received the degrees of Doctor of Philosophy and of Medicine at Padua in 1647. The rest of his life was spent in England. (Littlefield, Early Massachusetts Press, i. 70.)

[25] New England's First Fruits, (1643), Massachusetts Historical Society, Collections, 1st Series, i. 245.

[26] Ibid., i. 243. "When any schollar is able to understand Tully, or such like classicall Latine author extempore, and make and speake true Latine in verse and prose, ... and decline . . . . the paradigim's of nounes and verbes in the Greek tongue: Let him then . . . .be capable of admission."

[27] The endeavor of those interested in the college to ensure good teaching is shown by the following item from the Magnalia, ii. 14: "That brave old man Johannes Amos Commenius, the fame of whose worth hath been trumpetted as far as more than three languages (whereof every one is indebted unto his Janua) could carry it, was indeed agreed withal, by our Mr. Winthrop [the younger] in his travels through the low countries, to come over into New-England, and illuminate this Colledge and country, in the quality of a President: But the solicitations of the Swedish Ambassador, diverting him another way, that incomparable Moravian became not an American." Cf. Albert Matthews, Comenius and Harvard College, Publications of the Colonial Society of Massachusetts, xxi. 146-190.

liberal learning suffered common neglect.[28] Harvard at least
attempted to give as much culture as the English universities,
for, in the study of Greek, for example, the requirements
were: Etymologie, Syntax, Prosodia and Dialects, Grammar, Poesy, Nonnus, Duport, Style, Composition, Imitation, Epitome, both verse and prose.[29] One form of literary
activity practised at the English universities, the writing
and production of plays, was, of course, totally missing at
Harvard.

That the education to be gained at Harvard even in its
earliest days was the equivalent of that of Cambridge and

[28] Of Cambridge about 1600 J. B. Mullinger writes (History of the University
of Cambridge, p. 134), "Such are the chief features in the history of the university
in the reign of Elizabeth. It had been decided that Cambridge should be mainly
a school of divinity. . . . . The main interest having centred in the discussion
of theological questions, whatever was taught of liberal learning sank to an almost
lifeless tradition." Of Cambridge in the first half of the 17th century he writes
elsewhere (Cambridge Characteristics in the Seventeenth Century, p. 55 ff.),
"An attempt which he [Barrow] made to introduce the Greek tragedians to the
attention of his scanty auditory met with so little encouragement that he was
compelled to fall back on Aristotle. . . . . No mention appears to be made of
Thucydides as a college subject during this period. . . . . Æschylus is rarely
quoted, and Pindar . . . . still less. I find no instance of the employment of
Lucretius as a class-book. . . . . Of the inimitable beauties of the Latin poets
of the præ-Augustan school there is not a glimpse of anything like adequate
recognition. . . . . Indeed, if we except the names of Meric, Casaubon, Milton,
Herbert, Barrow, and Duport, it is doubtful whether we could point to any scholar
in England during the earlier part of the century, who possessed that refined form
of scholarship represented in the present day by so nice a sense of the beauties
and delicacies of Greek and Latin verse. . . . . Milton, indeed, stands in almost
painful contrast to his University from his superiority in this as in more important
traits." Of the latter Mullinger writes further (Ibid., p. 76), "In the case of Milton, for instance, beyond the culture of his classical taste, there is little reason for
supposing that Cambridge did much toward moulding his character, or, if so, it
would appear to be quite as much by the development of antagonistic as of sympathetic feelings. . . . . [p. 78.] However reluctantly, it would seem, therefore, that
we must forego that thrill of pride with which we should delight to trace, in the productions of the genius of John Milton, the fostering and guiding influence of his
university career." G. C. Brodrick, in his History of Oxford, p. 94, says, "Spenser
and other Elizabethan poets had received an University education; but such men
derived their inspiration from no academical source; their literary powers were
matured in a very different school."

[29] New England's First Fruits, Massachusetts Historical Society, Collections, 1st
Series, i. 244.

Oxford is best shown by the careers of some of its earliest graduates. Sir George Downing, of the first class, rose to distinction under Cromwell, acting as his minister at The Hague, a position which he retained under Charles II, who knighted him in 1660, and made him a baronet three years later.[30] Benjamin Woodbridge of the same class became one of the chaplains in ordinary to Charles II after the Restoration, and was given the choice of being canon of Windsor if he would conform,—which he refused to do.[31] Henry Saltonstall, also of the first class at Harvard, was given recognition at Oxford. Among the incorporations of 1652, according to the record in Wood's "Athenæ Oxoniensis," appears, "June 24, Henr. Saltonstal, a Knight's Son, Fellow of New Coll. by the favor of the Visitors, and Doct. of Phys. of Padua, was then incorporated. The said degree he took at Padua in Oct., 1649." Samuel Mather, the first graduate to be made a Fellow of Harvard, became chaplain to Thomas Andrews, Lord Mayor of London, about 1650. He was admitted by Cambridge, Oxford, and Trinity, Dublin, "ad eundem," and by the latter was offered a "baccalaureatus in theologia" which he declined, although he accepted an election as Senior Fellow. He also served as chaplain in Magdalen, Oxford, preaching sometimes in St. Mary's.[32] Increase Mather became a Master of Arts at Trinity, Dublin, and was well received by the scholars there, being offered a fellowship which he declined.[33] Before returning to Boston at the age of twenty-two,[34] he served for a time as chaplain at Guernsey.[33]

With the graduates of Cambridge and Oxford who returned to England when the Puritans came into power, went a number of Harvard men other than those mentioned above, all of whom seem to have been equipped to succeed

[30] Winthrop Papers, i. 536 note.
[31] Massachusetts Historical Society, Collections, 1st Series, x. 32 note.
[32] Magnalia, ii. 43.
[33] Wendell, Cotton Mather, p. 19.
[34] Magnalia, ii. 18.

in England.   One of them, Nathaniel Mather, wrote back
to his relatives in New England, in 1651, "Tis incredible
what an advantage to preferm[t] it is to have been a New
English man."[35]   It is with natural pride that Cotton Mather
remarks, "From that hour [the time of the founding of
Harvard] *Old* England had more ministers from *New*, than
our New-England had since *then* from Old."[36]

The satisfactory condition of scholarship at Harvard is
further shown by the fact that "in several instances youth
of opulent families in the parent country were sent over to
receive their education in New England."[37]

Colonial interest in education was not limited to the
higher education of the college, as is shown by the law
passed in Massachusetts in 1647:[38]

. . . . every township in this jurisdiction, after the Lord hath
increased them to the number of fifty householders, shall then
forthwith appoint one within their town to teach all such children
as shall resort to him to write and read, whose wages shall be paid
either by the parents or masters of such children, or by the inhabitants in general . . . . where any town shall increase to the
number of 100 families or householders they shall set up a grammar

[35] Massachusetts Historical Society, Collections, 4th Series, viii. 5. He reports
receiving, within three hours of landing in England, two offers of churches, one
worth £140 per annum.

[36] Magnalia, i. 237. In addition to those mentioned above, the following
Harvard men took advanced degrees: Benjamin Woodbridge (A.M., Oxford,
1648), James Ward (A.M., Oxford, 1648, M.B., 1649), William Stoughton (A.M.,
Oxford, 1653), John Glover (M.D., Aberdeen, 1654), Leonard Hoar (M.D., Cambridge, 1671), Isaac Chauncy (M.D.), Ichabod Chauncy (M.D.), Joshua Ambrose
(A.M., Oxford, 1656), and John Haynes (A.M., Cambridge, 1660). Publications
of the Colonial Society of Massachusetts, xviii. 210.

[37] Palfrey, History of New England, ii. 49. Palfrey gives Johnson's Wonder-
Working Providence as authority. Johnson writes, " . . . . some Gentlemen
have sent their sons hither from England, who are to be commended for their
care of them, as the judicious and godly Doctor Ames, and divers others." (p. 202,
Jameson ed.)   Among the "divers others" was Sir Henry Mildmay, who "sent his
Son *William Mildmay*, Esq; the Elder Brother of *Henry Mildmay*, Esq; of *Shaw-
ford* in *Hampshire*, to study here [Harvard]." (Neal, History of New England,
i. 206, 2d ed.)   Richard Lyon, who helped Dunster with the revision of the Bay
Psalm-Book, was the tutor of Mildmay. (*Ibid.*, p. 207).

[38] Littlefield, Early New England Schools, p. 77.

school, the master thereof being able to instruct youth so far as they may be fitted for the university. . . . .

Before this law was passed many towns had made provision for grammar schools.[39] Just how zealously the law was enforced it is impossible to determine, but there are records of towns being fined for failure to provide schools, as well as records of towns fining men for not teaching their children or apprentices to read and write.[40] The grammar schools were supplemented, as in England, by dame schools. The established endowed grammar schools of England were probably superior to the colonial schools, but not as numerous in proportion to the population, for England had no compulsory school law until two hundred years later, and illiteracy was common.[41]

Before 1645, also, two books for school use had been printed at Cambridge. One of these, of which no copy has survived,[42] is referred to as "The Spelling Books," printed by Stephen Day between 1642 and 1645. The other is John Cotton's catechism entitled "Spiritual Milk for Boston Babes in either England Drawn out of the Breasts of both Testaments for their soul's nourishment."[43] Such catechisms,

[39] Small, Early New England Schools, p. 30, gives the following dates for the founding of grammar schools:

Boston	1635–6	Braintree	1645–6
Charlestown	1636	Watertown	1650
Salem	1637	Ipswich	1651
Dorchester	1639	Dedham	1653
New Haven	1639	Newbury	1658
Hartford	1639	Northampton	1667
Cambridge	1640–3	Hadley	1667
Roxbury	1645	Hingham	1670

[40] Ibid., pp. 346 ff. Sometimes the towns escaped the fine upon the plea of inability to obtain a schoolmaster.

[41] In 1847 there were official statistics in England that one-third of the men and half the women who presented themselves for marriage were unable to sign their names. In 1856 it was reported that there were 700 teachers of the dame school type who could not write. De Montmorency, The Progress of Education in England, pp. 90, 94.

[42] Littlefield, Early New England Schools, p. 118.

[43] Ibid., p. 107. Printed before 1646.

it must be remembered, were commonly used as primers or first readers in day schools in both Old and New England in the seventeenth and eighteenth centuries. The shifting of religious education to Sunday and the Sunday-school was the work of the nineteenth century.

All the above evidence would seem to indicate that, as far as the possibilities and benefits of a satisfactory education were concerned, the early colonists and their children were under no serious disadvantage in comparison with those whom they had left behind in England.

Chapter II: Libraries and the
Circulation of Books.

ALTHOUGH the Pilgrims, as has been said, came from the lower ranks of society, and although they endured years of hardship from their first interrupted attempt to leave England until they were finally established in Plymouth nearly twenty years after, they were not without books. William Brewster, for example, left at his death in 1643 a library of nearly four hundred books,[1] and the old soldier, Miles Standish, left about fifty.[2] Among the latter are such interesting items as:

> The History of the World
> Turkish History
> A Chronicle of England
> The History of Queen Elizabeth
> The State of Europe
> Bariff's Artillery
> Caesar's Commentaries
> Homer's Iliad
> The Swedish Intelligencer
> The French Academy
> The Country Farmer
> Calvin's Institutions

Brewster's library is more interesting as well as larger. The fact that many of the books were published after 1620 shows that the cares of colonial life and the distance from book-stalls did not prevent the continued acquisition of books,—the steady acquisition, if we may be allowed to draw any conclusion from the fact that in his library every

[1] Massachusetts Historical Society, Proceedings, 2d Series, v. 37.
[2] New England Historical and Genealogical Register, v. 337.

year from 1620 to that of his death, with the exceptions of 1639 and 1641, is represented.[3] The following partial list will show the more literary tone of this collection:

Camden,	Britain
Camden,	Remains
Smith, J.,	Description of New England
Bacon,	Advancement of Learning
Bacon,	Declaration of Treasons of the Earl of Essex
Raleigh,	Prerogative of Parliament
Machiavelli,	Princeps
Richardson,	On the State of Europe
	The Swedish Intelligencer 1632
Cornwallis,	Essays of Certain Paradoxes
Prynne,	Anti-Arminianism
Prynne,	Looking-Glasse for all Lordly Prelates
Rainolds,	The Overthrow of Stage Plays
Hakluyt,	Principal Navigations
Wither, G.,	Works
Dekker, T.,	Magnificent Entertainment given to King James, March, 1603, with speeches and songs delivered
[?]	Adventure of Don Sebastian
[?]	Messelina (perhaps Nathaniel Richard's The Tragedy of Messalina,) acted by the company of His Majesty's Revels, 1640[4]
Herring,	Latin poem in honor of James I
Hornby,	Scourge of Drunkenness (verse)
Rich, R.,	Newes from Virginia, 1607 (verse)
Johnson, R.,	Golden Garland of Princely Pleasures
Brathwait,	The Description of a Good Wife (verse)
Smith,	Commonwealth of England and Government Thereof
Lodge, T.,	Translation of the works of Seneca
Cawdrey,	Treasurie of Similies
Keckerman,	Systema Geographicum

[3] Massachusetts Historical Society, Proceedings, 2d Series, v. 37.

[4] *Ibid.*, v. 37. If the identification of *Messalina* is correct, this and Dekker's *Magnificent Entertainment* are the earliest evidences we have of the existence of the drama in New England libraries. Another play, *Roxana Tragedia*, is mentioned in the John Harvard library.

Rathbone,	Surveyor
Norden,	Surveyors Dialogue
Standish,	New Directions . . . . for Increasing Timber

Governor Bradford left a library of about eighty volumes, including, in part, the following.[5] It is regrettable that so many were uncatalogued.

> The ffrench acaddamey
> The Guiciardin
> The history of the Church
> The history of the Netherlands
> Speeds generall Description of the world
> The method of phiscicke
> Taylers libertie of Phrophecye
> Gouges Domesticall Dutyes
> three and fifty smale bookes
> Calvine on the epistles in Duch with Divers other
>   Duch bookes

Very few of the Pilgrims were without books. The inventories of estates filed among the Wills in the Plymouth Colony Records give proof of this. Of over seventy inventories examined in the first two volumes of the Wills, only a dozen failed to make specific mention of books, and among these were some whose entire estates, including house and land, clothes and tools, amounted to only twenty-five or thirty pounds. Such people, among them single men who had evidently come to the new colony with almost nothing, probably uneducated, would not be likely to possess books in a frontier town even today. In many cases the books mentioned are very few, the exact number being hidden under such phrases as: "bookes," "all his bookes," "3 bibles and other books." Inasmuch as "all his bookes" were valued at only eighteen shillings,[6] and "3 bibles and

[5] Mayflower Descendant, ii. 232.
[6] Plymouth Colony Records, Wills, i. 31. Estate of John Bryant. In these volumes the numbers refer to sheets, not pages. Up to one hundred, and in a few cases beyond that, the sheets are numbered 11, 21, 31, or 651, 661, 671, when

other books" at six pounds,[7] the phrases are of little value in estimating the possible number. That even so small a collection as "1 bible, 1 book catechism, 1 book Practice of Christianity" was itemized[8] would seem to show their respect for the mere presence of a book. The valuation helps little to estimate the number where only value is given. Brewster's library of 400 volumes was appraised at £42.19.11,[9] which would give an average of ten books to the pound; but William Gibson's "1 bible and 10 other books" at £00.06.00,[10] and Thomas Pryor's "1 great bible 1 smale bible and 50 other bookes" at £01.10.00,[11] give a different ratio.

It is not possible, then, outside of a few lists in addition to those given, to estimate the number of books in the homes of the Pilgrims; but the following details will give some indication.

Name	Year	Total Inventory	Books
Steven Deans	1634	£ 87.19.06	£ 01.00.00
Thomas Pryor	1639	22.07.06	01.10.00
Nathaniel Tilden	1641	200.00.00	05.00.00
John Atwood	1643	186.14.00	09.00.00
John Jenney	1644	108.03.03	01.03.06
William Brewster	1644	150.00.07	42.19.11
Edward Foster	1644	42.03.00	06.00.00
Love Brewster	1650	97.09.01	05.12.04
Nicolas Robbins	1650	38.19.09	02.14.00
Henry Smith	1651	149.16.00	01.00.00
William Thomas	1651	375.07.00	08.05.00
John Hazell	1651	165.19.00	04.06.00
William Hatch	1652	95.03.04	01.10.00
Judith Smith	1650	120.06.00	01.00.00
Henry Andrews	1653	330.16.00	02.00.00

we would use 1, 2, 3, or 65, 66, 67. I have changed uniformly to the modern system.

[7] *Ibid.*, i. 60. Estate of Edward Foster.
[8] *Ibid.*, i. 29. Estate of William Palmer.
[9] *Ibid.*, i. 53–59.
[10] *Ibid.*, i. 35.
[11] *Ibid.*, i. 34.

Robert Waterman	1653	£ 78.00.00	£ 01.04.00
John Lothrop (Rev.)	1653	72.16.06	05.00.00
Ann Atwood	1654	24.00.03	07.00.00
William Phillips	1654	78.08.00	01.00.00
William [torn]	1654	157.09.00	01.10.00
James Pilbeame	1655	48.05.10	01.10.00
Elizabeth Pole	1656	188.11.07	02.00.00
Miles Standish	1656	358.07.00	11.13.00
John Gilbert	1657	200.00.00	02.00.00
William Bradford	1657	not given	15.00.00
Park Chittenden	1676	156.08.05	01.14.00
John Miles (Rev.)	1683	260.00.00	50.00.00

Where titles are itemized they are in most cases devotional or theological. In the inventory of Samuel Fuller, 1633, of the twenty-six given by title, but three are non-religious: a book on government, one on husbandry, and a "dixionary;" a volume of "notable things" might belong to either class.[12] There are also "other bookes" to the value of one pound. The inventory of John Atwood includes "Acts and Monuments" in three volumes, a history, Prynne's "Historio [sic] Mastix," and divers other books to the value of three pounds.[13] Ann Atwood possessed two of Prynne's works, unnamed, two French books and a French Testament, and "four and fifty smale bookes at 6ᵈ the piece."[14] John Hazell had Josephus and two history books.[15] Governor Thomas Prince owned, among books to the number of 187, valued at £13.18.08 in a total estate of £422.00.00, Laud's "Conference with Fisher the Jesuit," Prynne's "Account of Laud's Trial," Morton's "New England's Memorial," and the "Essays" of Sir William Cornwallis.[16]

Books and libraries were much more common among those who settled in the neighborhood of Boston and in

---

[12] *Ibid.*, i. 22.
[13] *Ibid.*, i. 47.
[14] *Ibid.*, i. 124.
[15] *Ibid.*, i. 101.
[16] F. B. Dexter, Proceedings of the American Antiquarian Society, xviii. 143.

Connecticut.   Each minister had at least a small library, and some who were not ministers had excellent collections of books, as, for example, John Winthrop, Jr., who, according to his father's Journal, had in New England, in the year 1640, a library of over 1000 volumes.[17]   Two years later the father, Governor Winthrop, was probably one of the magistrates who collectively gave to Harvard books to the value of £200;[18] and about 1660 he gave to Harvard's library some forty volumes more.[19]   The best example of the kind of library which the colonists brought with them is John Harvard's, which made a substantial part of his bequest in 1638 to the college then being built in Cambridge.   As Harvard had been in the colony but a year, he could not have added many books to those he had with him upon arrival.   Although naturally largely theological or expository, this collection contained a considerable number of books of a literary nature, as the following selected list will demonstrate:[20]

> Angloru prælia
> Aquinatis Opa. Conclusiones
> Aynsworts [Henry Ainsworth] workes
> Alstedij Physica Harmonia
> Aschamj Epistolæ
> Æsopi fabulæ
> Academia Gallica

[17] Journal, ii. 18. "Mr. Winthrop the younger, one of the magistrates, having many books in a chamber where there was corn of divers sorts, had among them one wherein the Greek testament, the psalms and the common prayer were bound together. He found the common prayer eaten with mice, every leaf of it, and not any of the two other touched, nor any other of his books, though there were above a thousand." It seems probable that these represented only a part of the library of John Winthrop, Jr. It does not seem likely that a man who prized books as he did would have left valuable books in a storeroom in which grain was kept.

[18] Chaplin, Life of Henry Dunster, p. 78. See pp. 40 and 41, below.

[19] Life and Letters of John Winthrop, ii. 438. College Book III, 32.

[20] Harvard Library, Bibliographical Contributions, No. 27, 1888, p.7. [Revised by A. C. Potter, Catalogue of John Harvard's Library, Publications of the Colonial Society of Massachusetts, xxi: 190-230. 1919. Ed.] His library contained over 300 volumes.

βασίλικον δῶρον
Bacons advancem[t]. Essayes
Camdens remaines
Calliopæia [rich store-house of . . . phrases.]
Duns Scotus in 8 Libros Arist. Phys.
Erasmj Colloquia
Epictetj Enchyridion
Elegant Phrases
Garden of Eloquence
Essayes morall & Theol.
Felthoms resolues
Homers workes in English[21]
Haylins Geography
Juvenalis
Isocratis Orat: Græc & Latin
Lightfoots Miscelanes
Lucanus
Londons complaint
Nichols mirrour for Magistrates
Plautus
Plutarchj [North's Translation] Vitæ Angl.
Porcensis orationes
Persij Satyræ
Poetarū flores
Quarles Poems
Roxanæ Tragedia[22]
Salustius
Terentius
Thesaurus poeticus
Tullij, opa in 2 Tomis. de officijs
Withers [Title not given]

The colonists, then, were not unfurnished with books
when they arrived; and there is much evidence that their
libraries were constantly increased by shipments from Eng-

[21] This may be Chapman's translation, a copy of which was in the Harvard
Library in 1723. Bibliographical Contributions, No. 27, p. 10.

[22] By W. Alabaster. In five acts and verse. Given at Cambridge. Published
1632.

land. Isaac Johnson was scarcely in New England before John Humfrey wrote to him from England,

I have sent you those new bookes that are lately come out, Dr. Ames' Cases to Mr. Governor[23] which I purpose to send you by the next, & now Dr. Sibs' Bruised Reede & Mr. Dike of Scandals to you.[24]

Henry Jacie wrote to John Winthrop, Jr., in January, 1631,

A book of the Northern Star (by Dr. Goad) was sent you to go herewith.[25]

Edward Howes wrote to John Winthrop, Jr., November 9, 1631,

The bookes Mr. Gurdon hath fetcht away, and the *Luna* is at your service; soe is [*sic*] both the books & *Sol*, & *quodcunque sub sole habet, vel habebit me, tuum.*[26]

The next year he wrote:

I havinge sent some bookes to James Downinge . . . . beinge incited thereunto by his father; . . . . I sent your honored father a booke of bookes among those to J. D.[27]

. . . & that your worthy father, with all my louinge frinds may reead at large the workinge of our God in these latter dayes, here I haue sent you the Swedish Intelligencer which speakes wonder to the world; withall I haue sent you your Archymedes and an Almenack, with a booke or two of other newes besides.[28]

Here in closed you shall find a booke of the probabilities of the North West passage.[29]

I have sent M[r] Samford the Instrument and sight ruler the Germaine bespoke for him, together with a booke to teach the

---

[23] Mr. Governor is John Winthrop, Sr.
[24] Winthrop Papers, i. 4.   December 9, 1630.
[25] Massachusetts Historical Society, Collections, 3rd Series, i. 241.
[26] Winthrop Papers, i. 472.
[27] Massachusetts Historical Society, Collections, 3rd Series, ix. 243.   April 3, 1632.
[28] Winthrop Papers, i. 477.   1632.
[29] *Ibid.*, p. 480.   November 23, 1632.   This book was by Howes himself.   The copy inscribed by him is in the collection of the Massachusetts Historical Society.

use thereof, namely Smyths Arte of Gunnery at folio 58 there the same Instrument is to be seene; I have likewise sent him Nortons Practise of Artillerie chosen by the Germaine for him; and alsoe diverse platformes of the latest invented forts and fortifications: For new bookes I writt to you of D[r] Fludds works and sent you a cattalogue of them by M[r] Hetherley; there is a booke lately come out of mathematicall conclusion and recreations, which I bought purposely for you, but M[r] Saltonstall hath borrowed it . . . . albeit I have sent you two other bookes viz[t] Malthus Fireworks, and the Horizontall Quadrant full of new devices; which I present to your kind acceptance.[30]

The same year F. Kirby wrote to the younger Winthrop at various times:

For the Catalogue of bookes from Frankfort I have sent you that of the Autumnall mart 1631. the next is not to be had the third not yet come by reason of Contrary wind, but I shall send it God willinge by the next ship. . . . . I have now received all your mony of Edward Howes which maketh in all 4li. 12sh. for the bookes and carriage of them.[31]

With this I enclose the Catalogue of the last vernall mart, the last autumnall is not yet to be had.[32]

I have sent you heer inclosed the Catalogue of the Autumnall mart 1632. all the former I have sent before.[33]

In the years that follow Edward Howes continued to send books.

. . . . in a bundle of clothes for your cosen Mary . . . . you shall find from him a cattalogue of the last marte bookes; and from your poore frind an exact and large and the latest dis-couery of the North West passage, made by a painfull and indus-trious gent., Capt. James, as a remembrance of my obliged loue.[34]

I haue bin held in hand at Mr. Fetherston's shop by his men,

---

[30] Massachusetts Historical Society, Collections, 3rd Series, ix. 255. March 18, 1632–3.

[31] *Ibid.*, p. 249. November 25, 1632.

[32] *Ibid.*, p. 252. December 3, 1632.

[33] *Ibid.*, p. 260. March 26, 1633.

[34] Winthrop Papers, i. 487. June 22, 1633.

euer since 8ber,[35] to be furnished with all those bookes you writt for, and now am forced to buy them where I can find them.[36]

The bookes I haue sent you, March, 1634.

2 Catalogues of printed bookes.

	li.	s.	d.
Dr. Fludds Macrocosme in 2 volumes	1	10	0
Isagoge Phisico Magico &c.	0	1	6
Petrus Galatinus de Arcanis Catholicæ veritatis	0	10	0
Phillippi Grulingij Florilegium	0	2	0

These are parte of them you writt for.

I haue here alsoe sent you a few others, which if you like not, I pray send them againe, or any of them.

Mercurius Rediuiuus per Norton	0	2	6
The Rarities of Cochin China	0	1	0
Wingates Logarithmes	0	4	6
An English Grammer	0	1	0
The Gunners Dialogue	0	2	0
Bedwells Messolabium	0	1	0

.   .   .   .

The rest I cast in to the bargaine, for you and your fancie to make merry withall.[37]

The bookes you writt for, I haue not mett with them as yet at the shopps where I haue bin.[38]

One consignment of books to the elder Winthrop may have failed to reach Boston. Robert Ryece wrote to him, January 17, 1636,

I wrotte vnto you the 17 of Maye laste, accompanied with a boxe of boocks, which I sente by my brother Samuell Appleton, to be convayed to hym for you. . . . . I do feare . . . . that the schippe with the passengers, mooche stuffe & goods, are all perished by the waye.[39]

There is no further record of this.

[35] October.
[36] Winthrop Papers, i. 496. March 29, 1634.
[37] Ibid., i. 497.
[38] Ibid., i. 506. April 14, 1639.
[39] Ibid., i. 394.

The London Port Books give other evidence of the shipment of books to Boston.

xvj Februar 1633[-34] In le Mary and John of London . . . .

j chest bookes.

Quinto Aprilis 1634 . . . . In le Elizabeth and Dorcas . . . . ij packes made clothes and bookes vj trunckes apparell and bookes for prouision for the passengers.[40]

Others than the Winthrops were receiving books from England, although unfortunately most of the records of these shipments have been lost.   President Dunster's father wrote to him, March 20, 1640–1, "Your brother Thomas remembers his love, and hath sent you two dozen of almanacks."[41] Henry Jacie wrote March 6, 1647–8, "I have sent to Mr. Cotton or Mr. Wilson a book for the Governors, of the present proceeds between the King & Parliament."[42]   The colonists seem to have been able to get books fresh from the English presses.   Roger Williams wrote in a letter which, although undated, undoubtedly belongs to the year 1650, "The Portraicture [Eikon Basilike], I guesse is Bp. Halls, the stile is pious & acute, very like his, & J. H. subscribes the Epitaph."[43]   And on February 15, 1654–5, he wrote of two books published in 1653, "We allso here that 2 of Mr. Dells bookes were lately burnt at the Massachusetts, (possibly) containing some sharpe things against the Presbyterians & Academians, of which I brought ouer one cald the Triall of Spirits."[44]

At least one comprehensive library was brought over for

[40] Massachusetts Historical Society, Proceedings, xlvii. 179, 183. Both shipments were consigned to John Winthrop, Sr.

[41] Chaplin, Life of Dunster, p. 22. It must be remembered in connection with this item that the almanac was in better esteem then than now, being the sole convenient handbook of scientific information, often containing useful tables of varied information besides the usual astronomical calculations and astrological prophecies, the latter often rhymed.

[42] Winthrop Papers, i. 465.

[43] Ibid., i. 282 and note.

[44] Ibid., i. 291. He returned from England in the summer of 1654.

sale in the early days, for Cotton Mather records with pride the fact that although the learned Dr. William Ames was prevented by death from coming in person to America, his library did come.[45]   A later historian says,

Harvard College being built, a Foundation was laid for a *Publick Library* . . . . The first Furniture of this Library was the Books of Dr. *William Ames*, the famous Professor of Divinity at *Franequer*.[46]

The return to England of a number of ministers during the Puritan régime undoubtedly deprived the colony of several libraries, but in some cases the libraries were retained in New England. Samuel Eaton, returning in 1640, gave to New Haven his library of over 100 volumes, including the following books:[47]

> Plutarch (perhaps North's translation)
> Virgil
> Sandys' metrical translation of Ovid[48]
> Dionysius of Halicarnassus
> More's Utopia
> Erasmus' Proverbs
> Raleigh's History of the World
> Foxe's Book of Martyrs
> Heylyn's Cosmography

A few years later John Eliot wrote,

And for my self I have this request (who also am short enough

---

[45] Magnalia, i. 236.

[46] Neal, History of New England, i. 202. It is not quite clear whether the historian means to imply that this purchase was made before Harvard left his library to the college, or was the first addition after that. If the gratuity granted to Mrs. Ames by the Colony in 1637 was a partial return for the library of her husband, that library preceded the books from Harvard's estate and formed the foundation of the Harvard library. See Publications of the Colonial Society of Massachusetts, xvii. 210, and page 40 note 62, below. The Ames library was almost entirely theological or philosophical.

[47] Proceedings of the American Antiquarian Society, xviii. 138.

[48] It is interesting to note that this product of the Virginia colony, and the finest piece of literary work which the first century of colonization produced, reached the northern colony within fifteen years, if Eaton had the complete edition.

in books) that I might be helped to purchase my brother *Weld* his books, the summe of the purchase (34 li.) I am loth they should come back to *England* when we have so much need of them here.[49]

The books were purchased for him in 1651 by the Corporation for New England.[50] Herbert Pelham, who returned to England in 1649, mentioned in his will (he died in 1676) "all other Brass, Beding, and Linnin with all my Books and other Utensills and moveables which I have in the Massachusetts Bay."[51] The Rev. Thomas Jenner, returning to England about 1650 because of trouble with the churches, was "compelled by poverty to sell his library, which seems to have been bought for Harvard College."[52]

Libraries were not limited to the studies of ministers, for Lion Gardiner wrote to John Winthrop, Jr., in 1650, in reference to the obtaining of a pastor for the small settlement of which he was leader,

Att present wee ar willing to giue this man you writ of 20*li.* a year, with such diat as I myself eat, til we see what the Lord will do with vs; and being he is but a yong man, hapily he hath not manie books, thearfore let him know what I have. First, the 3 Books of Martters, Erasmus, moste of Perkins, Wilsons Dixtionare, a large Concordiance, Mayor on the new Tstement; Some of theas, with othar that I have, may be vcefull to him.[53]

When William Tyng, merchant, died in 1653, leaving the largest estate recorded up to that time (totaling £2774.14.04), part of the estate comprised, according to the inventory, "Books as per schedule valued at 010 00 00."[54] The schedule

[49] Massachusetts Historical Society, Collections, 3rd Series, iv. 128.
[50] New England Historical and Genealogical Register, xxxvi. 371.
[51] *Ibid.*, xviii. 175.
[52] *Ibid.*, xix. 247, and Maine Historical Society, Collections and Proceedings, 2d Series, iii. 293 ff.
[53] Winthrop Papers, ii. 59.
[54] Publications of the Colonial Society of Massachusetts, xiii. 289.

lists nearly one hundred books, mostly in quarto, including the following:[55]

> Bookes of Martyrs in 3 volumes
> Books of Statutes at Large
> The Survey of London
> Speeds Chronicle
> Camdens Britannia
> Marchants Accompts
> Gecords Herball[56]
> Treatise of Magistracy—two
> Enonimous Tresure
> Apeale to Parliament
> Janua Linguarum
> a Duch Worke
> Circkle of Comerse
> abridgm[t] of Camden
> Singin Psalemes
> office of executors
> Imposts & customes
> logick & Rethoricke
> 16 Ciceroas orations
> Interest States & kingdomes

The will of Nicholas Busby, September 10, 1657, bequeathed

vnto my two Sonns *John Busby* & *Abraham*, my printed bookes, in manner following;
    to *John*

> all my Phisicke bookes, as
> *Glendall* practice,
> *Barrowes* method,
> Dutch Phisicke & garden of health
> Mr *Coggans* treatis, and
> the Dialogue of Phisicke Surgery, with
> *Plinnys* Naturall Hystory

[55] New England Historical and Genealogical Register, xxx. 432.
[56] Probably an error for Gerarde's.

Vnto *Abraham*,
> my bookes of Divinitie, vizt.
> Mr *Perkins*
> Mr *Willet* sinops and Comentary on the Romans, &
> M^r [sic] *Hieroms* two bookes;

as for the rest of my bookes of divinities, or Hystory, my desire is, they may Loveingly & Brotherly devide them betweene except the three Bibles.[57]

Governor Thomas Dudley, dying the same year, left a small but interesting collection of books, including in part:[58]

> General History of Netherlands
> Turkish History
> Livius
> Camden: Annale Regnante Eliza
> Commentaries of the wars in France
> Buchanan: Scot Hystory
> Abstract of Penal Statutes
> Vision of Pierc Plowman[59]
> Apology of ye Prince of Orange
> Baynes: Letters
> Swedish Intelligencer
> Mantuanii Bucolica [Virgil]
> The book of Laws
> 8 French books
> Several pamphlets
> New books
> Smalle writings[60]

While individual libraries were slowly growing by importations and gifts from England and, from as early as 1647,

---

[57] New England Historical and Genealogical Register, viii. 279.

[58] *Ibid.*, xii. 355.

[59] This is perhaps the most curious item in all the lists of colonial books. It would cast much light upon colonial culture if we could know how he came to own such a volume, and whether he ever read it. The latest edition he could have had is that of 1561.

[60] The last three items are typical of the vagueness of many of the comparatively few book records preserved. Complete lists would add much to our knowledge.

by purchase in the shop of Hezekiah Usher,[61] the Harvard College library was also growing from its beginning in the Ames library and the 320 volumes left by John Harvard.[62] Roger Harlakenden, dying in 1638, willed "to the librarye ten pownds & all my books wch are not usefull for my wife."[63] The first notable increase was the gift by the magistrates in 1642 of books from their own libraries to the value of £200.[64] If the appraisal of William Tyng's library of nearly 100 volumes at £10 were any criterion,[65] this must have meant a great addition; but doubtless a majority of these books were large and expensive theological folios, which would proportionately lessen the number of books added. There was still need for many more books, for we find President Dunster writing in 1645,

Seeing the public library in the College is yet defective in all manner of books, specially in law, physics, philosophy, and mathematics, the furnishing whereof would be both honorable and profitable to the country in general and in special to the scholars, whose various inclinations to all professions might thereby be encouraged and furthered; we therefore humbly entreat to use such means as your wisdom shall think meet for supply of the same.[66]

I have found no record of any results from this plea.

[61] In 1647 Usher is referred to in Aspinwall's Notarial Book as "Hezekiah Usher of Boston, bookseller." (Littlefield, Early Boston Booksellers, p. 67.) Samuel Danforth's Almanac for 1647 bears the imprint, "Cambridge printed by Mathew Daye; and to be sold by Hezekiah Usher, at Boston." (Thomas, History of Printing, i. 48 note.)

[62] Mr. Julius H. Tuttle, of the Massachusetts Historical Society, thinks that it may be inferred that the gratuity to Mrs. Ames from the General Court was in recognition of the use of the Ames library by the students of Harvard, and that a somewhat similar grant to the widow of the Rev. Jose Glover may indicate that his library was also used by the college just as his printing press was established in connection with it. (Publications of the Colonial Society of Massachusetts, xiv. 65, 66 note.)

[63] New England Historical and Genealogical Register, ii. 182.

[64] Chaplin, Life of Dunster, p. 78.

[65] See p. 37, above.

[66] Chaplin, Life of Dunster, p. 80. The letter was addressed to the Commissioners of the United Colonies of New England.

But books were being added by gifts both at home and from England. Joshua Scottow, of Boston, presented "Henry Stephen his Thesaurus in foure volumes in folio" with a curious proviso.[67] Sir Kenelme Digby, scientist and man of letters, in spite of his leanings toward Catholicism, twice sent books to the young Puritan college,[68] perhaps in-

[67] Chaplin, Life of Dunster, p. 79. The proviso follows. "Thes p^{r}sents witness^e, that wheras Joshuah Scottow, of Bostō, march^t, hath of his owne free accord procured for the library of Harvard Colle[ge] Henry Stephen his Thesaurus, in foure volumes in folio, and bestowe[d] the same thereon: it is on this condicōn, and wth this p[ro]mise following that if ever the said Joshuah, during his life shall have occasion to use the said booke, or any parcell thereof, he shall have free liberty thereof, and accesee thereto: and if God shall blesee the said Joshuah wth any child or childrē that shal be students of the Greeke tongue, thē the said bookes above specifyed shalbee unto them delivered, in case that they will not otherwise be satisfyed wthout it." Dated October 28, 1649. Thus were books esteemed! It might be assumed from this that Scottow, although there is no record that he was a university man, read Greek; if not, why should he reserve such a privilege? He certainly knew French, for he translated The Rise, Spring and Foundation of the Anabaptists, or Re-baptized of our Time. Written in French by Guy de Brez, 1565. . . . . And Translated for the use of his Countrymen, by J. S. [Joshua Scottow] Cambridge: Printed, and to be Sold by Marmaduke Johnson. 1668. (Green, Early American Imprints in Massachusetts Historical Society, Proceedings, 2d Series, ix. 424.)

A later item, undated, in the College Records shows that he availed himself of his reserved privilege. (College Book I, 260.)

"Recev^d of Mr Vryan Oakes p^{r}s[ident] ye above Expressed Thesaurus in foure volumes acc^{r}ding to Condition above: upon the demand of my sonn Thomas Scottow I say received p^r me this 30th of August
                                    Josh: Scottow"
Urian Oakes was president, acting or official, from 1675 to 1681. As in 1682 Cotton Mather includes a copy of this Thesaurus in a list of books which he had purchased from the duplicates in the Harvard Library, either the Scottows soon returned their set, or two others were presented to the library. (Ms. list in Mather's handwriting in possession of the American Antiquarian Society.) Thomas Scottow graduated from Harvard in 1677.

[68] Winslow, New England's Salamander Discovered. 1647. Massachusetts Historical Society, Collections, 3rd Series, ii. 117. "As for Doctor Childe hee is a gentleman that hath travelled other parts before hee came to us, namely Italy; . . . . he tooke the degree of Doctor in Physick at Padua. . . . . Hee comes [to New England] a second time, and not onely bestoweth some bookes on the Colledge, as Sir Kenelme Digby and many others commendably did. . . . ."

In 1654 Hugh Peter wrote from London to John Winthrop, Jr., "I haue sent you 2 peeces of black stuffe . . . . all by the hand of Mr. Norton of Boston, in a great chest of bookes sent agayne by Sir Kenelme Digby, who longs for you here." (Winthrop Papers, i. 116.)

fluenced by his acquaintance with John Winthrop, Jr.[69] There are two references in the College Records to Sir Kenelme's gifts. In College Book I there is a list of seventeen titles, mostly church fathers, given by him in 1655.[70] In College Book III, p. 31, under the date 1659, are mentioned several gifts to the college, the first item being "S.r Kenelme Digby gave to s.d Colledges Library, as many books as were vallued at Sixty pound." It is impossible to tell whether this refers to both gifts together, or to the more recent.

The other gifts recorded with Sir Kenelme's are:

S.r Thomas Temple Knight. gave two Globes a Caelestiall & Terrestriall to s.d Colledge.

M.r Thomas Graves gave some Mathematicall Books tow.ds the furnishing of the Library.

M.r Ralfe ffreck gave to s.d Library Biblia Polyglotta.

M.r John ffrecks gave some Books to the vallue of ten pounds.

M.r John Winthrop gave toward y.e furnishing s.d Library many choice books to the vallue of twenty pounds.

S.r Richard Daniel Knight gave many books to the Library.

Two undated book-lists in College Book I record other gifts.[71] One is a list of twenty titles given by Richard Bellingham. The other is a list of thirty-five titles given by Peter Bulkeley, perhaps at his death in 1658, but probably earlier, as it is not mentioned, as one might expect it would be, in the 1659 list with Sir Kenelme Digby's. Two other men are known to have contributed during this period,

[69] See end of note 68, above. Sir Kenelme wrote to John Winthrop, Jr., from Paris, January 26, 1656 n. s., "I beseech you present my most humble thankes to the President and fellowes of y.r college for the obliging Letter they haue bin pleased to send me. So small a present as j presumed to make them, deserued not so large a returne." (Massachusetts Historical Society, Collections, 3rd Series, x. 16.) Other letters among the Winthrop Papers testify to the correspondence between the two. See i. 116, ii. 588, 593; Massachusetts Historical Society, Collections, 3rd Series, i. 183. See also p. 66 ff., below.

[70] Harvard Library, Bibliographical Contributions, No. 27, p. 13.

[71] Ibid., pp. 13, 14.

Dr. Robert Child[72] and Ezekiel Rogers.[73]   In the inventory of college property made December 10, 1654, at the time the college was settling accounts with Dunster, who had just resigned as president, the "library & Books therin" were "vallued at" £400.[74]

Before the Harvard library was a quarter century old it had a rival in a public library in Boston. Robert Keayne, merchant, suggested in his will, dated August 1, 1653, the erection of a town-house (apparently a combination of a town hall and a neighborhood house) which should contain a market, a library and a gallery, rooms for divines and scholars, for merchants, for strangers, and so on, should his estate prove large enough to provide sufficient funds above his bequests to his family. Of his own books, "all English none Lattine or Greeke," his son and wife were to take their choice "whether Divinitie, Hystory, or Milletary;" the rest were to be looked over by John Wilson and John Norton, who were to choose out for his town-house library all fit books, selling any others. The will further provided that if the town-house was not built the books were to go to Harvard.[75] As the estate was not quite large enough, a sum of £300 was raised by subscription and the building begun in 1657.[76] Unfortunately there are no more records of this library for fifteen years, either in regard to nature, size, or growth; but it is an indication of the culture of the place that such an institution was in existence thus early in the history of the colony, and partly built by the people themselves. Of its subsequent history more will be said later.[77]

During these years there were some losses of books by

[72] See p. 41 note 68, above.
[73] New England Historical and Genealogical Register, v. 125, and p. 44, below.
[74] College Book III, p. 41.
[75] New England Historical and Genealogical Register, vi. 90. The will, the abstract of which covers eleven pages of the Register, the will itself covering 158 pages of the original record of Suffolk County Wills, gives striking evidence of the originality and individuality often found among the dissenters and Puritans.
[76] Publications of the Colonial Society of Massachusetts, xii. 120.
[77] See pp. 132 ff. and 179 ff., below.

fire. Stephen Bachiler wrote to John Winthrop, May 18, 1644, "I haue had great losse by fire, well knowne, to the vallue of 200*li*., with my whole studdy of bookes."[78]   In 1651, on the evening of his third wedding, Ezekiel Rogers lost his house and entire library by fire.[79]   In 1666 the Bradstreet house at Andover was burned. Simon Bradstreet thus records the loss in his diary:

July 12, 1666. Whilst I was at N. London my fathers house at Andover was burnt, where I lost my books. . . . . Tho: my own losse of books (and papers espec.) was great and my fathers far more being about 800, yet ye Lord was pleased . . . . to make up ye same to us.[80]

There may have been other losses of which record is lost;[81] but in general there was a steady increase in the number of books in New England. Simon Bradstreet's reference above to the making up of the lost books, and the fact that Ezekiel Rogers, having lost his entire library in 1651, at his death in 1660 was able to bestow upon Harvard College "his books wherewith he had recruited his library, after the fire, which consumed the good library that he had brought out of England,"[82] including Latin books valued at

[78] Winthrop Papers, ii. 107. The phrase "whole studdy of bookes" would seem to imply a considerable library.

[79] Winthrop Papers, ii. 205 note. New England Historical and Genealogical Register, v. 124.

[80] Ellis, Works of Anne Bradstreet, lxi.

[81] The house of Herbert Pelham, first treasurer of Harvard, was burned in December, 1640. Mr. Downing's house was burned in April, 1645, with a loss of household goods to the value of £200. The same week the house of John Johnson of Roxbury was totally wrecked by a fire and the explosion of gunpowder stored therein. (Winthrop's Journal, *passim*.) At the burning of Springfield by the Indians in 1674, "thirty-two houses, and amongst the rest, the minister's with his well-furnished library, were consumed." (Magnalia, ii. 565.) The library of William Blackstone, formerly of Boston, was destroyed during King Philip's War, when his house at Lonsdale, R. I., was burned by the Indians, shortly after his death. There were some 160 books in the collection. The house of Increase Mather was burned on November 27, 1676. (Massachusetts Historical Society, Proceedings, 2d Series, xiii. 373-374.)

[82] Magnalia, i. 412.

£47 and some of his English books to the value of £26,[83] demonstrate both the possibility and the fact of considerable book-buying within forty years of the founding of Boston. Although John Johnson's house was wrecked by fire and explosion in 1645, in 1647 he possessed books which Richard Mather was glad to borrow.[84] The church in Hartford, inviting Jonathan Mitchel to succeed Thomas Hooker, who died in 1647, as pastor, promised that they would "immediately upon his acceptance of their invitation, advance a considerable sum of money, to assist him in furnishing himself with a library."[85] The books were evidently to be procured in Boston before he left for Hartford. Thomas Mayhew, writing to John Winthrop, Jr., of his son, Thomas Mayhew, missionary to the Indians of Martha's Vineyard and Nantucket, who was lost at sea in 1657 while on his way to England, said, "He allso hath had of the Commissioners in all, besides his books, 160*li.*, his bookes were 37*li.*, as I take it."[86] It is not clear whether books to that value had been sent from England, or whether the money had been sent to buy books in Boston. In either case there is evidence that the colonists found it possible to procure books in considerable numbers.[87]

Books, largely gifts, continued to come from friends in England. John Winthrop, Jr., wrote to Robert Child, March 23, 1648–9,

I am glad to heare of those bookes coming forth, Paullin and

[83] Publications of the Colonial Society of Massachusetts, xii. 49.

[84] See p. 44 note 81, above, and p. 57, below.

[85] Magnalia, ii. 88.

[86] Winthrop Papers, ii. 35.

[87] Although Hezekiah Gay, who died in 1669, seems to have had but two books to will ("give my mother, Mr. Burrowes' Book and my sister Whiting that new book concerning Thomas Savage," New England Historical and Genealogical Register, xlviii, 324,) one of them had been published within a year: Gods Justice Against Murther, or the bloudy Apprentice executed. Being an exact . . . . relation of a bloudy murther committed by one T. Savage . . . . in Ratcliffe upon the maid of the house his fellow servant. London, 1668. *Cf.* Publications of the Colonial Society of Massachusetts, xx. 237-239.

Propugnaculi Fabri, and Helmonts workes, but how to be certaine
to procure thẽ I know not, except you please to doe me the favour
to send for thẽ where they are to be had, and desire Mr Peters,
or my brother in my name to lay out the price for me. I
desire also y^t in high Duch, Glauberus, if you approve of it, and
one more I desire you earnestly to procure for me; that is Vigineere
des Cyphres wch you know is to be had at Paris; . . . . I would
have one in this country before the impression be quite worn out.[88]

Stephen Winthrop wrote from England in 1649 to his
brother, John Winthrop,

.. . . . ye rest voted the triall of the King, who is since beheaded, ... but I canot inlarg to pticuler, passingers &
bookes will informe best.   I shall send my father some."[89]

Richard Saltonstall wrote to President Dunster from England where he was visiting,

This enclosed booke I must entreate you to accept insteade of
such lines as I should have added.[90]

Roger Williams wrote, February 21, 1656,

Sir Henry Vane being retired to his owne private in Lincolnshire
hath now published his observations as to religion, he hath sent me
one of his books.[91]

John Eliot wrote to Mr. Hord, October 8, 1657,

. . . likewise I did receive a smal packet of books from **Mr.**
Jessy according to Mr. Jessy's appointment.[92]

John Davenport wrote to the younger John Winthrop,
August 19, 1659,

[88] Winthrop Papers, iv. 41. "Vigineere des Cyphres" is the *Traité des Chiffres*
of Blaise de Vigenère.
[89] *Ibid.*, p. 209.
[90] Massachusetts Historical Society, Collections, 4th Series, ii. 194. The letter
is undated, but marked as received May 15, 1651.
[91] *Ibid.*, 3rd Series, x. 19.
[92] Massachusetts Historical Society, Proceedings, xvii. 246. Mr. Hord was
treasurer of the Corporation for Spreading the Gospel among the Indians. Mr.
Jessy was a minister in Southwark, England.

I have received letters & bookes, & written papers from my ancient & honored freinds Mr. Hartlib, & Mr. Durie, wherein I finde sundry rarities of inventions . . . . which I long for an opportunitie to communicate to your selfe . . . . They are too many to be transmitted unto you by passengers.[93]

The next year he wrote, July 20,

Sir, I humbly thanck you for the Intelligence I received in your letters, and for the 2 weekly Intelligences, which Brother Myles brought me.[94]

A few days later he wrote again (August 11),

M[r] Hartlib . . . . hath sent also sundry wrightings, and bookes, some to your selfe, some to me . . . . M[r] Drury also hath sent some papers and bookes to the 2 Teaching Elders at Boston, and to me.[95]

Samuel Hartlib wrote to John Winthrop, Jr., in 1661,

. . . . Mr. Davinport, to whom I cannot write for the present, but have sent him by these ships a smal Packet directed to his name with a Book or two of the Bohemian Ch-Government, & some Prophetical Papers. . . . . Some weekes agoe I sent you the Systeme of Saturne with all the Cuts, being Mr. Brereton's gift . . . . Hevelii Selenographia in fol. with excellent Cuts is no more to bee had . . . . Mr. Morian promised to send mee for you all the Glauberian Tracts with some other w[ch] are counted truer Adepts.[96]

In the same letter in which he urged John Winthrop, Jr., to write a "philosophical letter" to the Royal Society,[97] Henry Oldenburg, Secretary of the Society, wrote,

The Bearer hereof will doubtlesse give you the use of y[e] printed

[93] Winthrop Papers, ii. 504.   For Mr. Hartlib see p. 70, below.
[94] Massachusetts Historical Society, Collections, 3rd Series, x. 36.
[95] *Ibid.*, p. 38.
[96] Massachusetts Historical Society, Proceedings, 1st Series, xvi. 212.   It should be noted that this one letter mentions three different people as sending books to New England.
[97] See p. 72, below.

History of y[e] R. Society;[98] by w[ch] you will find what progres they have made hitherto . . . . I presume to transmit you some of the Transactions I monthly publish.[99]

He wrote again in 1669,

My letter, recommended to y[e] s[d] Stuyvesand [Peter] for you, was accompanied wth an Exemplar of the History of y[e] R. Society, and wth some of the Philosophicall Transactions. . . . . I send you herew[th] a Printed paper, w[ch] contains y[e] predictions of M[r] Bond for the variations of y[e] Needle for several years to come . . . you will take notice . . . how the variation varies in New England.[100]

John Eliot wrote in 1670 to Robert Boyle of "that worthy gift, which your honour is pleased to bestow upon me, viz. Pool's Synopsis, or Critica Sacra."[101] Presumably these are but chance records saved and indicate what must have been a general custom.

Books constantly came in with visitors or settlers from England, sometimes against the will of the government of the Colony. Upon the introduction of certain Quaker books, the General Court voted, August 22, 1654:

It is ordred, that all & euery the inhabitants of this jurisdiction that haue any of the bookes in their custody that haue lately bin brought out of England vnder the names of John Reeues & Lodowick Muggleton . . . . & shall not bring or send in all such bookes now in their custody, to the next magist[r], shall forfeit the sume of ten pounds for euery such booke that shalbe found. . . . [102]

William Baker, brought before the Middlesex Court in 1657, denied the possession of any Quaker books, saying that he disliked those which he had seen and had burned

[98] By Bishop Sprat.

[99] Massachusetts Historical Society, Proceedings, 1st Series, xvi. 230. Dated October 13, 1667.

[100] Ibid., p. 239.   Received May 6, 1669.

[101] Massachusetts Historical Society, Collections, 1st Series, iii. 177.

[102] Massachusetts Records, iii. 356.

them.[103]   In 1662 action was brought against Captain Robert Lord for bringing in Ann Coleman of the "cursed sect," who "came furnished wth many blasphemous & hæretticall bookes, which she had spread abroad."[104]

Reference to the wills and inventories of the time (some of which have already been quoted) shows not only the presence of many collections of books, large and small (chiefly the latter), but a keen appreciation of their value. Edward Tench, of New Haven, died in 1640, leaving a library of 53 volumes, appraised at £12.10.00 out of a total estate of £400.[105] John Tey, in 1641, ordered his books to be kept for his son in the hands of "Mr. Eliote, Teacher of Roxburye."[106] John Oliver, the same year, mentioned among his possessions books and geometrical instruments.[107]   In 1644 Israel Stoughton willed

to sonne *Israel* one fourth part of smale Library, & vnto *John* another fourth pt, & unto W^m the other halfe, for his incouragm[t] to apply himself to studies . . . . Provided also, concerning the Bookes, that my wife retaine to her vse during life what she pleaseth, & that my daughters chose each of them one for theire owne, that all may haue something they may call theire ffathers.[108]

George Phillips, minister of the church at Watertown, died July 1, 1644, leaving a "study of bookes" valued at £71.9.9.[109] William Brinsmade, in 1647, left to his son all his books.[110] In the same year Thomas Hooker left books appraised at £300.[111] John Cotton's will, dated November 9, 1652, states,

[103] Middlesex Court Records, i. 145. Quoted in Duniway, Freedom of the Press, p. 37 note.
[104] Massachusetts Records, iv. part 2, 55. Duniway, Freedom of the Press, p. 37 note.
[105] Proceedings of the American Antiquarian Society, xviii. 137.
[106] New England Historical and Genealogical Register, ii. 105.
[107] *Ibid.*, iii. 266.
[108] *Ibid.*, iv. 51.
[109] Mullinger, The University of Cambridge, iii. 176 note 3.
[110] New England Historical and Genealogical Register, iii. 266, 267.
[111] Palfrey, History of New England, ii. 45.

My books I estimate to y[e] value of 150 l. (though they cost me much more) and because they are of vse only to my two sonnes, *Seaborne & John*, therefore I giue them unto them both, to be devided by equal portions.[112]

John Ward wrote in his will, December 28, 1652,

My bookes I doe give to Thomas Andrews of Ipswich, and allso my chirurgery chest and all that is now in it.[113]

John Lothrop, of Barnstable, who died August 10, 1653, left his books to his children, in order of age, as they might choose, the rest to "bee sold to any honest man whoe can tell how to make use of them."[114]   Books were mentioned in the will of Thomas Rucke, Jr., about 1653.[115]   Daniel Maud, of Dover, N. H., wrote in his will, January 17, 1654,

what few books I have I leave [to my successor] for the use and benefit of such a one as may be fit to have improvement, especially of those in the Hebrew tongue; but in case such a one be not had, to let them go to som of the next congregation as York or Hampton: except one boke titled "Dei [illegible] w[ch] I woul have left for Cambridge library, and my little Hebrew bible for Mr. *Brock*.[116]

In the inventory of the estate of Nathaniel Rogers, pastor at Ipswich, taken August 16, 1655, books were listed at £100 out of a total estate of £1497.[117]   Peter Bulkeley bequeathed the following books, April 14, 1658:[118]

to Sonne John,   Mr. Cartwright upon the Rhemish testament
                . & Willets Sinopsis
to Sonne Joseph, Mr. Hildersham upon the one & fiftieth psalme
                  History of the Councell of Trent in English
                  Cornelius Tacitry [!] in English
                  Mr. Bolton on Gen. 6

[112] New England Historical and Genealogical Register, v. 240.
[113] *Ibid.*, xxii. 32.
[114] *Ibid.*, v. 260.
[115] *Ibid.*, v. 295.
[116] New England Historical and Genealogical Register, v. 241.
[117] Records and Files of the Quarterly Courts of Essex County, iii. 232.
[118] New England Historical and Genealogical Register, x. 167.

[to others]   Dr. Twisse against the Arminians
                   Mr. Rutherfords treatise upon the woman of
                   Canaan
                   Mr. Rutherfords upon the dying of Christ
                   Rutherford upon John 12
                   Mr. Cooper on the 8th chapter to the Romans
                   Mr. Dike on Jeremiah 17th
to Sonne Edward, All Piscators Commentaries on the bible
                   Dr. Willett on Exod. & Levitt. on Sam. 1. 2. &
                   on Daniell
                   Tarnovius in 2 vollūms upon prophetas minores
                   Dr. Owen, against the Arminians . . . .
                   One part of the English anotations upon the
                   bible, the other part to be to my Son Gershom
                   Mr. Aynsworth notes upon the 5 books of Moses
                   & upon the psalmes.

Bulkeley's library was appraised at £123.[119] In 1658 Ralph
Partridge left a collection of 420 volumes valued in his
inventory at £32.09.00.[120] The library of John Norton, according to the inventory of April 24, 1663, contained 159
books in folio, valued at £187.19, and 570 smaller books
valued at £112.1, or a total value of £300.[121] The same year
Samuel Stone left books valued at £127.[122] John Wilson, in
1667, wrote in his will,

   To my son, *John Wilson*, I give all my old Bookes and my new
Bookes lately bought of *Mr. Usher* or of any others in New England.[123]

[119] Proceedings of the American Antiquarian Society, xviii. 140.
[120] *Ibid.*, p. 141.
[121] New England Historical and Genealogical Register, xi. 344.
[122] Palfrey, History of New England, ii. 45.
[123] New England Historical and Genealogical Register, xvii. 343. Other wills
might be quoted in this connection, from Edward Holyoke's, 1658, referring to
a considerable library, "As for my books and wrightings, I giue my sonn *Holyoke*
all the books that are at Linn . . . . and the bookes I haue in my study that
are *Mr Beanghans* works I giue him . . . . and my dixinary . . . . and A
part of the New testament in Folio, with wast paper betwin euery leafe, and the
greate mapps of geneolagy," (*Ibid.*, ix. 345), to such as John Coggan's careful
bestowal of his single book: "My booke of Martires I giue vnto my sonne *Caleb*,
my dau. *Robinson* & my dau. *Rocke*, the Longest Liuer of them, to enjoy the

The library of John Davenport was inventoried in 1670 at
£233.[124]

One excellent indication of the kind of library to be found
in the colonies toward the end of this period is given in a
manuscript list of his books made out by Increase Mather
in 1664, from which the following titles are selected:[125]

Milton	Defence of Smectymnuus
Milton	defensio Populi Anglicani
Fuller	Lives of Fathers
Fuller	Lives of Englands Worthyes
Herbert	Poems[126]
Camden	[No title given; probably Britannia]
Camden	Remaynes
Verulamus	de Augmentis scientiarum
Februn [?]	Body of Chymistry
Alstedii	encyclopædia
Child	History of Waldenses
Prideux	Introduction to History
de Laet	America descriptio
Sands	his Traveles
Purchases	Pilgrimage
. . . . .	Rerum Anglicarum Scriptores post Bedam
Bacon	Natural History
Howes	History of England
Mortons	History of New England
Raleigh	The Prerogative of Parliaments
Burtons	Pryns and Bastwicks Trial
. . . . .	Sr. H. V[ane's] Trial

same wholly"—in the meantime they were to divide it as they best could. (*Ibid.*,
ix. 36). Many wills simply mention books, from which no deductions as to size
can be made; but the almost general reference to books in the wills emphasizes
the reverence in which they were held.

[124] Palfrey, History of New England, ii. 45.

[125] Proceedings of the American Antiquarian Society, xx. 280.

[126] In the New England Historical and Genealogical Register, xxvii. 347, A. E.
Cutler records his ownership of the third edition of Herbert's "Priest to the Temple;
or, the Country Parson," London, 1675, which contains the dated Latin autograph
of Increase Mather: Crescentius Matherus, 1683. This cannot be the same volume
as the one in the 1664 list; evidently he had two volumes of Herbert's poems in
1683, or had given away the earlier one.

. . . . .	Against Actors showing of stage plays
Josephus	His works
⎰ Juvenal et	cum Lvbini Commentar.
⎱ Persius	
Plautus	
Senecæ	Tragæd.
Sophocles	Tragæd.
Poetæ Minores	
Demosthenes	Orat.
Horatius	
Ovidii	Amorum Libri
Æsopi	Fabulæ
Lucani	dialog.
Grotius	de imperio Majestatis
Verstegan	English Antiquities

Another interesting list of books is that given in the inventory of the estate of Thomas Grocer, "stranger," who died in Roxbury February 2, 1665. Grocer was a London trader who had dealt with Barbados. The books may have been his private library but were more likely brought as a venture, even though the lack of duplicates among the item-ized books might seem to support the first theory. The books mentioned by title number 202; 384 books of various sizes are given as a single item, with a value of £28.16.00, and similarly "120 sticht bookes" are valued at £1. Among the titles given the following are of interest:[127]

> Burtons Melancholy
> Journey of Fraunce
> a Booke of Jests
> Character of King Charles
> 4 uolumes of poems *at* 4s.
> Mountignes Assayes
> Purchase right ordering of the Bees
> Bancrofts epigrammes
> Lilly anatomye of witt
> Golden remaines

[127] Ford, The Boston Book Market, p. 71 ff.

Epicures Morals
greens farewell to Follye
Relation of a Uoyage to Guiana
9 paper Bookes of Manuscripts
Heywood [The Hierarchie] of Angells
German Dyet
Treatise of Fruit trees

It is impossible to prove that the colonists had as large libraries as their contemporaries in England, or as they themselves would have had if they had remained in England; but the evidence given above would seem to show that the early settlers did not suffer for books, either old or new, since the good libraries they brought with them were constantly increased by importations. Furthermore, the comparative nearness of the various settlements made it possible for the colonists to increase their range of reading by borrowing, or to assist their friends by lending. Such libraries as that of John Winthrop, Jr., were almost circulating libraries. The following extracts from colonial letters are characteristic.

I vmblie pray you that when you haue perused the followinge treatise, that you will restore it to mee againe.[128]

Lent to M.ʳ Williams, 18. 8, my blew manuscr̃., my relac̃on, the brevᵗ of Cambridge, Nath. Wiggins Reasons, & the printed relation of the Martyrs.[129]

I have therefore bene bold to send you the Medulla and the Magnalia Dei.[130]

By this bearer . . . . I received your booke, & had by the same returned it, but that I desire to reade it ouer once more, finding it pleasant & profitable, & craue the sight of any other of that subiect at your leisure, kindly thancking you for this inclosed.[131]

---

[128] John Blackleach to John Winthrop, 1637. Winthrop Papers, ii. 149.

[129] Thomas Lechford, Note-Book, p. 4. 1638. Mr. Williams is probably **Roger** Williams. The numbers give the date, October 18th.

[130] Roger Williams to John Winthrop, Jr., 1645. Massachusetts Historical Society, Collections, 3rd Series, ix. 268.

[131] Roger Williams to John Winthrop, Jr., 1649. Winthrop Papers, i. 267.

He [Mr. Caukin] tells me of a booke lately come ouer in Mr. Pynchon's name, wherein is some derogation to the blood of Christ. The booke was therefore burnt in the Market place at Boston, & Mr. Pynchon to be cited to the Court. If it come to your hand, I may hope to see it.[132]

Dr. Choyse hath none of the bookes mentioned in your note.[133]

I pray you to read & returne this Jew. I haue allso an answere to him by a good plaine man, expounding all which the Jew takes literally, in a spirituall way: & I haue (in a discourse of a Knight (L'Estrange) proving Americans no Jewes) another touch against him . . . . [134]

My deere Frend,—I had yours, and truly doe loue you hartily, though I haue bin some tymes troubled at my busines having no returnes, & you selling my house for 20*l*, & lending out my bookes & things & sending home nothing to mee.[135]

I send you, by this bearer, such books of Intelligence, as were sent me.[136]

I would now (with very many thanks) have returned you youre Jesuits maxims but I was loath to trust them in so wild a hand, nor some tidings which I have from England.[137]

Deare S[r],—I have herewith sent you two of a sort of those bookes I promised you; to the intent you may reserve one by you, and yet pleasure your freinds either by loane or gifte with the other. I have also sent you the dementions of a furnace hearth. But I can not at present find the booke it is in, it being packed away in some trunke amongst other things. I shall mynd it, and send it to you by the first opportunity . . . . [138]

[132] Roger Williams to John Winthrop, Jr., 1650. *Ibid.*, i. 285.

[133] John Davenport to John Winthrop, Jr., evidently in reply to a request for certain books. 1654. *Ibid.*, ii. 488.

[134] Roger Williams to John Winthrop, Jr., 1654–5. *Ibid.*, i. 291.

[135] From Hugh Peter, then living in England, to Charles Gott, deacon of Salem, evidently his agent. This library was circulating too freely to satisfy its owner! 1654. Winthrop Papers, i. 116.

[136] John Davenport to John Winthrop, Jr., 1654–5. Massachusetts Historical Society, Collections, 3rd Series, x. 7.

[137] Roger Williams to John Winthrop, Jr., 1655–6. *Ibid.*, p. 11. The "wild hand" indicates that an Indian was the bearer.

[138] Richard Leader of Piscataway to John Winthrop, Jr., 1655. Massachusetts Historical Society, Proceedings, 2d Series, iii. 192.

Sir) I thanck you for the 2 bookes you sent me to peruse, which I am reading dilligently.[139]

I am much obliged vnto your Worshipp that at last you were myndfull of me, & sent the boke soe much desyred by goodman Staythrop, by which I haue gott much satisfaction.[140]

More workes of the same, I would gladly see . . . . I pray you parte not with my booke.[141]

. . . . many thancks for . . . . the Almanack, which I had not seene before, though, since my receite of yours, the president of the Colledge sent me one.[142]

The booke concerning bees, which you desired, I now send you, by John Palmer, & with it 3 others, viz., 1. An Office of Address, 2. An Invention of Engines of Motion, 3. A Discourse for divisions & setting out of Landes. . . . . I shall add unto them a 4th booke in 8°, called Chymical, Medicinal, & Chirurgical Addresses. These are a few of many more which are sent to me. I hoped for an opportunity of shewing them to you here, & shall reserve them for you til a good opportunity.[143]

Sir, I humbly thanck you for the Intelligence I received in your letters, and for the 2 weekly Intelligences, which Brother Myles brought me.[144]

I shall send the an answer to John Nortons booke . . . . if I cann procuer it.[145]

I make bold wth you to transmitt by your hand to Colonell Temple those books [*illegible*] wch you will receive heerw[th] (want of fitt artists heere must be my excuse that they appeare in that dessolate forme); they were sent me before winter, from the great intelligence of Europe, Mr Samuell Hartleb, a Germã

[139] John Davenport to John Winthrop, Jr., 1655. Massachusetts Historical Society, Collections, 3rd Series, x. 14.
[140] Jonathan Brewster to John Winthrop, Jr., 1656. Winthrop Papers, ii. 72. The book referred to is one on alchemy.
[141] Jonathan Brewster to John Winthrop, Jr., 1656. *Ibid.*, ii. 78, 81.
[142] John Davenport to John Winthrop, Jr., 1659. Massachusetts Historical Society, Collections, 3rd Series, x. 23.
[143] John Davenport to John Winthrop, Jr., 1659. Winthrop Papers, ii. 509.
[144] John Davenport to John Winthrop, Jr., 1660. Massachusetts Historical Society, Collections, 3rd Series, x. 36. The *Intelligence* is probably the *London Intelligencer.*
[145] William Coddington to John Winthrop, Jr., 1660. Winthrop Papers, ii. 287.

gentlemã, as conteinig something of novelty. That they are yet in sheets may have this convenience, that, being divers distinct relations, the Govern[r], Mr Wilson, & Mr Norton (if there be any thing worth their notice), or any other friends he please, may have the pvsall of some p̃ts [*illegible*] whiles the other parts are reading.[146]

I humbly thank your Worship for your last present, viz[t] those printed papers of Intelligence referring to the philosophical transactions of the Royall Society of the Virtuosi: I did according to your order to me acquaint M[r] Danforth of Roxbury and others with them; the communication thereof renders us all, but especially myself greatly indebted unto your Honour.[147]

In connection with this, mention must be made of the list in his own handwriting of 90 books borrowed by Richard Mather from John Johnson and William Parks of "Rocksbury," January 10, 1647–8. These are all theological except "Seneca his works."[148]

Additional information in regard to books owned or read by the early settlers may be gained from a study of their references to or quotations from books. Ezekiel Rogers, in his epitaph on Thomas Hooker, written about 1647, wrote the following:[149]

> America, although she do not boast
> Of all the *gold* and *silver* from that coast,
> *Lent* to her sister Europe's need or pride;
> (For that repaid her, with much gain beside,
> In one *rich pearl*, which Heaven did thence afford,
> As pious Herbert gave his honest word;) . . . .

The reference is evidently to the passage in Herbert's

---

[146] John Winthrop, Jr., to Thomas Lake, 1661. *Ibid.*, iv. 73.

[147] Thomas Shepard to John Winthrop, Jr., 1669. Massachusetts Historical Society, Collections, 3rd Series, x. 71.

[148] Massachusetts Historical Society, Collections, 4th Series, viii. 76. Johnson and Parks were both laymen, and yet had libraries of theological books, at least, from which as prominent a minister as Richard Mather found it worth while to borrow books in considerable numbers! See p. 45, above.

[149] Magnalia, i. 351.

"Church Militant" beginning at line 235, which refers to the Puritan movement toward America.[150]

Governor Bradford, in his polemical writings, quotes authorities freely, and sometimes cites authors or volumes which are not mentioned in the extant lists of his own library or any contemporary Plymouth library. Such names may furnish a clue to the identity of some of the uncatalogued books in his library. The following are quoted, some more than once.

[Whittingham?]	A Brieff discours off the troubles begonne at Frankford . . . . 1554.[151]
Baylie, R.	A Dissuasive from the Errors of the Time, 1645.
Cotton,	Answer to Mr. Baylie
Eusebius,	Ecclesiastical History
Fulke,	On Romans the xi.
Robinson, J.,	Apology
Robinson, J.,	A Justification of Separation
Speed,	Cloud of Witnesses
Taylor,	The Liberty of Prophesying, 1647.[152]
Anderton, L.,	The Triple Cord, or a Treatise proving the Truth of the Roman Religion, 1633.
Bale, John,	Acts of English Votaries
Barnes, R.,	On the Keyes
Beza,	Confessions
Bullinger,	Not stated
Burton, H.,	A Vindication of Churches commonly called Independent, 1644
Calvin,	Not stated
. . . . .	Centuries of Madgeburg
Fox,	Abridgment of Acts and Monuments
Gillespie, G.,	Aaron's Rod Blossoming, 1646
Grosthead, R.,	Not stated

[150] See p. 137, below.

[151] Quoted in the Introduction to the Ecclesiastical History of the Church at Plymouth.

[152] The references in this group are quoted in "A Dialogue, or the sum of a Conference between some Young Men born in New England and sundry ancient men that came out of Holland and Old England, Anno Domini 1648."

Gualter, R.	On Acts
Guicciardini,	History of the Wars of Italy
[?]	An Harmony of the Confessions of Faith, 1643
Jacob, H.,	Attestation
Jewell, J.,	Not stated
Mantuanus,	Quotes poetry
Peter Martyr,	Commonplaces
Mornay, Philip,	Mysterie of Iniquity
Mornay, Philip,	Fowre Books of the Institutions
Pareus,	Commentary on Revelation, 1644
[?]	The Reasons presented by the Dissenting Brethren against certain Propositions, 1648
Serres, J.,	Generall Historie of France, 1624 [English edition]
Socrates,	Church History
Symson, P.,	Historie of the Church
Tindall, W.,	Not stated
Vives, Lud.,	Edition of Augustine's De Civitate Dei
Whetenhall,	Discourse on the Abuses in the Church of Rome
Whitgift,	An Answere to a certain Libell
Whittaker,	Not stated
Willett, A.,	Commentary on Jude.[153]

Richard Mather quoted the following:[154]

Bullinger,	Decad. 5, Serm. 9.
Ames,	Cases of Conscience, 1. 4, C. 28. Q. 1.
Alsted,	Encyclopædia, p. 25
Alsted,	de Casibus, c. 8. reg. 3, memb. 12
Calvin,	Institutions, (Several)
Martin,	Loci Communes, Clas. 4, c. ii. Q. 14

[153] References in this group are quoted in "A Dialogue or 3d Conference, between some yonge-men borne in New-England; and some Ancient-men, which came out of Holand and Old England concerning the church." This was probably written in 1652. It is noticeable that many of these books, the dates of which I have added in the list, were published after the Pilgrims came to America, and that some were used by Bradford within a year or two of the time of publication. It is evident that even in Plymouth, which had no bookseller, and was in general far behind Boston in culture, books fresh from the press were not unknown. See pp. 25 and 26, above.

[154] Mather Papers, p. 74.

Musculus,	Loci Communes, de Cœna
Mead,	Inst. Loc.
Pareus,	On 2 Corinthians, 11: 26
Zepper,	de Polit. Eccles. L. 1, c. 14

Anne Bradstreet in her poems referred to various writers:

> To whom the old *Berosus*[155] (so much fam'd)
> His Book of Assurs monarchs dedicates.

> No *Phoenix* pen, nor *Spencers* poetry,
> Nor *Speed's* nor *Cambden's* learned History[156]

> If *Curtius* be true in his report[157]

> He that at large would satisfie his mind,
> In *Plutarch's* Lives his history may find.[158]

> Which makes me now with *Sylvester* confess,
> But *Sidney's* Muse can sing his worthiness.[159]

References to DuBartas, author of the "Divine Week," and to Sylvester, who turned DuBartas' poems into English, are frequent in her poems, one of which is "In Honour of DuBartas." According to J. H. Ellis, who edited her poems, much of her historical material was taken from Raleigh's "History of the World"; his evidence is satisfactory.[160]

Nathaniel Morton, in his "New England's Memorial," occasionally drew upon history for illustrations, giving in each case his authority and generally the page reference. Authors cited include Carion, Languet, Peter Martyr, Pliny, Purchas, and Socrates.

[155] The Works of Anne Bradstreet in Prose and Verse, edited by J. H. Ellis, p. 317. Berosus, a Babylonian historian of about 260 B. C., was probably met by Mrs. Bradstreet in the pages of Raleigh's History.

[156] *Ibid.*, p. 358. Camden's Annales Rerum Anglicarum . . . . Regnante Elizabetha was published in 1615. English versions appeared in 1625 and 1635. Speed's History of Great Britain was published in 1623.

[157] *Ibid.*, pp. 257, 265. Quintus Curtius, Roman Historian.

[158] *Ibid.*, p. 297.

[159] *Ibid.*, p. 349. In An Elegie upon that Honourable and renowned Knight, Sir Philip Sidney, she has much to say of his work as a poet.

[160] *Ibid.*, pp. xlvii–xlix.

It would seem, then, from the foregoing evidence, that, as the colonists brought with them many good libraries, constantly added new books, and supplemented their own libraries by borrowing freely from their neighbors near and remote, they were not without the means of culture and had access to a moderate amount of real literature. It must be remembered that we possess only fragmentary records of private life in the colonies; more comprehensive records would almost certainly give added proof of the possession of books and libraries. It seems fair to assume that, although the colonists were at a disadvantage in this respect compared with their English contemporaries who lived in or near London or either university, they were under no greater handicap than if they had been living in some remote place in the north or west of England.

Chapter III: Intercourse with England and English Literary Men.

IT is a mistake to think of New England colonists as practically cut off from the outside world, dwellers in a lonely desert place. Our popular histories have created this impression by their over-emphasis on the dramatic elements of the hardships of the first years of settlement, especially at Plymouth. The settlers of Plymouth had few friends in England and were, perhaps, isolated from the world until the Massachusetts Bay settlements were established. The latter, however, were always in close touch with England. John Josselyn, coming to Boston in 1638, presented his "respects to Mr. *Winthorpe* [*sic*] the Governour, and to Mr. *Cotton* the Teacher of *Boston* Church, to whom I delivered from Mr. *Francis Quarles* the poet, the Translation of the 16, 25, 51, 88, 113, and 137. Psalms into *English* Meeter, for his approbation."[1] Mention has already been made of early graduates of Harvard who returned to England to engage in public life there.[2] Twenty-seven of the ministers who came to the colony in the early years returned to England, some of whom became colonists again at the Restoration.[3] Business trips to England were such ordinary affairs as to call for no comment; in all of my reading I have found no reference to them either as difficult or as unusual.[4] The colonists thought of themselves as Englishmen, further

[1] Josselyn, Two Voyages to New England, p. 20. The last phrase is interesting.
[2] See p. 18, above. Others not Harvard men also returned to active life in England, such as Giles Firmin, who, born in England, accompanied his father to New England, was educated and married here, but later returned to England to spend his life. Such people were a bond between the old and the new.
[3] Magnalia, i. 588.
[4] John Wilson went to England in 1631 and again in 1635. (Winthrop's Journal, i. 80, 145.) Edward Winslow went to England in 1635 as agent for Plymouth,

away from London, the heart of England, than if they had
stayed in Old England, but still living in a part of England,
New England.   Edward Johnson, in his "Wonder-Working
Providence," used the phrase "our Countreymen" to refer to
people in England,[5] and seemed eager to have his readers
think of himself and his colonial neighbors as interested
essentially in the welfare of England.[6]   The affection felt
by New England for Old England is also shown in Anne
Bradstreet's poem, "A Dialogue between Old England, and
New England," and by a statement of John Dunton in one of
his letters.   He spoke of his own love for England, adding,
"And 'twas thus with the first Planters of this Country,
who were, even to their 80th year, still pleasing themselves
with hopes of their Returning to England."[7]

During the period of the Commonwealth they felt perhaps even more strongly their ties to the mother country,
for their friends, and in many cases their neighbors or
members of their families, were taking an active part in
English affairs.   Dr. Palfrey writes,

Hugh Peter and Thomas Welde, sent over by Massachusetts to
look after its affairs, both rose to influence with Cromwell, and

and in 1646 as agent for Massachusetts. (Magnalia, i. 115.) William Hibbens
of Boston accompanied Hugh Peter and Thomas Welde to England in 1641,
returning the next year alone. (Winthrop's Journal, ii. 32, 71.) In 1646 Samuel
Gorton and two of his followers went to England to complain of their persecutions
at the hands of the Massachusetts authorities. (Ibid., ii. 282.) John Wheelwright
visited England during the Protectorate and was well received by his old friend
the Protector. (Ibid., i. 197 note.) John Winthrop, Jr., made three trips to
England; his brother Stephen also made repeated visits to the mother country.
(Winthrop Papers, iv. 199 note.) Daniel Gookin went to England in 1650, 1654,
and 1657. (Gookin, Life of Daniel Gookin, p. 81 ff.). Henry Wolcott of Windsor,
Connecticut, crossed the ocean for business in 1654, 1663, and about 1671. (Wolcott, Memorial of Henry Wolcott, pp. 36–38.)

[5] "the learned labours of this Souldier of Christ [John Norton] are obvious to
our Countreymen." (p. 103.)   "Many pamphlets have come from our Countreymen of late, to this purpose." (p. 173.)

[6] "for Englands sake they are going from England to pray without ceasing for
England.   O England! thou shalt finde New England prayers prevailing with
their God for thee." (p. 53.)

[7] Letters, p. 62.

the former, as his chaplain, walked by the Protector's Secretary, John Milton, at his funeral.[8]

Hugh Peter married Mrs. Reade, the mother of the wife of John Winthrop, Jr.;[9] her first husband, Edmund Reade, had been a colonel in the parliamentary army.[10]   Stephen Winthrop, brother of John Winthrop, Jr., and Fitz-John, the latter's son, both served in that army.   Stephen Winthrop, on a visit to England in 1646, accepted a commission in the Parliamentary army.   He rose rapidly to the rank of colonel.   Roger Williams, writing from England to John Winthrop, Jr., in 1656, mentioned the fact that "Your brother Stephen succeeds Major-General Harrison."   In this same year he represented Banff and Aberdeen in Parliament.   He married one sister of Colonel Rainsborough of the Parliamentary army, another becoming the fourth wife of his father, Governor Winthrop.[11]   Fitz-John Winthrop went to England in 1657, having been offered commissions by two of his uncles, Stephen Winthrop and Thomas Reade. He accepted a lieutenancy in Reade's regiment of foot, rose to a captaincy, and at one time was governor of Cardross in Scotland.[12]   Samuel Desborough, the first magistrate of Guilford, Connecticut, returned to England and became, under Cromwell, Lord Keeper of the Great Seal of Scotland.   His brother John had married Cromwell's sister Jane.[13]   John Hoadley, also of Guilford, became one of Cromwell's chaplains at Edinburgh, and afterwards chaplain to General Monck.[14]   Samuel Mather, brother of Increase, was chaplain to Thomas Andrews, Lord Mayor of

[8] History of New England, i. 586.

[9] Dictionary of National Biography; Massachusetts Historical Society, Proceedings, xlii. 169.

[10] Dictionary of National Biography.

[11] Winthrop Papers, iv. 199 note; Dictionary of National Biography.

[12] Massachusetts Historical Society, Proceedings, 2d Series, i. 118 ff.; Winthrop Papers, ii. 203; iv. 266 note.

[13] Dictionary of National Biography.

[14] Steiner, History of Guilford and Madison, p. 43.

London, and later was chosen to accompany the English Commissioners to Scotland. Still later Henry Cromwell took him as one of his chaplains on his Irish expedition.[15] Francis Higginson, second son of the Reverend Francis Higginson of Salem, studied at Leyden, conformed to the Church of England, and spent his life as a vicar in Westmoreland.[16] The two sons of Governor John Haynes by his first wife had stayed in England when he emigrated; both are said to have drawn "their swords in the great Civil War,—the elder for the King, the younger for the Parliament."[17] John Haynes, Jr., son of Governor Haynes by his second wife, after graduating from Harvard in 1656, went to England in 1657 with Fitz-John Winthrop. Instead of going into the army, he went to Cambridge, where he took the Master's degree in 1660. He remained in England and, having conformed, spent his life as rector of the Church of England in Suffolk and Essex.[18]

Several others returned to enter the Parliamentary army. Major Robert Sedgwick of Charlestown rose to the rank of Major-General, and was employed by Cromwell in the expedition against the West Indies, succeeding General Fortescue as Governor of Jamaica.[19] Captain George Cook, who had been active in the Massachusetts militia, became a colonel in Cromwell's army.[20] Israel Stoughton, whose son William was lieutenant-governor under William and Mary, became a lieutenant-colonel among the Ironsides.[21] Captain John Mason, hero of the Mystic fight, was urged by Sir Thomas Fairfax, his old comrade in arms, to join the army of Parliament, but he did not return to England.[22]

[15] Massachusetts Historical Society, Collections, 1st Series, x. 26 note.
[16] Dictionary of National Biography. See p. 153, below.
[17] Massachusetts Historical Society, Proceedings, 2d Series, i. 118.
[18] *Ibid.*, i. 118 ff.
[19] John Hull's Public Diary, p. 174 note.
[20] Winthrop's Journal, ii. 140 note.
[21] *Ibid.*, i. 147 note.
[22] *Ibid.*, i. 218 note.

John Collins, Harvard 1649, was a chaplain in Monck's army;[23] and William Hooke, of New Haven, was one of Cromwell's chaplains, his wife, a sister of General Whalley, being a cousin of the Protector.[24]   He was also probably Master of the Savoy.[25]   Edward Hopkins, of New Haven, was active in public life during Cromwell's régime.[26]   Edward Winslow, having gone to England as agent of Massachusetts in 1646, remained in England and later became one of the Grand Commissioners of Cromwell's expedition against Hispaniola.[27]   Daniel Gookin, on his third visit to England, served for a time (1658–1659) as collector of customs at Dunkirk, being appointed later Deputy Treasurer of War there.   He was acquainted with Cromwell, and it was through him that Cromwell gave his invitation to the New Englanders to remove to the balmier climate of Jamaica.   On his return to Boston in 1660 he was accompanied by Goffe and Whalley, the regicides.[28]

Mention has already been made of the friendship between John Winthrop, Jr., and Sir Kenelme Digby.[29]   There are several references to this in letters to Winthrop from William Hooke, then in London.   He wrote, April 13, 1657, "For Sir Kenelme Digby is in France, and when he will return I hear not.[30]   Again, April 16, 1658, "Sir Kenelme Digby is not, as yet, returned, & therefore I can give you no account of him."[31]   And again, March 30, 1659, "As for Sir Kenelme Digby, I have not heard of him a long time.   He is not (for ought I heare) in England.   He is a greate schollar, but I

[23] John Hull's Diary, p. 159 note 3.
[24] Dictionary of National Biography.
[25] *Cf.* Massachusetts Historical Society, Proceedings, xli. 304.
[26] Winthrop's Journal, i. 223 note.   He was successively First Warden of the Fleet and a Commissioner of the army and navy.
[27] Magnalia, i. 115.
[28] Gookin, Life of Daniel Gookin, *passim.*   Tyler, History of American Literature, i. 152.
[29] See pp. 41 and 42, above.
[30] Massachusetts Historical Society, Collections, 3rd Series, i. 183.
[31] Winthrop Papers, ii. 588.

heare no good of him by any."[32] One letter from Sir Kenelme himself gives further evidence of a friendship which would seem to have been close, to judge both by the eagerness with which Winthrop was making inquiry for Sir Kenelme through his London correspondent, and by Sir Kenelme's evident desire to serve Winthrop. The opening sentences refer to his second gift to the Harvard Library.

Paris 26. Jan. 1656. new stile.

. . . . I beseech you present my most humble thankes to the President and fellowes of yʳ college for the obliging Letter they haue bin pleased to send me. So small a present as j presumed to make them, deserued not so large a returne. . . . . I haue searched all Paris for Blaise Viginere des Chiffres. I had it in my library in England: But att the plundering of my house, j lost it wᵗʰ many other good bookes. I haue layed out in all places for it: and when j gett it, it shall be for you by the first conueniency of sending it to you.[33]

John Winthrop, F. R. S., grandson of John Winthrop, Jr., in a letter to Cotton Mather written in 1718, referred as follows to this friendship:

The famous & learned Sʳ Kenelme Digby (then at Paris) earnestly solicited my honʳᵈ granfather to returne back to England, urging that America was too scanty for so great a philosopher to stay long in. My good ancestor modestly answered, '*Res angusta domi*, my duty to a numerous family, will not permitt it.'[34]

Hugh Peter would seem to have been acquainted with Sir Kenelme also, for it is he who first sent word to Winthrop that the knight was sending a great chest of books to Harvard.[35]

Cromwell had a college mate in the colonies, John Wheelwright, B. A. of Sidney Sussex in 1614, and M. A. in 1618. Of him he later said,

[32] *Ibid.*, ii. 593.
[33] Massachusetts Historical Society, Collections, 3rd Series, x. 15.
[34] Winthrop Papers, vi. 384 note.
[35] *Ibid.*, i. 116. See p. 41 note 68, above.

I remember the time when I was more afraid of meeting Wheelwright at foot-ball, than I have been since of meeting an army in the field, for I was infallibly sure of being tripped up by him.[36]

Cromwell was also well acquainted with John Cotton, if we may judge from the friendly tone of a letter which has been preserved.[37] John Oxenbridge was another colonial friend of Cromwell, and of Milton and Marvell as well.[38] If conditions in England had differed upon one occasion, Cromwell himself would have come to New England. He told Lord Falkland in 1641 that if the Remonstrance had not passed, "he would have sold all he had the next morning, and never have seen England more."[39] Cotton Mather mentions Cromwell, with "Mr. Hambden, and Sir Arthur Haselrig," among those who were forcibly detained from coming.[40] This legend lacks satisfactory proof; in fact, at the time they were supposed to have been stopped, Hampden was in the midst of his legal contest against the shipmoney, and it is hardly believable that he would have deserted in the heat of the fight. But that it was believed by the next generation and has been accepted quite generally ever since gives evidence of its truth in probability, if not in fact. New England did not seem far away to those who desired asylum from political oppression in England; nor, as we have seen, did England seem far away, when political conditions changed, to those on this side of the water who desired a larger field for action than the colonies seemed to afford. Chance, or beliefs, or both, had much more to do with determining who came than ability. The men who

36 Memoir of John Wheelwright, p. 2.

37 New Hampshire Historical Society, Collections, i. 258.

38 Publications of the Colonial Society of Massachusetts, xii. 121. When Marvell was tutoring William Dutton, Cromwell's ward, he went to live, upon Cromwell's advice, with Oxenbridge, then a fellow at Eton. Marvell wrote the epitaph upon the first wife of Oxenbridge. Marvell's poem "Bermudas" was probably suggested by Oxenbridge, who had lived there for a time. (Dictionary of National Biography, and Poems of Andrew Marvell, Muses' Library edition.)

39 Clarendon, Rebellion, Book IV. §52.

40 Magnalia, i. 79.

settled New England, it must be remembered, were not an inferior class.

The feeling of unity between New and Old England at the time of the Commonwealth is well illustrated by the behavior of the authorities of Massachusetts in the case of the burning, in 1650, of William Pynchon's "The Meritorious Price of our Redemption." When the General Court found it to be "erronyous and hereticale," and ordered it to be burned, it was careful to issue a " Declaration" of its detestation of the heresy.

The "Declaration" was immediately sent to England to be printed and circulated there, in order that the Court might set itself right with its Christian brethren, while John Norton was entreated to answer Mr. Pynchon's book with all convenient speed, and his answer was also to be sent to England to be printed.[41]

At the Restoration New England once more became the place of refuge for exiles from England. Cotton Mather mentions fourteen ministers who came to avoid persecution at this time,[42] and refers also to "some eminent persons of a New-English *original*, which were driven back out of Europe into their own country again, by that storm."[43] Among these exiles were some who, as the highest judges of England, had tried even a king. It is interesting at this point to speculate upon the possibility that, had he been accorded harsher treatment, Milton himself might have followed the Regicides to America, in which case "Paradise Lost" would have been written in New England,—or not at all. Which is the more probable of these two possibilities will be discussed elsewhere.[44] At least he would have found friends here; Roger Williams seems to have been on intimate

[41] Duniway, Freedom of the Press in Massachusetts, p. 32.
[42] Magnalia, i. 237. The ministers are James Allen, John Bailey, Thomas Baily, Thomas Barnet, James Brown, Thomas Gilbert, James Keith, Samuel Lee, Charles Morton, Charles Nicholet, John Oxenbridge, Thomas Thornton, Thomas Walley, and William Woodrop.
[43] *Ibid.*, i. 238.
[44] See pp. 93 and 94, below.

terms with him during his visit to England from 1651 to 1654,[45] as was also the Reverend John Clarke of Newport, R. I.;[46] and Milton knew and corresponded with John Winthrop, Jr.[47] Winthrop probably became acquainted with Milton through their mutual friend, Samuel Hartlib, author of many works on agriculture and natural history, to whom Milton addressed his tract "Of Education" with every evidence of close acquaintance, and with whom Winthrop had an extensive correspondence.[48] Theodore Haak, said to have been the founder of the "London Club, or Invisible College of Natural Philosophers," from which the Royal Society developed, and Henry Oldenburg, for several years Secretary of the Royal Society, were also friends and correspondents of Winthrop, and friends of Milton.[48]

It was through these friends that Winthrop became one of the early fellows of the Royal Society, being nominated as fellow in 1662,[48] when the Society was less than two years old.[49] Winthrop's interest in science was evidently strong before he came to New England, as a reference to

[45] Williams wrote to John Winthrop, Jr., July 12, 1654, having just returned from England, "It pleased the Lord to call me for some time and with some persons to practice the Hebrew, the Greeke, Latine, French and Dutch: The Secretarie of the Councell, (M[r] Milton) for my Dutch I read him, read me many more Languages." It is probably in this way that Milton became acquainted with the Dutch Lucifer by Vondel. Williams seems to have discussed education with Milton, for he says further in this letter, "Grammar rules begin to be esteemd a Tyrannie. I taught 2 young Gentlemen a Parliament mans sons (as we teach our children English) by words phrazes and constant talke &c. I have begun with mine owne 3 boys." (Massachusetts Historical Society, Collections, 3rd Series, x.3.) See Milton's criticism of the time wasted in the study of grammar, in Of Education.

[46] Clarke lived in England from 1651 to 1663. He was also acquainted with Sir Henry Vane and the Earl of Clarendon. It was through the latter that he obtained from Charles II the remarkable Rhode Island Charter of 1663, granting religious freedom. (Early Religious Leaders of Newport, p. 16.)

[47] Philosophical Transactions of the Royal Society of London, xl. 1741. Dedication.

[48] Massachusetts Historical Society, Proceedings, 1st Series, xvi. 207. See p. 47, above.

[49] The Society was founded in 1660, and incorporated in 1662. Encyclopedia Britannica.

the titles of books sent him by his friends in England shows.[50] That theology was not the all-exclusive factor in colonial life that it is often pictured as being is shown by the fact that a busy colonial governor found the time to keep up his study of science after the experimental method newly discovered by Bacon, and was considered by English scientific men worthy to become their associate in research, and even to serve on two committees of the Royal Society in 1664.[51] His friendship with Sir Kenelme Digby may easily have resulted from their common interest in alchemy. The letter of Sir Kenelme from which quotation has already been made was largely made up of explanations and discussions of wondrous liquids, potent medicines, and especially Digby's favorite sympathetic powder.

Winthrop's correspondence with scientific and literary men in England and on the Continent was extensive. Dr. Cromwell Mortimer, Secretary of the Royal Society, in dedicating the fortieth volume of the Transactions of the Society to John Winthrop, F. R. S., grandson of John Winthrop, Jr., referred to "the great Treasure of curious Letters on various learned Subjects" written to the earlier Winthrop and then in the possession of the younger, and listed over eighty of the writers of these letters.[52]

[50] See pp. 32–34, above.

[51] Massachusetts Historical Society, Proceedings, 1st Series, xvi. 206 ff.

[52] The following names are characteristic of the list:

Earl of Anglesey	Robert Hooke
Earl of Arundel	Ch. Howard, Duke of Norfolk
Elias Ashmole	Joh. Keppler
Robert Boyle	Dr. Lovell, Oxon.
Tycho Brahe	Earl of Manchester
Lord Brounker	John Milton
Dr. Browne [probably Sir Thomas]	Sir Rob. Moray
Jo. Camden	Lord Napier
Lord Clarendon	Isaac Newton
Comenius	Dr. Pell
Charles II	Earl of Pembroke
O. Cromwell	Pet. Peregrinus, Romæ
Ernestus Coloniæ, Episc.	Alb. Peterson, Amstel.

His friends of the Royal Society expected from him valuable contributions to knowledge, and were not disappointed. Henry Oldenburg, Secretary of the Society, wrote in 1667:

SIR,—So good an opportunity as this I could not let passe w[t]hout putting you in mind of y[r] being a member of y[e] Royall Society, though you are in New-England; and that even at so great a distance you may doe that Illustrious Company great service. . . . . We know y[r] ingenuity, experience, and veracity, y[e] best qualities of a man and a Philosopher; . . . . And, since you have now been from us severall years, give us at last a visit by a Philosophicall letter.[53]

In a postscript he discussed the value of the experimental method of searching "the works of God themselves." Early in 1669 he wrote again in regard to scientific equipment in America, and requested certain experiments performed:

Giue me leaue . . . . to inquire . . . . Whether you haue any good Telescopes, to compare the Phænomena from that Coast wth the Accompts of Hevelius, Ricciolo, Cassini, etc. What advance of Harverd Coll. in y[r] Cambridge? Whether you are furnisht wth the modern books of ye most Ingenious and famous Philosophers and Mathematicians [of whom he gives a list] . . . .

I send you herew[th] a Printed paper, w[ch] contains y[e] predictions of M[r] Bond for the variations of ye Needle for several years to

Joh. Espagnet
Dr. Everard
Gal. Galileo
J. R. Glauber
Dr. Goddard
Princeps Gothar
Dr. Grew
J. B. van Helmont
J. F. Helvetius
Lord Herbert [of Cherbury?]
Hans Albrecht, Dominus Herberstein
Joh. Hevelius
Sir. Jo. Heydon
Frederick Princeps Holsatiæ et Dominus Slesvic

Conrad Roves, Dominus Rosenstein, Margrav. in Croatia
Prince Rupert
Dr. Sackville
Earl of Sandwich
J. Slegelius
Sir Rob. Southwell
Bishop Sprat
Princeps Sultsbergensis
Dr. Tanckmarus
J. Tradescant
Dr. Wilkins
Dr. Willis
Dr. Witherly
Sir Henry Wotton
Sir Christopher Wren

[53] Massachusetts Historical Society, Proceedings, 1st Series, xvi. 229, 230.

come. . . . . you will take notice . . . . how the variation
varies in New England . . . [54]

The next year Oldenburg wrote to thank Winthrop for
a collection of curiosities sent to the Society with a written
account of them:

SIR,—Y^r Kinsman, Mr. Adam Winthrop, hath acquitted himself faithfully of ye trust you had reposed in him, in delivering
into my hands both y^r letter and ye American Curiosities accompanying the same. . . . . His Maj^{ty} himselfe, hearing of some of
ye rarer things, would see y^m, and accordingly the Extraordinary
Fish, the dwarf-oaks, ye gummy fragrant Barke, wth knobbs, y^e
silken podds, ye baggs wth litle shells in them, etc., were carried
to Whitehall, ... [55]

Winthrop's account of these things was published soon
after in the Transactions of the Society, with drawings of
some of the curiosities including the "extraordinary fish,"
which was a starfish.

In a letter to Henry Oldenburg written November 12,
1668, Winthrop mentioned sending seeds, roots, and such
things to Robert Boyle, Lord Brereton, Charles Howard,
Dr. Goddard, Dr. Merret, Dr. Whistler, Dr. Benjamin
Worsley, and Dr. Keffler.[56]

John Davenport also seems to have been interested in
science, for he too was corresponding with Hartlib, receiving
from him "bookes, & written papers . . . . wherein I
finde sundry rarities of inventions. . . . . you [Winthrop]
will finde some particularities among them, which may be
advantagious to your private proffit, in the improvement of
your Fishers Island."[57] The last clause would indicate that
some of these books and papers were on Hartlib's favorite
subject, scientific farming. In another letter to Winthrop,

[54] *Ibid.*, xvi. 239, 242. The undated letter was received May 6, 1669. See p. 48,
n. 100, above.
[55] *Ibid.*, xvi. 244. Letter dated March 26, 1670.
[56] Winthrop Papers, iv. 129.
[57] *Ibid.*, ii. 504. See p. 47, above.

given on page 56, above, Davenport mentions four scientific books as "a few of many more which are sent to me." These may have been from Hartlib.

Thomas Shepard thanked Winthrop for copies of the Transactions of the Royal Society, which he had passed on to others to enjoy,[58] and in the same letter reported some astronomical observations.

Besides all these who had a true interest in science (and the list could be extended, did more data survive), Connecticut boasted one genuine alchemist. Jonathan Brewster, who was glad to borrow books on chemistry from Winthrop, and willing to lend his own in return,[59] was searching to find the true elixir. He reported to Winthrop that the latter's books had been of great service to him, enabling him to understand some operations "which before I understode not, ... as the head of the Crowe, Vergines milke, &c." With this help he felt sure that his elixir, already well started, would be perfected in five years, provided that the Indians did not burn down his house or otherwise interfere with his work.[60] If the statement of Secretary Mortimer is accurate, it was only chance which prevented the founding of a colony of experimental scientists in Connecticut, to keep Winthrop and Brewster company. He writes:[61]

In Concert with these [Boyle, Wilkins, Oldenburg] and other learned Friends, (as he often revisited *England*) he was one of those, who first form'd the Plan of the *Royal Society;* and had not the Civil Wars happily ended as they did, Mr. *Boyle* and Dr. *Wilkins*, with several other learned Men, would have left *England*, and, out of Esteem for the most excellent and valuable Governor, JOHN WINTHROP, the younger, would have retir'd to his new-born Colony, and there have establish'd that *Society for promoting Natural Knowledge*, which these Gentlemen had formed, as it were, in *Embryo* among themselves; but which after-

[58] See letter on p. 57, above.
[59] See letter on p. 56, above.
[60] Winthrop Papers, ii. 79.
[61] Philosophical Transactions of the Royal Society of London, xl. Dedication.

wards receiving the Protection of King CHARLES II. obtain'd the style of ROYAL . . . .

Robert Boyle, member of the Royal Society and at one time its president, and, with the possible exception of Sir Isaac Newton, the most representative English scientist of his day, also had considerable correspondence with the leading men of New England. This was not primarily scientific, however, but rather missionary in character, Boyle being for years Governor of the Corporation for the Spread of the Gospel in New England.[62]

There were other links between the colonists and the men in active life in England. Sir Thomas Temple, proprietor of Nova Scotia (together with Colonel William Crowne), resided here for several years during the Interregnum, acquiring property and business interests, part of which he sold in 1653 for £5500.[63] At about this time John Crowne, "Starch Johnny" Crowne (son of Colonel William), poet and dramatist of the Restoration period, was living in Boston. He resided for a time, at least, (about 1660) with the Reverend John Norton, and studied at Harvard.[64]

It would seem certain, then, that the inhabitants of New England, during the first half century of their colonization, were able, as far as they desired, to keep in touch with political, scientific, and literary men and activities in England; and that, beyond any other of England's colonies, at any time in her history, during the period of colonization, they felt a desire for these things. Their life may have been simple, or even rough; luxuries or comforts may have been lacking; but there is no evidence of any lack of intellectual eagerness or of the means to satisfy such eagerness.

[62] Dictionary of National Biography.

[63] Massachusetts Historical Society, Collections, 1st Series, vii. 229, and manuscript copy of the deed in the Ewer MSS., in the library of the New England Historical and Genealogical Society. It is Sir Thomas who is said to have told Charles II that the tree on the pine-tree shilling was the royal oak which had preserved His Majesty's life at Worcester, thereby turning away the King's anger at the colonists for daring to coin money without the King's consent.

[64] Calendar of State Papers, Colonial Series, America and West Indies. 1661–1668. No. 161, p. 54.

Chapter IV: Other Phases of Culture.

THE early settlers of New England were not only well educated and furnished with libraries, but in many cases came from families of distinction and even of title, and brought with them considerable wealth. Among those who came with John Winthrop in 1630 were Isaac Johnson and his wife, the Lady Arbella, sister to the Earl of Lincoln. These two did not live long enough to influence the life of the colony, but that they desired to come is significant. Three years later the Lady Arbella's sister, Lady Susan, and her husband, John Humfrey, joined the colonists.[1] Lady Alice Apsley Boteler, widow of Lord John Boteler and daughter of Sir Edward Apsley of Sussex, married Mr. George Fenwick just before he embarked for America, and accompanied him to Connecticut.[2] Sir Richard Saltonstall also boasted a title, and was the son of a Lord Mayor of London.[3] John Winthrop had been a magistrate and man of affairs in England, and his father, Adam Winthrop, was also a magistrate and, for a number of years, auditor of Trinity College, Cambridge.[4] Edward Johnson, town clerk of Woburn and author of "The Wonder-Working Providence," was the son of the parish clerk of St. George's, Canterbury, and possessed a considerable estate in Canterbury and elsewhere in Kent.[5] Thomas Dudley had been steward for the Earl of Lincoln and managed the large estate successfully.[6] Simon Bradstreet, Dudley's son-in-law, had succeeded him in the management of the

[1] Winthrop's Journal, i. 127.
[2] Steiner, History of Guilford and Madison, p. 22.
[3] Winthrop's Journal, i. 25 note.
[4] Diary of Adam Winthrop, in the Life and Letters of John Winthrop, i. 405 ff.
[5] Jameson, Johnson's Wonder-Working Providence, p. 5.
[6] Magnalia, i. 133.

affairs of the Earl of Lincoln, and later had been steward for the Countess of Warwick.[7] Governor William Leet of Connecticut was by education a lawyer, and by employment a register in the Bishop's court.[8] John Wilson was a grandnephew of Edmund Grindal, Archbishop of Canterbury.[9] Mrs. Anne Hutchinson was second cousin to the poet Dryden.[10] President Chauncy's wife was granddaughter of Bishop Still.[11] President Hoar married a daughter of Lord Lisle, one of the Judges of Charles I.[12] Theophilus Eaton had been employed by the King of England as envoy to the King of Denmark, and had been successful in business as a member of the East Land Company.[13] The list might be extended to considerable length, but one quotation will perhaps be sufficient to show the type of people who helped to settle New England. Speaking of one town, and that not one of the largest, Scituate, Deane writes:

Many of the fathers were men of good education and easy fortune, who had left homes altogether enviable, save in the single circumstance of the abridgment of their religious liberty. In 1639, this town contained more men of distinguished talents and fair fortune than it has at any period since. They were "the men of Kent," celebrated in English history as men of gallantry, loyalty and courtly manners. Gilson, Vassall, Hatherly, Cudworth, Tilden, Hoar, Foster, Stedman, Saffin, Hinckley, and others had been accustomed to the elegancies of life of England.[14]

There are numerous evidences of wealth among the pioneers. John Winthrop had sufficient property so that the mismanagement and defalcation of his steward to the amount of over £2000 did not ruin him, although it was a

[7] Ellis edition, The Works of Anne Bradstreet, p. xxii.
[8] Magnalia, i. 156.
[9] Winthrop's Journal, i. 51 note 3.
[10] New England Historical and Genealogical Register, xx. 366.
[11] Ibid., x. 253.
[12] Massachusetts Historical Society, Collections, 1st Series, vi. 100 note.
[13] Magnalia, i. 151; Winthrop's Journal, i. 223 note.
[14] Quoted by Chaplin, Life of Henry Dunster, p. 205.

great loss.[15] John Harvard left an estate of £1600, besides his books.[16] Thomas Flint brought with him an estate of £2000.[17] Peter Bulkeley brought £6000.[18] William Tyng, dying in 1653, left a property inventoried at £2774.14.04.[19] The estate of Henry Webb, inventoried September 25, 1660, amounted to £7819.[20] Edward Breck "died in the year 1662, leaving an estate, the value of which ran into hundreds of pounds sterling, a large sum for his day."[21] The

[15] Life and Letters, ii. 253; also Massachusetts Historical Society, Collections, 4th Series, vii. 224 ff. In considering the question of wealth in the colonies, the difference in the value or purchasing power of money must be kept in mind. The highest salary paid to any minister around Boston in 1657, according to a report made by a special committee to the General Court, was £100, and the average of the twelve listed in the report was £65, only three out of the twelve receiving over £60. The families to be supported on these salaries averaged seven in number. Some had farms in addition to the salary, but they could hope for no other income, as marriages they considered a civil function, to be performed only by the magistrates. The cost of labor also illustrates the high value of money at that time. A report to the General Court of Connecticut in 1680, signed by William Leet, Governor, and John Allen, Secretary of the Colony, complains that "labour is dear, being from 2s to 2s6 a day for a labourer." (Massachusetts Historical Society, Collections, 1st Series, iv. 222.) Evidently labor had been cheaper in the early days of the colony; but accepting this figure, and comparing it with present (1916 pre-war) prices of from $1.50 to $2.50 for unskilled labor, we get a ratio of about four to one. An estate of £1000 then would thus be equivalent to one of $20,000 today, and John Eliot's £60 salary as pastor of the church at Roxbury would amount to $1200. As the Connecticut report also quotes pork at 3d a pound, beef at 2¼d, and butter at 6d, the ratio of four to one does not seem too high. F. B. Dexter (Proceedings of the American Antiquarian Society, xviii. 137) calls £300 equivalent to perhaps six or seven thousand dollars with us.

[16] Thomas Shepard's Autobiography, p. 63.

[17] Peter Bulkeley wrote (to whom is not known, as the name is missing from the letter), "I . . . . do further entreat you would please, both of you, to take into consideration the condition of Mrs. Flint, the widow of worthy Mr. Flint deceased, who served in the same office of magistrate many years, and never received of the country any recompense. . . . . And some things there are which may persuade on this side more effectually, both in regard of a great family of children, and the great decay of his estate which he brought into this country, (being about £2000,). . . . " (Massachusetts Historical Society, Collections, 3rd Series, i. 47.)

[18] New England Historical and Genealogical Register, xxxi. 155.

[19] Ibid., xxx. 432.

[20] Ibid., x. 180.

[21] Dr. Edward Breck in Publications of the Colonial Society of Massachusetts, xiv. 49 ff. He adds, "It is significant of the degree of refinement obtaining among

Reverend John Norton's estate was appraised, April 24, 1663, at £2095.[22] The Reverend John Wilson left £419 in addition to a farm valued at £1300.[23] John Endicott's estate, 1665, totalled £2269.[24] John Bracket was worth £1021, according to inventory of February 22, 1666;[25] and the same year Henry Shrimpton, brasier, left assets of £11,979, and debts to the amount of £5743.[26] The estate of Hezekiah Usher, who died in 1676, was appraised at £15,358.[27] These are just some of the larger estates, and the Suffolk and Essex Probate Records contain many inventories of estates appraised between £500 and £1000.

There is further interesting testimony in regard to the existence of men of wealth in New England in the sarcastic reference to them made by John Josselyn, an English merchant, in his account of his two voyages to New England:

The grose *Goddons*, or great masters, as also some of their Merchants are damnable rich; generally all of their judgement, inexplicably covetous and proud.[28]

Elsewhere he wrote of Boston as it was in 1663:

The buildings are handsome, joyning one to the other as in London; with many large streets, most of them paved with pebble stone. In the high street towards the Common, there are fair buildings, some of stone; and, at the east end of the town, one amongst the rest, built by the shore by Mr. Gibs, a merchant,

---

even the earliest pioneers of New England [Breck came in 1635], that in the inventory of Edward Breck's estate occurs the mention of a bath-tub."

[22] New England Historical and Genealogical Register, xi. 344.

[23] *Ibid.*, xvii. 344.

[24] *Ibid.*, xv. 128. This inventory, as perhaps some of the others, includes farm lands; but as one farm of 550 acres is appraised at just £550, I do not think the inventories are "padded" with undeveloped land.

[25] *Ibid.*, xv. 250.

[26] *Ibid.*, xv. 78. The expenditure for his funeral amounted to £134.05.06 ($2500.00 in modern equivalent). It must have been an elaborate ceremonial to have cost that much!

[27] Littlefield, Early Boston Booksellers, p. 68.

[28] Josselyn, Two Voyages to New England, p. 180.

being a stately edifice, which it is thought will stand him in little less than £3,000 before it be fully finished.[29]

In the matter of wealth, as in other things already noted, Plymouth was far behind the rest of New England. Estates above £500 were rare, and £200–£300 was the usual figure, as will be seen by reference to pages 28 and 29, above. The settlers of New England, then, were not without some wealth, just as they were not without either libraries or means of education. And they possessed one other element of culture at a surprisingly early period in their history: a printing-press was brought over and set up at Cambridge in 1638, before Boston was ten years old.[30] This may not seem at all remarkable until we compare Cambridge with other cities both in England and in other colonies. Printing was begun in Glasgow one year later than in Cambridge. It was first practiced in Rochester in 1648, or ten years later, and at Exeter in 1668, thirty years later. There was no printing in Manchester until 1732, and none in Liverpool until after 1750.[31] The first press in Pennsylvania[32] was William Bradford's, established about 1686. Bradford moved to New York in 1693 to establish the first press there.[33] A press was running in Virginia in 1682, but was quickly suppressed, there being no further printing in that colony until 1729.[34] There was no press in Canada until 1751, when Bartholomew Green, Jr., brought one from Boston to Halifax.[35] Another was es-

[29] Josselyn, New England's Rarities Discovered, p. 1. $60,000 (in modern equivalent) for a house!

[30] Massachusetts Historical Society, Collections, 4th Series, vi. 99.

[31] Truebner, Bibliographical Guide to American Literature, p. ix.

[32] Thomas, History of Printing, i. 208. The Quakers, like the Puritans, showed their interest in books by the early establishment of a press, within five years of the granting of the charter.

[33] Ibid., i. 291.

[34] Ibid., i. 331. In 1671 Governor Berkeley remarked, "I thank God we have not free schools nor printing." (Ibid., i. 330.)

[35] Ibid., i. 357.

tablished in Quebec in 1764, and one in Montreal in 1775.[36]
One press did not satisfy New England long, for a second
press was established in 1674, in Boston, followed by several
others before 1700, and one was set up at New London in
1709.[37]   Some of the productions of the New England
presses will be discussed in the following and later chapters.

[36] *Ibid.*, i. 362; Truebner, Bibliographical Guide, p. viii.
[37] Thomas, History of Printing, i. 184.

Chapter V: The Production of Literature.

AS the preceding chapters have shown that the culture of New England in its earlier years did not differ greatly from that of England during the same period, it is necessary to discuss and explain the seeming inferiority of New England's literature to contemporary English literature. To do this it will be necessary not only to consider the literary production of the colonists,—its kind, its extent, and its quality,—but also to compare it with that of the English Puritans and account for such actual differences as are found.

An indication of the nature of the literary activity during this period may be obtained from the following tabulation of the output of the press at Cambridge from its establishment through the year 1670.[1]

Total number of publications	157
Almanacs (many contained verse)	26
Books in the Indian language	19
Religious books (prose)	58
Religious books (verse)	5
Lists of Harvard theses	12
Laws and official publications	22
School books	3
Poetry	4
History, Biography, etc.	8

This list, however, fails to give an accurate impression of the extent of their production of books. It must be remembered that the colonists thought of themselves as Englishmen primarily,[2] and in any important book would wish to

---

[1] These figures are based upon the list of publications given in Evans' American Bibliography.

[2] See pp. 62, 63, above.

address their countrymen who still lived in England as much as, if not more than, their New England neighbors. All books before the press was established at Cambridge in 1638, and the more important books after that time, were sent to London for publication. Roger Williams' "The Bloody Tenet of Persecution for Cause of Conscience," written by Williams while visiting in London, was published there in 1644. A copy soon reached the library of John Cotton in Boston, who saw fit to reply to it. The reply, "The Bloody Tenet washed and made white in the Blood of the Lamb," was sent to London, where it appeared in 1647. When this reached Williams in Rhode Island he wrote a second book to reply to Cotton's argument, "The Bloody Tenet yet more Bloody, by Mr. Cotton's Endeavor to wash it white in the Blood of the Lamb." This also crossed the ocean for publication in 1652. Thus did men living within fifty miles of each other argue over a range of six thousand miles because they were writing for all Englishmen to read. Similarly, elegies and books of religious verse for local use, such as "The Bay Psalm Book," were printed at Cambridge; but the first volume of poetry written with literary intent, Anne Bradstreet's "The Tenth Muse, lately sprung up in America," was sent to London for publication in 1650.

To the productions of the press at Cambridge, then, must be added the many books published abroad. These were fewer in number, but really amounted to more, since many of the Cambridge volumes were merely sermons, or thin pamphlets, whereas the books sent to England were generally full-fledged books.

Religious books were numerous among those printed in England, but were perhaps exceeded by a class of books almost unknown to the Cambridge press, descriptions of America or of life in America. These range from such discussions of the natural history of the region as Wood's "New England's Prospect" and Josselyn's "New England's Rarities Discovered," to such defenses against those who published un—

favorable reports of conditions, either physical, political, or religious, in New England as Winslow's "Good News from New England" and Johnson's "Wonder-Working Providence."

To the products of the presses on both sides of the ocean certain other writings must be added if we are to get a fair estimate of the activity of New England pens during these years. Several books, among them some which rank highest in modern estimates of the period, were not printed until years or even centuries had passed. Such are Bradford's "History of Plymouth Plantations," Winthrop's "Journal,"[3] and Mason's account of his fight with the Pequots at Mystic. Considerable verse also escaped publication, some until Cotton Mather wrote his "Magnalia Christi," and more until antiquarian interest set people to hunting through ancestral records.

In quantity, it is evident, the literary output of the early colonists was considerable. Its quality is less marked, how much less depending upon the standards by which it is tested. Tested in comparison with the best which England produced in the seventeenth century, it is certainly deficient. Tested in comparison with the bulk of the writings of English Puritans during the same period, its deficiency is not very marked. Surely the latter test is the fairer one, and William Prynne a more typical author with whom to compare the New Englander than John Milton.

If we eliminate poetry from the discussion, the best that New England produced is not greatly inferior to Milton's work. In Governor Winthrop's "Journal" there are many eloquent passages, in spite of the fact that much of it was evidently written in great haste at odd moments. Governor Bradford's style in his "History" is remarkably simple and direct, and the same may be said of Winslow's in his narratives.[4] Roger Williams and John Winthrop, Jr., also wrote

---

[3] Sometimes called Winthrop's History of New England. This was first printed in part in 1790, and as a whole in 1825. Bradford's History was printed in 1856.

[4] It must be remembered that Dryden was the first to write a prose which can

effective prose.   As for religious literature, it is impossible to distinguish between that produced in the colony and in the mother country, partly because so many of the leading divines preached and published their sermons with equal satisfaction to hearers and readers in either country.   That so many books written in New England were published in London is further evidence that a voyage to America did not affect either the ability or the popularity of a writer.   If no great literature was produced by the Puritans in New England, it may be not because they were in New England, but because little great literature was produced by the Puritans anywhere.

It is only when we turn to conscious literature, to belles-lettres and especially to poetry, that we find any decided inferiority in New England.   Milton, Marvell, and Wither have no rivals there, although the worst of Wither has perhaps nothing to distinguish it from the better colonial poems. But we must not forget that to compare Anne Bradstreet with Milton may be unfair; it would seem more just to compare her with Mrs. Katharine Philips (Orinda), her English contemporary.   If it is true that Mrs. Bradstreet is remembered only as a curiosity of American literature, it seems just as true that Mrs. Philips is not remembered at all.   This is not to imply that the poetry of Mrs. Bradstreet or of her neighbors is good poetry, but to warn the reader against the common tendency to rate it lower than it deserves in comparison with the general output of Puritan poetry in England at the same time.

Funeral elegies were a custom of the time, a custom faithfully observed in both New and Old England.[5]   Of English

be called modern, that is, which does not seem somewhat strange to a modern ear, and that his first separate prose publication, the Essay of Dramatic Poesy, did not appear until 1668, practically at the end of the period under discussion.

[5] Samuel Stone of Hartford wrote to Thomas Shepard of Cambridge, July 19, 1647, "If I have the whole winter, you may think whether it may not be comely for you & myselfe & some other Elders to make a few verses for Mr. Hooker & inscribe them in the begin^g of his book, as if they had been his funerall verses." (Mather Papers, p. 546.)

elegies of the period most of us know only "Lycidas" and perhaps Marvell's "Poem upon the Death of his Late Highness
the Lord Protector," and when we read the colonial elegies we
compare them with these, forgetting that these are quite
exceptional.   And the fact that the colonial elegies (because
so many of them were preserved for us by Morton in his
"New England's Memorial" and by Cotton Mather in his
"Magnalia Christi," whereas much fugitive poetry undoubtedly perished) form an abnormally large part of the whole
body of colonial poetry gives us a false impression of the
whole.   It might be fairer to disregard them entirely in our
estimates of colonial poetry, as we practically do disregard
the English elegies of the same period when we consider English poetry of the seventeenth century.[6]   But if we must consider them, let us compare them with similar elegies produced in England.   The colonial ministers wrote elegies
not because they felt themselves to be poets, but because
it was the fitting way to pay tribute.   English ministers did
the same for the same reason.   Did they succeed any better?   To get some answer to this question, I examined the
works of an English Puritan divine, well known and popular
both as a preacher and as a writer and perhaps typical, to
see whether he ever attempted verse or not.   I discovered
that Richard Baxter had not only written but published a
volume of verse which went through three editions in the
seventeenth century, and was reprinted in 1821.   One of
the first poems I read was an elegy, part of which I venture
to copy here for comparison with one of the colonial elegies
which Professor Tyler[7] used as an example of the "elaborate

[6] Who ever reads the other elegies to Edward King published with Lycidas?
No criticism of colonial verse is more severe than Professor Masson's remark
(Globe ed. Milton, p. 432), "All the more striking must it have been for a reader
who had toiled through the trash of the preceding twelve pieces (I have read them
one and all, and will vouch that they *are* trash) to come at length upon this opening
of a true poem:—

'Yet once more, O ye laurels . . . . '"

[7] A History of American Literature, i. 269.

and painful jests" and the "ingenuities of allusion" which characterized them.

Upon the Sight of Mr. VINES his Posthumous Treatise on the Sacrament, Octob. 18, 1656. who dyed a little before.

> While thou grew'st here, thy fruit made glad
> The hearts that sin and death made sad:
> Lest we would surfeit of thy fruit,
> Thy Life retired to the root.
> Desiring with us first to keep,
> A Passover before thy sleep:*
> Weary of Earth, thou took'st thine Ease,
> Passing into the land of Peace:
> The threatned Evil we foresee,
> But hope to hide our selves with Thee.
> Though thou art gone, while we must fight,
> We'll call it *Victory*, not *Fight*.
> When God hath taken up this VINE,
> We thought no more to taste its Wine,
> Till in the Land of *Salem's* King,
> We drink it new, even from the Spring:
> But unexpectedly we find,
> Some Clusters which are left behind:
> This Mantle from thy Chariot fell;
> We know it by the pleasant smell:
> Who knows but from this little seed
> Some more such fruitful *Vines* may breed?
> The *Tree of Death* bears precious Fruit,
> Though in the Earth it have no Root.

> . . . . . .

> The Soul imboided [imbodied] in those Lines,
> Doth make us say, that, This is VINES:
> And if our Hearts with you could be;
> Our Lord would say, that there are we.
> But as according to desert,
> The Heavens have got thy better part;

* He dyed suddenly on the Lords Day at night, after he had Preacht and Administred the Sacrament. [Author's note.]

And left us but some of the Wine,
Whilst they have taken up the *Vine:*
So we look up, and wait, and pray,
And yet still feel, we live in Clay.
Here we are keeping sin's account,
While some small sparks do upward mount,
Crying "How long, Holy and True."
Till we are taken up to you.
Thus also we must follow LOVE*,
To find our HEAD and LIFE above.
He that is made by the New-Birth,
A *Burges* of the Church on Earth,
And then by Faith can rise so high,
In Divine LOVE to live and die,
Shall be translated to your soil,
Remov'd from sin, and fear, and toil;
And from this House of Worms & Moles
Unto that Element of Souls.
Where every Branch becomes a VINE;
And where these clods like stars will shine
God is not there known by the Book!
You need not there the pruning-hook:
There you have Wine without the Press;
And God his praise without distress.

.   .   .   .   .

A Threnodia upon our churches second dark eclipse, happening July 20, 1663, by death's interposition between us and that great light and divine plant, Mr. Samuel Stone, late of Hartford, in New England.[8]

Last spring this summer may be autumn styl'd,
Sad withering fall our beauties which despoil'd;
Two choicest plants, our Norton and our Stone,

* Mr. A. *Burgesse* was Minister at *Lawrence* Church: Mr. *Love* succeeded him, and was beheaded by the Remnant of the Long Parliament, which cut off the K. for sending Money to some about the present King. Mr. *Vines* succeeded him. [Author's note.]

[8] Chronicles of the Pilgrim Fathers, p. 197.

Your justs threw down; remov'd, away are gone.
One year brought Stone and Norton to their mother,
In one year, April, July, them did smother.
Dame Cambridge, mother to this darling son;
Emanuel, Northampt' that heard this one,
Essex, our bay, Hartford, in sable clad,
Come bear your parts in this Threnodia sad.
In losing one, church many lost: O then
Many for one come be sad singing men.
May nature, grace and art be found in one
So high, as to be found in few or none.
In him these three with full fraught hand contested,
With which by each he should be most invested.
The largest of the three, it was so great
On him, the stone was held a light compleat,
A stone more than the Ebenezer fam'd;
Stone splendent diamond, right orient nam'd;
A cordial stone, that often cheered hearts
With pleasant wit, with Gospel rich imparts;
Whetstone, that edgify'd th' obtusest mind;
Loadstone, that drew the iron heart unkind;
A pond'rous stone, that would the bottom sound
Of Scripture depths, and bring out Arcan's found;
A stone for kingly David's use so fit,
As would not fail Goliah's front to hit;
A stone, an antidote, that brake the course
Of gangrene error, by convincing force;
A stone acute, fit to divide and square;
A squared stone became Christ's building rare.
A Peter's living, lively stone (so reared)
As 'live was Hartford's life; dead, death is fear'd.
In Hartford old, Stone first drew infant breath,
In New, effused his last; O there beneath
His corps are laid, near to his darling brother,[9]
Of whom dead oft he sighed, Not such another.
Heaven is the more desirable, said he,
For Hooker, Shepard, and Hayne's company.

                      E. B.*

[9] Thomas Hooker, Stone's colleague, had died in 1647.
* Supposed to be Edward Bulkley.

Both poems are unquestionably bad, and for the same chief cause, the tendency to overdo the fantastic. Of the two, I do not feel that the colonial poem is the worse, for it seems to me that it has more form and that the playing upon the word *stone* is better managed and more effective than that upon the word *vine*.

In another and even humbler form of verse, that which appeared in the almanacs of the day, a form generally, and perhaps deservedly, neglected by students of literature, the colonial writers were also not inferior to those of the mother country. A comparison of the incomplete file of seventeenth century British almanacs in the Massachusetts Historical Society library with the almanacs published in Massachusetts during the period under discussion, shows that more colonial almanacs in proportion contain verse, that they average more lines of verse per almanac, and that in general this verse exhibits more originality. No New England almanac maker found it necessary to repeat, with slight changes, the verses which he had used the year before, as Edward Pond did in his almanac for 1611, nor to reprint verse which he had used over twenty years before, as Ralph Partridge in 1705 drew upon his own "Merlinus Redivivus" of 1684. Most of the verse on both sides of the water is mechanical rhyming upon the trite topics of the changing seasons, the influence of signs of the zodiac, astrological advice, or the possibilities of the coming year. Three of the American almanacs, however, show some originality. Samuel Danforth's "An Almanack for the Year of our Lord 1649" contains an eighty-eight line poem followed by an eight line prognostication, the whole planned to fit the almanac with eight lines at the head of each month. The poem is an elaborate and not ineffective (though not very poetical) allegorical account of the settlement of New England and the trials of the colonists. Hurricanes, Indian uprisings, the "antinomian" errors of Mrs. Hutchinson, plagues of pigeons and army worms, and even echoes of the troubles in England, are brought into this account of the "Orphan" driven from "England's armes" into the wilderness. Josiah Flint's "Almanack" for 1666 contains a history of the Jews in rhyme. John Richardson's "Almanack" for 1670 furnishes an example of a quality generally lacking in colonial literature —humor. "The Countryman's Apocrypha," as the main poem is called, is a satire upon the vulgar belief in and love of marvels. The satire is exaggerated and the humor is blunt;[10] but there is nothing trite or conventional about the poem. Neither English nor colonial almanacs printed selections from real poetry at this time; that custom was not established until the second quarter of the eighteenth century. Those who depended upon the annual almanac for their literature had meager fare; but they were at no disadvantage if they lived in New England.

In attempting to determine the quality of the literature produced by the people of New England it must not be forgotten that in so far as they were consciously writing, they were writing for their contemporaries, and that, in consequence, it should be judged by their standards. To us

[10] The following lines are characteristic:

> The Moon is habitable, some averre;
> And that some Creatures have their Dwelling there;
> Judge what you please; but yet 'tis very true,
> This year the Moon a Pair of Horns will shew.

The satire at the expense of the ignorant aroused the ire of Samuel Bailey of Little Compton, who wrote in reply The College Ferula, the almanac, printed at Cambridge, being considered a college product. Bailey's poem, sent to John Whipple, town clerk of Providence, lay hidden in manuscript among the town records until 1840. It is a better poem than the other. It concludes:

> These are grave sophisters, that are in schools
> So wise they think their aged fathers, fools
> That plough and cart; and such they are indeed
> Or else they would not work so hard, to breed
> Their boys to flout them; but I cannot stay
> Foddering of asses thus; I must away
> And give my sheep their breakfast, who, I fear,
> Wait at the stack, while I write verses here.

The entire poem is printed in the New England Historical and Genealogical Register, ix. 356.

much that they wrote seems absurd, and such effusions as "The Bay Psalm Book" and Wigglesworth's "The Day of Doom" are held up for ridicule in almost every history or collection of American literature. Yet contemporary England found nothing absurd in them. "The Day of Doom" was twice reprinted in England,[11] and "The Bay Psalm Book" passed through eighteen editions in England, the last in 1754, and twenty-two editions in Scotland, the last in 1759.[12] The latter was popular in the mother country long after Tate and Brady's version had supplanted it in some of the New England churches.[13] Perhaps New England taste was not abnormal or even peculiar; perhaps it is only the popular taste of seventeenth century England on either side of the water which seems so strange, and which, met almost solely in the poetry of New England (since few read the equivalent poetry written in England, there being so much that is better), gives us a false impression of colonial taste and literary culture.

We expect too much of early New England literature, then, if we attempt to compare it solely with the best of contemporary literature; and we are also unfair to New England when we compare its production with that of all England—the colony in its earliest years with the mother country. It would be fairer to compare the colonies with some district of England,—to compare Boston in New Eng-

[11] At London in 1673, and at Newcastle in 1711.

[12] Truebner, Bibliographical Guide to American Literature, p. viii. Thomas Prince wrote in the preface to the version of 1758, "I found in England it was by some eminent Congregations prefer'd to all Others in their Publick Worship, even down to 1717, when I last left that Part of the British Kingdom." (Sewall's Diary, iii. 16 note.)

[13] "A sing lecture att ye north Brick. Mr. Coleman preached from those words "They sung a new song" . . . Sung Tate & Brady 4 psalms . . ." (Diary of Jeremiah Bumstead, September 21, 1722, in the New England Historical and Genealogical Register, xv. 196.) An edition of Tate and Brady's Psalms, "for the use of her Majesty's Chapel in America," was published at Boston in 1713. (Thomas, History of Printing, ii. 367.) Copies of the English version were on sale in Boston as early as 1700, five copies being listed in the inventory of the estate of Michael Perry, Bookseller. (Ford, The Boston Book Market, p. 176.)

land and the district around it with Boston in Old England and the surrounding county of Lincolnshire. Thomas Fuller in his Lincolnshire section of "The Worthies of England" mentions the following as writers since the Reformation: Edmund Sheffeild, Peter Morwing, Anthony Gilby, John Fox, Dr. Thomas Sparks, Dr. Tighe, and Fines Morison. The editor of the 1840 edition of the "Worthies" adds a list of writers since Fuller's time. The only names in that list which come within the period of the entire first century of colonial life are Susannah Centlivre and Sir Charles Cotterell, the translator of "Cassandra." Such limited literary activity as these names represent would not indicate that New England was, by comparison, sterile soil for literature.

The preceding attempt to determine a fair standard by which to judge of the quality of colonial writings partly explains why the early colonists did not produce a finer literature than they did; they were producing the literature which, in general, their class in England produced. The earlier chapters have shown that their education and literary culture were not greatly affected by their removal to a new land. For just that reason their literary activity was little affected by their change. If no fine poetry was produced, it was because the Puritans had few poets of ability and of them none chose to come to New England. Poets of little ability seem to have been uninfluenced by emigration. John Wilson wrote much poor poetry in New England; but there seems to be no evidence that the volume which he published in England in 1626 before he came contained any better poetry. If a poet of real ability had come to Boston, he would not have ceased to be a poet. If John Milton, for instance, had been driven over by the Restoration, I see no reason why he could not have developed "Paradise Lost" as well as in England. There is a possibility that the busy life of a young colony might in some cases have militated somewhat against the production of poetry, but that would not have affected Milton, whose blindness would have ensured to him the leisure necessary for his work.

The really remarkable thing about the literature of New England in its earliest days is that there is as much of it as there is, and that it is as good as it is. There were certainly many things which might have hampered and probably did hamper literary work. The lack of leisure time, already mentioned, might have hindered some, although the ministers and some of the wealthier men would have been free from this handicap. The necessity of sending all material, at first, to England for publication, and of sending much even after a press was established at Cambridge, may have been a restraining influence. Still another was the rigid censorship of the colonial press, little used during this period, as far as the records show, but nevertheless always in existence, as shown by the fining of Marmaduke Johnson for printing without authority in 1668,[14] and by the stopping of a partially printed edition of Thomas à Kempis in 1669.[15] The narrowness of some of the leaders may have had a repressing influence upon freedom of expression.[16] There was no literary circle for the mutual encouragement of those who might be interested in the production of literature, and no

[14] Johnson, associated with Bartholomew Green at the Cambridge Press, printed without authority The Isle of Pines, a pamphlet of the Baron Munchausen order, already popular in England. For this offence he was fined £5. (Massachusetts Historical Society, Proceedings, 2d Series, xi. 247–249.)

[15] "The Court, being informed that there is now in the presse, reprinting, a booke, tī Imitacōns of Christ, or to yᵗ purpose, written by Thomas a Kempis, a Popish minister, wherein is conteyned some things that are less safe to be infused among the people of this place, doe comend it to the licensers of the press, the more full revisall thereof, & that in the meane tjme there be no further progresse in that worke." (Massachusetts Colony Records, iv. Part II, p. 424.) As no copy of an Imitatio Christi printed in New England at this time has ever been discovered, the licensers evidently decided that suppression was preferable to revision. (Diary of Cotton Mather, ii. 582 note.)

[16] Thomas Shepard found it necessary to write to Governor Winthrop, "Your apprehensions agaynst reading & learning heathen authors, I perswade myselfe were suddenly suggested, & will easily be answered by B: Dunstar, if yow should impart them to him." (Winthrop Papers, ii. 272.)

sufficient home market for any work of a purely artistic nature. In spite of all this, a great deal was written, and a large part of what was written was in the form of verse. Professor Tyler remarks,[17] with perhaps unnecessary sarcasm, upon the almost universal tendency to attempt to write verse. If they did not succeed in writing much good verse, it was not for lack of effort. That they wrote some real poetry must be acknowledged.[18]

It seems safe to conclude that the early New England colonists wrote more than they would have written had they remained in England, and that the quality of their work was not lowered by their removal, or by any lack of opportunities for culture in the new home.

[17] History of American Literature, i. 267.

[18] Anne Bradstreet's Contemplations and some of her shorter pieces, Wigglesworth's Vanity of Vanities and certain stanzas of The Day of Doom, Edward Johnson's From Silent Night, True Register of Moans, are instances of poems which have poetic merit.

Part II:
The End of the Seventeenth Century.
1670-1700.

Chapter VI: Education.

WHEN President Charles Chauncy of Harvard died in 1672, the college ceased to be in the control of those who had been educated in England, and was managed thereafter by its own graduates. Leonard Hoar, his successor, had taken his first degree at Harvard in 1650, and his three successors, Urian Oakes, John Rogers, and Increase Mather, had graduated there, the first two in 1649, and the third in 1656.[1] The change seems to have had little effect upon the quality of the work done in the college, partly, perhaps, because even before this Harvard graduates, as tutors, had done much of the teaching.[2] Another reason for the slight effect of the change may have been that three of the four successors of President Chauncy had either studied or lived in England after finishing their courses at Harvard. Leonard Hoar went to England in 1653 and preached for some time at Wanstead. He later studied medicine at Cambridge, taking the degree of Doctor of Medicine in 1671.[3] While living in England he married the daughter of Lord Lisle.[4] Urian Oakes went to England soon after graduating, and there became pastor of a church at Titchfield. Being silenced at the Restoration, he accepted the call of the church at Cambridge, Massachusetts, and was soon after chosen President.[5] Increase Mather studied at Trinity College, Dublin, gaining the Master's

---

[1] Magnalia, ii. 30.

[2] Ibid., passim. George Downing and John Bulkly, Harvard 1642, had been the first tutors.

[3] Massachusetts Historical Society, Collections, 1st Series, vi. 100 note; Magnalia, ii. 14.

[4] Ibid. Mrs. Hoar's mother was the unfortunate Lady Alice Lisle, cruelly beheaded at Winchester in 1685 for giving refuge to fugitives from Monmouth's defeated forces.

[5] Ibid., ii. 115, 116.

degree, and being offered a fellowship which he declined. He also preached in the island of Guernsey before returning to New England.[6]

The arrival of Charles Morton in 1686 and his appointment in 1692 as fellow and in 1697 as vice president of Harvard brought to the colony and the college a valuable cultural influence, for Morton had been a fellow of Wadham College, Oxford, and for years a successful teacher in London. When he was appointed vice president it was planned that in time he should succeed to the presidency,[7] but he died in 1698 while Increase Mather was still president. Upon his arrival he read lectures on philosophy at his own home; but the lectures attracted so many from the college that he was requested to abandon them.[8]

Such contact with England and English scholastic life must have had considerable effect in keeping the college from becoming too provincial. Its standing was still sufficiently good to attract at least one student from England. Nathaniel Mather of Dublin wrote to his brother Increase, then newly chosen president, December 31, 1684:

. . . one Mr. Rich. Lob, merchant in London, who married my sister Thompson, desyres me to write in behalf of this gentleman, the bearer, his kinsman Mr. Penhallow of Falmouth in Cornwall, who designs to spend a year or two in New England, in the Colledg, for the perfecting of his learning, hee having lived 3 or 4 years under the instructions of one Mr. Morton . . . who is constreyned to withdraw by reason of Capias's upon an Excommunicaçon.[9]

One unfavorable picture of Harvard during this period

[6] See p. 21, above.

[7] Massachusetts Historical Society, Collections, 2d Series, i. 158 ff; Eggleston, Transit of Civilization, p. 45; Dictionary of National Biography. One of his pupils in England had been Daniel Defoe. He brought two students with him. At his death Morton left a sum of £50 to Harvard, and his funeral was attended by the officers and students of Harvard in a body.

[8] See Mather Papers, pp. 111, 112, for the letter requesting him not to compete with the college.

[9] Mather Papers, p. 59.

exists in the account of the visit to it of Jasper Danckaerts, a Dutch scholar, in 1680. In reading this it must be remembered that when the visit occurred Harvard had been four years without a president, and had not recovered from the disturbances and quarrels which led to the resignation and death of President Hoar. Urian Oakes, referred to at the end of the account, had been chosen president, but was not yet installed. The graduates of 1680 were but five, and in 1682 none took degrees.[10]

We reached Cambridge about eight o'clock. It is not a large village, and the houses stand very much apart. The college building is the most conspicuous among them. We went to it, expecting to see something unusual, as it is the only college, or would-be academy of the Protestants in all America, but we found ourselves mistaken. In approaching the house we neither heard nor saw anything mentionable; but, going to the other side of the building, we heard noise enough in an upper room to lead my comrade to say, "I believe they are engaged in disputation." We entered and went upstairs, when a person met us, and requested us to walk in, which we did. We found there eight or ten young fellows, sitting around, smoking tobacco, with the smoke of which the room was so full, that you could hardly see; and the whole house smelt so strong of it that when I was going upstairs I said, "It certainly must be also a tavern." We excused ourselves, that we could speak English only a little, but understood Dutch or French well, which they did not. However, we spoke as well as we could. We inquired how many professors there were, and they replied not one, that there was not enough money to support one. We asked how many students there were. They said at first, thirty, and then came down to twenty; I afterwards understood there are probably not ten.[11] They knew hardly a word of Latin, not one of them, so that my comrade could not converse with them. They took us to the library where there was nothing particular. We looked over it a little. They pre-

---

[10] Magnalia, ii. 31.

[11] The number was exactly thirty, seventeen undergraduates and thirteen graduates, according to Cotton Mather's lists of the graduates of the classes then in Harvard, Urian Oakes of the class of 1678 having died in 1679. (Magnalia, ii. 31).

sented us with a glass of wine. This is all we ascertained there. The minister of the place goes over there morning and evening to make prayer, and has charge over them; besides him, the students are under tutors or masters.[12]

As for the inadequacy of the Harvard Latin so severely criticized by Danckaerts, the fault may have been in Dutch ears, in different methods of pronunciation, or in youthful shyness in the presence of strangers. Cotton Mather, who had taken his first degree at sixteen just two years before this, and at this time was pursuing advanced studies, states that pupils were required to speak true Latin, and to write it in verse as well as prose, before they could enter Harvard; and he boasts that commencement orations were delivered in Latin, Greek, and Hebrew, and even in verse of all three.[13] No one familiar with his writings can doubt Mather's fluency—at least in quoting Latin.

It is worth mention here that two members of the class which was to have degrees conferred upon it in a few days after this visit, William Brattle and John Leverett, later became tutors of Harvard and, during Increase Mather's three and one-half years' absence in England, had complete charge of the teaching. Among the men whom they taught in those years were Paul Dudley, later Attorney General of the Colony, Samuel Mather, who became pastor of a church in England, Benjamin Wadsworth, later president of the college, and Benjamin Colman, leader in the religious and literary activities of Boston during the next two generations. The students whom Danckaerts pictured so unfavorably were capable of training men of ability, and Leverett himself was later chosen president of Harvard; both Lever-

[12] Journal of Jasper Danckaerts, p. 266, under date of July 9. Danckaerts' whole account of conditions in and around Boston is marked by an evident lack of sympathy and a willingness, if not an eagerness, to find faults.

[13] Magnalia, ii. 12. More than half of the students who were in Harvard at this time became clergymen, and as such they would have to have some fluency in speaking Latin.

ett and Brattle were honored by election as Fellows of the Royal Society.[14]

The following criticism of Cambridge University, England, in 1710—forty years later—also by a foreigner, one Uffenbach, a German savant, as given by Mullinger, should be taken into consideration when attempting to judge of conditions at Harvard.

[This] keen-eyed traveller, in visiting the other colleges [besides Trinity, whose hall he found dirty and "smelly"], could not but be struck by the indifference evinced for the higher interests of learning. At Caius College he found the manuscripts placed in "a miserable garret under the roof," and lying "thick with dust" on the floor. At Magdalene all the books were "entirely overgrown with mould." . . . At Trinity Hall, the library appeared to him "very mean, consisting only of a few law books." At Emmanuel, the books, though "respectable in number," stood "in entire confusion." At Peterhouse, the manuscripts were "buried in dust" and in the greatest disorder. At the University Library, a rare codex of Josephus being "torn at the end," the library-keeper obligingly presented him with a leaf![15]

Nathaniel Mather, of Dublin, writing in 1686, seems well satisfied with the scholarship of Harvard, although he criticizes some details:

The method of these, & the last years Theses is in my judgm̃t better than an[y] I have seen formerly. But the grammar of some of [them] might bee mended, e. g., in Thes. 2, . . . it should have been *producant*, not *producerent;* . . . But I perceive the Cartesian philosophy begins to obteyn in New England, & if I conjecture aright the Copernican System too. There should also in a thing coming out from scholars in an university, have been more care taken of orthography. e. g. Thes. Phys. 28, *nitrolis* for *nitrosis;* and *Phillipsius* should not bee with a double p.[16]

There is little evidence in this period of the attitude of

---

[14] Publications of the Colonial Society of Massachusetts, xiv. 291; Sibley, Harvard Graduates, iii. 183.

[15] Mullinger, History of Cambridge, p. 168.

[16] Mather Papers, p. 63.

the English universities toward Harvard; for after the
Restoration few Harvard men were tempted to England
either for study or to seek for churches. Cotton Mather
and Thomas Brattle, like William Brattle and John Leverett, were honored by being chosen Fellows of the Royal Society;[17] the former was given the degree of Doctor of Divinity by the University of Glasgow in 1710;[18] and Jeremiah
Dummer, Harvard 1699, was given the degree of Doctor of
Philosophy at Utrecht in 1703.[19] Benjamin Colman, Harvard 1692, was also given the degree of Doctor of Divinity
by the University of Glasgow in 1731.[20] Samuel Myles,
Harvard 1684, and William Vesey, Harvard 1693, received
the degree of Master of Arts from Oxford in 1693 and 1697.[21]
One other possible evidence of Harvard's standing in the
world of scholarship is found in a statement of Increase
Mather writing of the college in 1689:

. . . the Learned Men there have a corresponding communication with other Learned Men in divers parts of the World,
where the Reformed Religion is professed, and by them [are]
highly reverenced for their Learning and Sobriety.[22]

In this period, then, Harvard had come to hold a much less
important place in the English speaking world than it had
held in the first period, and to that extent had become provincial; but this change had not greatly affected the quality
of scholarship, and had, if anything, increased the influence
of the college in the colonies. There were few Oxford or

[17] Publications of the Colonial Society of Massachusetts, xiv. 81 ff; Narratives
of the Witchcraft Cases, p. 167.
[18] Sibley, Harvard Graduates, iii. 39.
[19] Sewall, Letter-Book, i. 302.
[20] Turell, Life of Benjamin Colman, p. 157.
[21] Publications of the Colonial Society of Massachusetts, xviii. 210, n. 1. The last
two degrees were awards to men who had adopted Episcopalianism, and that to
Colman was given at the request of Governor Belcher. If they were not always
rewards for scholastic ability solely, at least they showed that the British universities were willing to recognize Harvard officially through such honors to her graduates.
[22] A Brief Relation of the State of New England, Andros Tracts, ii. 162.

Cambridge men to compete with the Harvard men.   Cotton Mather, speaking of the influence of Harvard in 1696, states that of 87 ministers in Massachusetts, 76 were Harvard graduates, and of 35 in Connecticut, 31 were from Harvard.[23]

As to the quality of the scholarship, one or two more illustrations may be given.   Nathaniel Mather, brother of Cotton Mather, graduating from Harvard in 1685 at the age of sixteen, was sufficiently skilled in mathematics and astronomy to figure out the statistics and calculations of almanacs for the years 1685 and 1686, which he published.[24]   Samuel Sewall, Harvard 1671, seems to have had a sound classical training.   Dr. William Everett, in referring to Sewall's original English and Latin poems, says,

. . . in the latter, at least, the metre is irreproachable, according to the rules of quantity as recognized by the scholars of his time.   An exhaustive examination of the verses in the Diary leaves no doubt on this subject.[25]

Sewall also shows his scholarship elsewhere.   In a letter he writes:

There is mention made of a new Translation of the Bible: If it go forward, I would propound One Word of amendment: John, 10. 16.   The Word (Fold) in the latter part of the verse ought to be changed for the word(Flock).[26]   The new French Translation has it (*Un seul tropeau*) I have a Latin Testament printed *Parisijs ex officina Rob. Stephani typographi Regij M. D. XLV*.   He seems to be scrupulous in departing from the Vulgar Latin; yet has this Marginal Reading (*ut fiat unus grex*) Beza in his latter edition, has (*grex*) Tremellius his Translation of the Syriack, runs thus (*fietq[u]e totus grex unus*)   In reading Austin

[23] Magnalia, i. 86.

[24] The Boston Ephemeris, an Almanack for the year 1685 [and the same for 1686].   Many of the Boston almanacs of the seventeenth century were compiled by the graduates of Harvard who were continuing their studies in residence after graduation.   Such resident bachelors specialized in astronomy and mathematics.

[25] Massachusetts Historical Society, Proceedings, 2d Series, iv. 80.

[26] This change was made in the revised version of 1881, as the editors of the Letter-Book pointed out.

upon the Psalms, I have often met with, (*Unus grex, unus pastor*) Psal. 71. Col. 780. Psal. 77. Col. 852. Psal. 78. Col. 878. *ter legitur.* I do not see that the word is any where else translated (Fold). In Act. 20. 28, 29, and 1 Pet. 5. 2, 3, the word is of the same Origination, though of the Neuter Gender, and is still rendred (Flock).[27]

On one occasion he reports that he and a friend spent the evening reading Latin verse to each other.[28]   In another letter he discusses the "enetymology" of the word "Lordane, by Corruption, Lurdane; . . . . Though your English Dictionary carrys it another way."[29]   The following memorandum in his "Letter-Book" also indicates his interest in study:

To Mr. Stretton, to buy Bellarmine, two volumes, polemical works, fair print. Some Spanish Books; Barthol. de las Casas in Spanish, and in English too; Gramar and Dictionary, if to be had; and what else you shall see convenient for my purpose of getting a Smattering of the Spanish tongue.[30]

Somewhat later Cotton Mather also became interested in Spanish, as is shown by his own account:

About this Time, understanding that the way for our Communication with the *Spanish Indies*, opens more and more, I sett myself to learn the *Spanish Language*. The Lord wonderfully prospered mee in this Undertaking; a few liesure Minutes in the Evening of every Day, in about a Fortnight, or three weeks Time, so accomplished mee, I could write very good Spanish. Accordingly, I composed a little Body of the *Protestant Religion*, in certain Articles . . . This I turn'd into the Spanish Tongue.[31]

[27] Letter-Book, i. 297.

[28] "Mr. Bradstreet read to me Chrysostom's going out of Constantinople into Banishment; and I read his Return; both in Latin, very entertaining. 'Twas occasion'd by my mentioning the two folios I had given him. I offered to give Dr. Mather's Church History for them and put them into the Library. It seems Mr. Bradstreet has all the Eton Edition." (Diary, iii. 163.)

[29] Letter-Book, i. 18.

[30] *Ibid.*, i. 123.   In the year 1691.

[31] Diary, i. 284.   January, 1698–9.   He confessed in the Diary that the task gave him a terrible headache!

In the "Magnalia" he quoted one proverb in Spanish.[32]   He
also wrote at least one tract in French.[33]   In a day in which
the education of woman was neglected, he taught his daughter
Katherine both Latin and Hebrew.[34]   Evidently the scholarly spirit was not lacking in this period of the colonial
life.

Nor was the period without scientific spirit.   Nathaniel
Mather's letter, given on page 103, refers to the growing
influence of the Cartesian philosophy in the Colonies.
Thomas Brattle also refers to this in a letter which he wrote
at the time of the witchcraft troubles.

> The Salem justices . . . are so well instructed in the Carte-
> sian philosophy, and in the doctrine of *effluvia*, that they undertake
> to give a demonstration how this touch does cure the afflicted
> persons.[35]

It had become established at Cambridge not long before
this.[36]   The Reverend Deodat Lawson, whose lecture at
Salem Village, March 24, 1692, was largely responsible for
the beginning of the witchcraft persecutions, had been educated in England, where he had spent six years at the English
universities, whence he had brought the current beliefs of
English scholars.[37]   The Copernican theory was accepted
with some hesitation, but slowly gained way.   It was stated
and explained as early as 1659 in Zechariah Brigden's "Almanack" for that year.   Alexander Nowell in his "Almanack"
for 1665 defended it.   In 1665 Samuel Danforth published
"An Astronomical Description of the late Comet, or Blaz-

[32] Magnalia, ii. 581.

[33] Diary, ii. 651.   It was entitled *Grande Voix du Ciel à la* France *sous La Verge
de Dieu.*

[34] Wendell, Cotton Mather, p. 257.

[35] Massachusetts Historical Society, Collections, 1st Series, v. 63.

[36] Mullinger in his History of Cambridge, *ca.* p. 158, speaks of it as attracting
great attention and interest around 1660.

[37] Littlefield, Early Boston Booksellers, p. 164.   It must be remembered that the
colonists in their beliefs in witchcraft were not behind the times, but rather accepting the latest ideas as expressed by Joseph Glanvil and Henry More of Cambridge.
See p. 142 and p. 160, below.

ing Star," in which he maintained that the orbit of the comet was elliptical, and that its center was not the earth.[38]   In 1675 John Foster's "Almanack" advanced strong arguments for the theory.   In Nathaniel Mather's "Almanack" for 1686, already referred to, Robert Hook's discovery of a sensible parallax of the earth's orbit among the fixed stars was cited as proof of the truth of the new system.[39]

The influence of Harvard in this period, then, may have been more provincial; but there seems to be no proof that this change was attended by any appreciable decline in scholarship.   Harvard was still training men satisfactorily for the ministry; its graduates were achieving distinction in political life, Samuel Sewall, Paul Dudley, Benjamin Lynde, and Gurdon Saltonstall, for example; and two other graduates of this period, Cotton Mather and Thomas Brattle, received recognition for their scientific writings by the publication of their articles in the Transactions of the Royal Society as well as by election to that Society.[40]

Of common school education during this period there is no detailed information.   School books were imported in large numbers,[41] and some were printed in the colony.   Marmaduke Johnson testified in 1668 that he had printed a primer;[42] and before or by 1690 Benjamin Harris had pub-

[38] Eggleston, Transit of Civilization, p. 35.   This was reprinted in England.

[39] Sewall, for all of his classical learning, was somewhat skeptical of the new science.   As late as 1714 he wrote in his Diary (iii. 31), "Dr. C. Mather preaches excellently from Ps. 37.   Trust in the Lord &c. only spake of the Sun being in the centre of our System.   I think it inconvenient to assert such Problems."   Sewall's earlier credulity in accepting the spectral evidence in the witchcraft cases reacted upon him to make him cautious of things not too evident.

[40] Thomas Brattle was recognised for his ability as a mathematician and astronomer, Mather for his writings reporting natural (and sometimes, in the eyes of the modern reader, unnatural and absurd) phenomena.   The seeming absurdity of some of these articles must not blind us to the fact that they did not seem absurd at the time and were not at all out of place in the most learned periodical of the time.   "The Relation," commented the astronomer Halley, as editor, writing of one of the most absurd, "seems to be well attested."   (Publications of the Colonial Society of Massachusetts, xiv. 82.)

[41] See book lists in the following chapter.

[42] Massachusetts Historical Society, Proceedings, 2d Series, xi. 247.

lished the famous "New England Primer."[43] That primers such as these and catechisms like Cotton's "Spiritual Milk for Boston Babes"[44] sufficed for a primary education equivalent to that obtainable in old England is shown by the statement of John Locke in his "Thoughts Concerning Education," written in 1690, that the method of teaching children at that time in England "was the ordinary road of Hornbook, Primer, Psalter, Testament, and Bible."[45]   Mr. Littlefield's statement seems to sum up the situation accurately: "The writer is very strongly of the opinion that the facilities for instruction in the colonial and provincial periods were greater than is generally supposed."[46]

[43] Littlefield, Early New England Schools, p. 148; Ford, Boston Book Market, p. 29.

[44] See p. 23, above.

[45] Littlefield, Early New England Schools, p. 92.

[46] *Ibid.*, p. 328. That Massachusetts was interested in the enforcement of her public school law is shown by the fact that when she assumed authority over the province of Maine she applied to that territory the school law, and in 1675 the towns of Kittery, Cape Porpus, Scarboro, and Falmouth were all presented because they did not as towns take care to have their youth taught their catechism and educated according to the law. Maine Historical Society, Proceedings, 2d Series, iv. 192.

Chapter VII: Books and Libraries.

THE flow of books to the New England colonies increased rather than diminished during the second period. Gifts and shipments to individuals continued to come from England; booksellers became numerous; and both the Public Library and the Harvard Library grew in size.

As in the earlier period, John Winthrop, Jr., was one of the chief recipients of books. In 1670 Henry Oldenburg, returning to Winthrop the thanks of the Royal Society for curiosities which he had sent, wrote,[1]

And y^t this returne may not be altogether verbal, you are to receiue wth it some few books lately printed here by several Fellows of ye Society, viz.:

1. Mr. Boyles Continuation of ye Experimts concerning the Spring and weight of the Aire.
2. Dr. Holders Philosophy of Speech.
3. Dr. Thurston *de Respirationis usu primario.*
4. The Transactions of the last year.

In 1671 he wrote,

I herewith send you a few philosophical Books, lately printed here; viz.:—

1. Mr Boyl's New Tracts about ye wonderful rarefaction and Condensation of the Air, etc.
2. Monsr Charas's New Experiments vpon Vipers.
3. The Transactions of 1670.

To these I adde a small discourse . . . . against y^t great Sorbonist, Monsr Arnaud, touching ye Perpetuity of ye Romish Faith about the Eucharist.[2]

[1] Massachusetts Historical Society, Proceedings, 1st Series, xvi. 244.
[2] *Ibid.*, xvi. 251..

A year later he wrote,

I cannot but thank you for the particulars contained in y[r] letter; for w[ch] I have nothing to return . . . . but the Transactions of y[e] last year. . . . . The Discourse of Mr. Boyle concerning the Origine and Vertue of Gems is not yet printed off: when it is, you shall not faile, God permitting, of hauing a Copy of it sent you by y[e] first ship y[t] shall goe for y[r] parts after its publication.[3]

Similarly Samuel Petto of Suffolk, England, wrote to Increase Mather in 1677,

I also intend to send with it [his letter], D[r] Owen of the reason of faith.[4]

and again in 1678,

I have herewith sent you three books *Christianismus Christianandus*, and M[r] Ny's paper, of a question which is much debated here, . . . also M[r] Troughton of Divine Providence, ... If I knew what other such bookes would be acceptable to you, I would send them.[5]

Four years later he wrote,

I did also direct a few lines to you, with M[r] Stockton's book entituled Consolation in Life & Death. . . . . I intend to send you another of M[r] Stockton, entituled The best Interest when it is finished.[6]

Others were sending books, too. T. Jollie of England wrote in 1679,

I have sent you herewith 2 treatises, which severall yeares agoe I drew up when I was a prisoner.[7]

Abraham Kick of Amsterdam wrote in 1683 to Increase Mather,

I hope the bookes sent by Mr. John Pecke came safe to your hand . . . .[8]

[3] *Ibid.*, xvi. 248.
[4] Mather Papers, p. 341.
[5] *Ibid.*, p. 343.
[6] *Ibid.*, p. 348.
[7] *Ibid.*, p. 325.
[8] *Ibid.*, p. 598.

Samuel Baker of England wrote, September 2, 1684,

> I have given Mr. Epps order to send you,
>
> 1. An Acc⁰ of the present state of the Prot. Religion, supposed by Dr. O [wen] , though I guess you have it, for which reason I do not send you his Meditations of Glory.
> 2. A defence of his 12 arguments in answer to Baxter.
> 3. The Dr's Escot reprinted, with a Catalogue at the end, of all the Dr's books.
> 4. A little book against Health-drinking.
> 5. The life of one Mr. Henry Dorney . . . .⁹

He wrote again later,

> I . . . return my acknowledgmᵗ for the books I haue recᵈ. . . . I know not what return to make in this kind more acceptable than of Dr. Burnett's Lʳˢ,¹⁰ herewith sent.¹¹

Jonathan Tuckney of Hackney, England, sent books to Increase Mather from time to time, as the following letters indicate.

> I wrote to you about two months since & therewith sent you two bookes of my father's laboʳs, one English sermons, the other Latin Prelections & Determinations (as also two for my Cous. Whiting and two for my Cous. your Br. John Cotton), which I hope may be come to hand.¹²
>
> . . . . your kind letter of May 8, together with your new peece of Illustrious Providences . . . . whereas you desire to see Dr. Spencer of Prodigies, I have procured it you, & herewith send it. . . . .¹³
>
> . . . I have thought (since my writing that letter of August 29, (wherein I inclose this) myself, to read over Spencer of Prodigies before I part with it from me. . . . . And I desire you to accept from me in Exchange (which (you know the old saying is) that it is no robbery) another Latin piece

⁹ *Ibid.*, p. 513.

¹⁰ Rev. Gilbert Burnet's Travels through Switzerland, Italy, and some parts of Germany.

¹¹ Mather Papers, p. 513.

¹² *Ibid.*, p. 352.   September 9, 1679.

¹³ *Ibid.*, p. 354.   August 29, 1684.

of the same author's concerning *Urim & Thummim:* what they were.[14]

The following letter to Increase Mather from John Leusden, Professor of Hebrew and Jewish Antiquities at Utrecht, January 1688–9, is an example of the correspondence with learned men abroad to which Mather referred in the passage quoted on page 104.

Most Reverend, Much to bee Respected Sr,—I sought you in America,[15] and thither on the 30th of March I sent some books, vizt a New Lexicon, a Compendium of the Greek New Testament, two Psalters in Hebrew and English, and one in Hebrew & Latine. The Psalmes in Hebrew & English, I dedicated to Mr Eliot, & those four and twenty Preachers, lately heathens, now christians.[16] The Psalmes in Hebrew & Latine I have inscribed to your Revd name. . . . I lately received moreover two American[17] Bibles, two American Grammars, & other American books, as also the Indian's A.B.C. and some others, . . . You now desyre fifty Hebrew Psalters for the use of the students in Harvard Colledge; which I would now have sent, but because you doe not express what kind of Psalters it is which you desyre, whether Hebrew & Latine, or Hebrew & English . . . .[18]

Increase Mather sent home books from London during his residence there. His nephew, Warham Mather, wrote to him in 1688,

I delivered the Books I received from yourself according to order. . . . I am yet made a greater debter, by those for me.[19]

Cotton Mather recorded in his diary, January 7, 1698, "Arrives to mee, a Book in *Folio*, this year published in *London* . . . . a Collection of *Remarkable Providences;*"[20] and again, ". . . . some such Thing as to read a little

---

[14] *Ibid.*, p. 355. September 3, 1684.
[15] At this time Increase Mather was in London.
[16] Indian converts.
[17] *American* seems to be used here as equivalent to *Indian*.
[18] Mather Papers, p. 678.
[19] *Ibid.*, p. 671.
[20] Diary, i. 246.

Book, *De Satana Colaphizante*, which I received from *Holland*, the day after I was taken sick."[21]

Such items give some indication of the way in which books constantly came to America through private gifts. Even more striking is the increased importation of books through the regular channel of the booksellers' shops. Before this period opened there was at least one well-established bookseller in Boston, Hezekiah Usher, who died in 1676, "leaving a goodly fortune and two sons to quarrel over it and evoke the aid of the law."[22] His son, John Usher, carried on the business, but not without considerable competition. When John Dunton, a London bookseller, arrived in Boston in 1686 for the double purpose of collecting bad debts[23] from New Englanders who had bought books of him and of disposing of surplus stock, he found several booksellers established here, and three others soon followed him. He speaks of some of them thus:

This Trader [Mr. Usher] makes the best Figure in *Boston*, he's very Rich, adventures much to Sea; but has got his Estate by BOOKSELLING; he proposed to me the buying my whole Venture, but wou'd not agree to my Terms. . . . Mr. *Philips*, *my old Correspondent* . . . I'll say that for SAM (*after dealing with him for some Hundred Pounds*) he's very just, and (as an Effect of that) very Thriving. . . . I rambled next to visit *Minheer Brunning*,[24] he's a *Dutch* Bookseller from *Holland*. . . . *Brunning* is vers'd in the Knowledge of all sorts of Books, and may well be stil'd *a Compleat Bookseller*. . . . From the DUTCH, I went to the SCOTCH Bookseller, one *Duncan Cambel*. . . . The next I'll mention shall be *Andrew Thorncomb*, Bookseller from *London* . . . ,[25]

. . . tho' I have first broke the Ice, in bringing hither a Cargo of Books; yet by some Letters I receiv'd by the Rose Frigot [*sic*] . . . I perceive I shall not be the last. [He proceeds to report

[21] *Ibid.*, i. 365.
[22] Days and Ways in Old Boston, p. 95. See pp. 40 and 79, above.
[23] To the amount of £500. Dunton, Life and Errors, p. 101.
[24] Otherwise known as Joseph Browning.
[25] Dunton, Life and Errors, p. 127 ff.

the coming of Benjamin Harris and the How brothers, Job and John.][26]

The following list will give an idea of the number of men who engaged in the book business in Boston up to the year 1700, besides the Ushers and Dunton, who have already been mentioned.[27]

1672. John Tappin published at least one book. Books were incidental to his business in general merchandise as is shown by the inventory of his estate in 1678: Books, £16.00.00, other stock, £4777.07.07.

1673. Edmund Ranger established himself as bookseller, bookbinder, and stationer. He did little bookselling, his name appearing in three books, but was called bookseller in a legal document.

1675. John Foster took over Marmaduke Johnson's press when the latter died. He combined bookselling with printing until his death in 1681, when Samuel Sewall succeeded him.

1677. Henry Phillips, after seven years' apprenticeship with Usher, opened a bookshop in the Town House. Upon his death in

1680. Samuel Phillips, his brother, succeeded to the business. Although his shop was burned down in the great fire of 1711 and he did not resume business, he died wealthy in 1720.

——. Duncan Campbell. Date of arrival unknown; probably before 1679.

1679. William Avery married the widow of John Tappin and took over the bookshop which she and her son, Joseph, had carried on after her husband's death. When Avery died in 1687, the widow continued the business. She died in 1707.

---

[26] Dunton, Letters, p. 144.
[27] The list is summarized from Littlefield, Early Boston Booksellers.

1679. John Griffin's name first appeared as publisher of a book. He died in 1686. Benjamin Harris may have taken over his shop when he arrived that same year.

1681. Samuel Sewall succeeded John Foster. He gave up the press and shop in 1684.

1681–2. John Ratcliff, who came over to work on the Indian Bible, published some books.

1682. Joseph Browning arrived from Amsterdam. He died in 1691.

1684. Richard Wilkins arrived from Limerick, where he had sold books. He opened a shop opposite the west end of the Town House. Dunton used his shop as headquarters and upon leaving put in his hands his collections amounting to £300. Wilkins retired in 1704.

1684–5. James Cowes opened a shop. He returned to England three years later.

1685. Andrew Thorncomb arrived. After the reference to him by Dunton, quoted above, there are no records. He may have returned to London.

1686. Job How arrived. Further detail is lacking except his name in one book as publisher.

1686. Benjamin Harris, a London bookseller, driven out of London because of anti-Catholic publications, set up a shop in Boston. He visited London in 1687 and again in 1688. In 1695 he closed his business in Boston and returned to London.

1690. Nicholas Buttolph opened a bookshop. His shop was burned down in 1711, but he continued the business.

1694. Michael Perry began business in Samuel Phillip's old shop when the latter moved to a new location. Upon Perry's death in 1700 his widow continued the business.

1698–9. Benjamin Eliot began a business which was very successful. He died in 1741.

Two others who carried books with other merchandise were

Elkanah Pembroke, who opened a shop in 1689 at the Head of the Dock, and Joseph Wheeler, who had a shop in Dock Square, and published one book in 1697.

Samuel Sewall, even after he disposed of the printing and book shop, continued to do business in books. During his visit to England, 1688–1689, he recorded at different times payments for books which total over £30; and an invoice records that, among other freight:

Samuel Sewall hath aboard the America, Wm. Clark, Commander:

> Punchin Books
> Barrel of Books
> A Map of England and London.[28]

His "Letter-Book" under date of April 25, 1698, contains a memorandum of an order per Capt. Thos. Carter to Amsterdam which includes a "Ream of Marbled paper, Spanish Bible of Cypriano Valero, Deodats Italian Bible."[29] In his diary, in 1700, he recorded:

The President[30] desires me to send for the above mentioned Books [which are here written below]:

1. A Narrative of the Portsmouth Disputation between Presbyterians and Baptists at Mr. Williams's Meeting-house.
2. B[isho]p of Norwich's Sermon of Religious Melancholy.
3. Amintor, a defence of Milton with Reasons for abolishing the 30th Jan.y; [Two of them.]
4. An Account of the first Voyages into America by Barthol de las Casas 4s. [Two of them].
5. Account of a Jew lately converted . . . at the Meeting near Ave Mary-Lane [Four of them].[31]

[28] Sewall, Diary, i. 288. At about the same time he recorded in his diary (i. 284), "Mr. Matthew Wotton, Bookseller, sends me by his Servant a parcell of Englands Duty, which are 25, the Sale of which in N[ew]. E[ngland]. I am to warrant. . . . . [They] Are sent to Mr. Joseph Brañing [Browning], at Boston."
[29] Sewall, Letter-Book, i. 199.
[30] Presumably the president of Harvard.
[31] Sewall, Diary, ii. 13; Letter-Book, i. 239.

At the same time he copied into his letter-book the following:

> The books I would have bought are
> Ars Cogitandi.   2.
> Le Grands Philosophy, Latin.
> Heerboordi Meletomata.   3.
> Dr. Charletons Physiologia.
> D: Moors Imortality of the Soul.
> Metaphysicks, Ethicks
> Glanvils Sceptis Scientifica
> Dr. Wilkins's nattural Principles, and Duties.   His World in
>   the Moon.
> Stallius his Regulæ Phylosophicæ
> Stierij Questiones Physicæ cum Praeceptis Philosophiæ.
> Burgerdicius, Logick with Heerebords Notes.
> The great Hist. Geographical, and Poetical Dictionary being
>   a curious Misscellany of Sacred and Prophane History
>   printed at London for Henry Rhodes.   If there be an
>   Edition since 1694, Send the best Two of them.
> Francis Turretini Institutio Theologiæ Elencticæ . . .
> Turretini Disputationes de satisfactione Christi.
> Poles Synopsis criticorum . . . if [you] light on them a
>   peniwoth.
> A K[ing] Edward 6th, his Common Prayer Book
> Queen Eliz[abeth] [her Common Prayer Book]
> Queens Bible, If . . . reasonable.[32]

He added to this order:

> If the Money doe more than hold out, send in School Books;
>   Esops Eng[lish] and Lat[in],
>   Corderius Eng[lish] and Lat[in],
>   Terrence Eng[lish] and Lat[in],
>   Ovid de Tristibus,
>   Metamorphosis,
>   Virgil,
>   Tullies de Officijs,
>   Grammars,
>   constr[u]ing Books.[33]

[32] Sewall, Letter-Book, i. 237.   June 10, 1700.
[33] Ibid., i. 238.

Later in the year he ordered:[34]

> Pole's Synopsis Criticorum if to be had under five pounds:
> as much cheaper as you can,
> A Ream of good Marble Paper.
> A gross of Horn-books.
> Two Cambridge Concordances.
> Octavo Bibles.

and a few days later:[35]

> Duz. of Dr. Bates's Harmony of the divine Attributes,
> 6. Flavels mental errors,
> 2 Mordeus Geographie rectified,
> 12. Colsons Seamans Kalendar.
> 6. Wakely's Compass rectifier.
> 6. Norwoods Epitome of Navigation.
> One great Histor. Geograph. and Poetical Dictionary of the
> newest Edition . . . .[36]

There were, evidently, plenty of channels through which the people of Boston and vicinity could obtain the latest books; and they made good use of their opportunities. With all the competition from the established bookshops Dunton seems to have found a good market; he wrote with satisfaction,

> . . . having stock'd the Town of Boston with my Books; (some having bought more, I'm afraid, than they intend to pay for)[37] and having still a Considerable Quantity left, Several Gentlemen have given me great Encouragement . . . to send a Venture to Salem . . . .[38]

and there also he had success.

It is a mistake to think of these booksellers as carrying only theological or devotional works. No doubt such books

[34] *Ibid.*, i. 248.
[35] *Ibid.*, i. 247, 248.
[36] See list on page 118, above.
[37] His sale of books on credit alone amounted to £300. See p. 116, above, under Richard Wilkins.
[38] Dunton, Letters, p. 248.

were an important part of their stock in trade, perhaps even
the larger part; but this would have been just as much so
in England. We do not know, unfortunately, just what
books Dunton brought with him from England, or what he
took back with him unsold; but one item in his "Letters" may
throw some light on the matter. He wrote of one customer,

The chief Books she bought were Plays[39] and Romances; which
to set off the better, she wou'd ask for Books of *Gallantry*.[40]

Plays and romances are hardly in keeping with the common notion of Puritan life in 1686, and it might seem necessary to reject this statement as one of the many untruths
in Dunton's very unreliable "Letters"[41] were it not for the
fact that recently discovered invoices of book shipments to
New England show that such books were on sale in Boston
even before Dunton came. In 1682 Robert Boulter, a London bookseller, sent to John Usher as a venture, "without
ordre," a shipment of nearly 800 volumes under about 125
titles. As Mr. Usher in October, 1680, was owing Mr.
Boulter £370, he evidently had traded with him for some
time, and therefore Boulter's consignment was not a blind
venture but a shipment of books to a market with which he
was familiar.[42] For that reason the items included in the list
are of value as an indication of the probable taste of Boston
readers. Some of the more interesting titles follow.[43]

3 faramond [*Pharamond*, Or The History of *France*. A Fam'd
    Romance . . .]
2 last part of the english rogue
2 parismus [The most Famous . . . History of *Parismus*, the
    most renowned Prince of *Bohemia*]

[39] A dancing master had set up in Boston in 1681, and a fencing master in 1686.
See p. 155, below.
[40] Dunton, Letters, p. 116.
[41] See C. N. Greenough's account of the plagiarisms in the Letters and his evidence
of their untrustworthiness as historical material: Publications of the Colonial
Society of Massachusetts, xiv. 213 ff.
[42] Ford, The Boston Book Market, p. 9 ff.
[43] *Ibid.*, p. 88 ff. Fuller lists of the items in these invoices are given in the
Appendix.

1 destruction of troy
1 Valentyn and orson [The Famous History of *Valentine* and *Orson*, the two sons of the Emperour of *Greece*]
4 esops in english
2 felthams resolves
16 Cap of gray haires [A Cap of Gray hairs for a Green head, or The Father's Counsel to his Son, an Apprentice in *London*]
2 Clelias [A four volume translation from Scudery]
9 argalus and parthenia [The pleasant and delightful History of *Argalus* and *Parthenia*,]
1 pembrooks arcadia [Sir Philip Sidney's *Arcadia*]
2 reynolds on Murther [The Triumphs of God's Revenge against the . . . Sin of Murther, Expressed in Thirty several Tragical Histories.]
2 perfect politician [or A . . . Life . . . of *O. Cromwell*.]
2 temples miscellanea [By Sir William Temple]
1 Bacons works
1 Cambdens Elizabeth
1 Miltons history [The History of *Britain*]
6 Guy of Warwick
6 Reynard fox
12 dr Faustus [The History of . . . Dr. *John Faustus*]
12 Joviall Garland [. . . containing a Collection of all the newest Songs and Sonnets used in Court and Country]
12 Crown Garland
6 Garland of delight
6 fortunatus [The right pleasant, and variable Tragical, History of *Fortunatus*]
6 royall arbours [A Royall Arbor of Loyall Poesie, consisting of Poems and Songes, digested into Triumph, Elegie, Satyr, Love, and Drollerie]
8 Soggins jests [Scoggings Jests]
4 Mandevills travells
4 pack cards

The four other invoices, all of ordered books, show no such proportion of the light reading of that day, but do show that some real literature was imported into Boston. In connection with these items it must be remembered that these invoices report only the purchases of one Boston book-seller through a single ship captain (excepting those listed above sent by Boulter without order) in a period of less than two years.

Invoice of September 5, 1683.[44]

 1 Hacklutes Uoyages
 1 Mori Utopia
 1 Felthams Resolues
 7 Accademy Compliments [. . . with many new Additions of Songs and Catches à la mode]
 1 Shaftsburys Life
 1 Poeticall History [a mythology]
 7 Accademy Compliments, another sorte.
30 History of Dr. Faustus

Invoice of March 3, 1683–4.[45]

 2 Erle of Rochesters Poems
 4 Miltons Paradise Lost
 6 Lestranges Erasmus in English
 1 Baker's Chronicle [of the Kings of England]
 1 Pembrooks Arcadia
 3 Accademy of Compliments
 6 Nuga Uenales [. . . being new Jests . . .]
 3 Present State of England
18 Dr. Faustus
 6 Wilds Poems
 6 Argulus and Parthenia
 5 Oxford Jests

Invoice of May 29, 1684.[46]

 4 State of England
 3 Markhams way to get wealth
 2 History of Parismus

 [44] *Ibid.,* p. 108 ff. In this and in the next list it is reported that certain volumes ordered could not be supplied. Some of the items are designated for individuals not booksellers.
 [45] *Ibid.,* p. 121 ff.
 [46] *Ibid.,* p. 133 ff.

20 Gentle Craft [. . . with Pictures, and Variety of Wit and Mirth]
 2 Wonders of the Femall world [. . . or A general History of Women]
 1 Her and His [*Haec et Hic*, or The Feminine Gender more worthy than the Masculine.]
10 Second Part of the Pilgrims Progress.
 2 Two Journeys to Jerusalem
 2 London Bully [or The Prodigal Son; displaying the principal Cheats of our Modern Debauchees]
 2 Informers Doome [. . . with the Discovery of the Knavery and Cheats of most Trades in *London*]
 3 Uenus in the Cloyster

Invoice of April 13, 1685.[47]
 2 Glissons Common Law Epitomized
 8 Jure Maritimo
 2 Terms of the Law
 3 Daltons Justice [The Country Justice]
 2 Keebles Statutes
 2 Cooks Reports Engl. [By Sir Edward Coke]
 3 Blounts Law Dictionary
 1 Sheppards Grand Abridgement [of the Common and Statute Law of England]
 1 Hobbarts Reports [law]
 3 Miltons Logick
 6 History of Dr. Faustus
 2 Rochesters Life [Burnet's Life of the Earl of Rochester]
 2 Pulton of the Common Pleas Engls.
 5 Sheppards Sure Guide [for his Majesties Justices of Peace]
10 Wonderful Prodogies

From these invoices and certain references to bills and indebtedness Mr. Ford estimates that in the years 1679–1685, inclusive, John Usher imported books to a value of £567. Such a figure is a minimum rather than a maximum; he bought that much and he may have bought more through

[47] *Ibid.*, p. 140 ff.

other captains and of other London booksellers, record of the transactions having disappeared, even as these invoices vanished for centuries. One other invoice of the period has survived, together with a letter from the shipper to Increase Mather. The shipper was Richard Chiswell of London, whom Dunton calls "the Metropolitan Bookseller of England." He seems to have had a large trade in New England; the last four invoices above were of consignments from him. The letter and invoice follow; unfortunately the latter is not complete, including only the books sent to Dr. Mather, and not those to Usher which accompanied them.

S^r,—I rec'^{d} yours of July 19th, & have in Mr Vsher's Cask p^r Anderson, in the Ship Blessing, sent you all the books you wrote for, & have returned 8 of your Principles, which I cannot sell . . .

I have added a few new things of good note which I hope you will be pleased with, the first of them is an answer to a Pamphlet I sent you in the last pcell, & which makes no small stir here at present. Hales of Eaton, & Stillingfleet are very famous. Walker of Baptism is said to be very learned & exceedingly well done. The two books of Contemplations were writ by the Lord Cheif Justice Hales, a person who for all kind of learning, Philosophy, Physick, Mathematicks, &c., as well as Law, (his proper profession,) and for most exemplary piety . . . has not le[ft] his fellow, . . . the whole nation mournes for the loss of him. That Great audit or Good Steward's account, in the first vollume, is a most lively & exact character of his life. . . . I know not any two books have come forth these 20 yeares, that have sold so great a number in so short a time, as these two vollumes of his,[48] . . . I have sent a few books to Mr Vsher without order, which I put in to fill up the Cask. You may see them at his shop, & I hope may help some of them off his hands, by recomending them to your publick Library, especially the new ones, which cannot be there already, pticularly Dr Caves Lives of the Fathers,

[48] This letter has been given so fully because of its interesting testimony to the fact that the colonists were not entirely dependent upon their own tastes, or their knowledge of contemporary books. Their London correspondents tried to keep them abreast of current works.

& Dr Cary's Chronologicall account of ancient time, which are both exceeding well esteemed by the most learned & ingenious men here.[49]

A Coppy.

	£ s. d.
Postage . . . Letters . . .	0. 1. 0
Dr Tuckneys Sermons, 4°	0. 8. 0
Straight gate to heaven, 12° bound,	0. 0. 8
Hotchkis reformation or ruine, 8°	0. 2. 0
Discovery of Pigmies, 8°	0. 1. 0
Horologicall Dialogues, 8°	0. 1. 0
Hornes Cause of Infants maintained, 4°	0. 1. 0
Whiston on Baptism, all 3 parts, 8°	0. 5. 6
State of Northampton, 4°	0. 0. 3
Tozer's Directions to a godly life, 12°	0. 1. 0
Barbets Chirurgery, 8°	0. 6. 0
Leybournes Dialling, 4°	0. 3. 0
Hook's Motion of the Earth, 4°	0. 1. 0
Stephenson's mathemat. compendium, 12°	0. 2. 6
8 First principles of New England, 4° returnd[50].	0. 8. 0

ADDED.—

Pacquet of advices to the men of Shaftsbury, 4°	0. 1. 6
King & Ld Chancellor's Speeches.	0. 0. 6
Dr Stillingfleet's Letter to a Deist, 8°	0. 2. 6
Mr Hales (of Eaton) his Tracts, 8°	0. 2. 6
Hornecks Law of Consideration, 8°	0. 3. 6
Walker of Baptism, 12°	0. 3. 6
Rules of Health, 12°	0. 1. 0
Family Physitian, 12°	0. 1. 0
Judge Hale's Contemplations, 2 Vol. 8°	0.10. 0
24 Warrs of New England, 4° [51]	————
Catalogue No. 7. 8. 9. 10, fol.	————

[49] Mather Papers, p. 575. The letter was written in February, 1677.

[50] This was a book by Increase Mather which proved to be a poor seller, and so the left over copies are returned.

[51] Chiswell had reprinted this book by Increase Mather, and is sending these copies as a gift to the author, although he has been disappointed at not selling more than 500.

126 Literary Culture in Early New England.

Besides the regular booksellers, there were hawkers of books whose influence cannot be estimated for lack of information. Ballads, broadsides, popular books such as "Pilgrim's Progress" and Wigglesworth's "Day of Doom," and almanacs doubtless made up much of the hawker's stock in trade. Cotton Mather's busy brain saw opportunity for good here, for he recorded in his diary in 1683, "There is an old *Hawker* who will fill this Countrey with devout and useful Books, if I will direct him."[52]

There were, evidently, sufficient opportunities for the growth of private libraries. A letter from Increase Mather to Joseph Dudley, November 10, 1684, gives additional testimony of this fact. Writing of a letter containing defamatory matter to which his name had been forged to discredit him (probably by Edward Randolph),[53] he says:

He pretends as if I sent to Amsterdam for the New Covenant of Scotland, Carill upon Job, and Mr. Owen's last works. Now herein he has so grossly played the fool, soe as to discover the letter to be a meer peece of forgery. As for the new Covenant of Scotland, I never heard of such a thing, . . . Carill have been in my study this fiveteen years, & if I had him not, it is likely that I should send to Amsterdam, for Mr. Carill & Doct. Owen's works, which are here sould in Boston.[54]

The best of the private libraries of New England were undoubtedly those owned by the Mathers, father and son. Of the latter's Dunton wrote in 1686, when Cotton Mather was but eight years out of college:

. . . he shew'd me his Study: And I do think he has one of the best (for a Private Library) that I ever saw: Nay, I may go farther, and affirm, That as the Famous Bodleian Library at Oxford, is the Glory of that University, if not of all Europe, . . . so I may say, That Mr. Mather's Library is the Glory of New-

[52] Diary, i. 65. For later importance of hawkers of books see pp. 191-193, below.
[53] This is a part of the long quarrel between the Mathers and Randolph.
[54] Mather Papers, p. 101.

England, if not of all America. I am sure it was the best sight that I had in Boston.[55]

Of this library Cotton Mather wrote in his diary, October 16, 1700:

[A widow] had a Parcel of Books, which once belong'd unto the Library of our famous old Mr. *Chancey;* and if I would please to take them, she should count herself highly gratified, in their being so well bestowed. I singled out, about *forty Books,* and some of them large Ones, which were now added unto my Library, that has already between two and three thousand in it.[56]

An extensive private library was brought to New England in 1686 by Samuel Lee, pastor of the church at Bristol from that year to 1691. Returning to England in 1691 he was taken prisoner by the French and died in France. The books which he left in Bristol were put on sale in Boston in 1693 at the shop of Duncan Campbell. The catalogue of these books, printed by Campbell, contains, besides pages of theological titles, the following titles:[57]

Subject	Number
Physics	124
Philosophy	83
Mathematics and Astronomy	48 (in Latin)
	13 (in English)
History	112 (in Latin)
	45 (in English)
School authors	60
Law books	8
Unclassified	327

The following partial list will give an idea of the range of this library:

Paracelsi	Opera
Paracelsi	de Vita Longa

[55] Dunton, Letters, p. 75.
[56] Diary, i. 368.
[57] *Titles,* not volumes.

Reolani	Anatomia
Willis	Anatomia cerebri
Helmontii	Opera
Helmont[ii]	dies Aurora rubra
Roger Bacon	perspect. per Combas.
————	Theatrum Chemicum vols. 1-4
Platonis	Opera
Seneca	Opera
Luciani Phylosoph:	Opera
Xenophon	Philosoph.
Aristotilis	[several]
Bacon	de augment [atione] Scientiarum
Cartesii	Metaphisica
Petri Rami	prælectiones
Archemedis	omnia opera
Tychobrachy	opera omnia
Joan: Stadii	Ephimeridis
Evevautii	Ephimerid.
Newtons	Trigonometry
Newtons	Astronomy
Dugdal.	Monast. angl.
Duckdales	Antiquities of Warwickshire
Stout's	Survey of London
Hollinshead's	Chronicles of Scotland
————	England & Ireland in 3 vols.
Fox's	Acts and Monuments
Rawleigh's	History of the World
Eabran's	Cronicles
Crackinthorp's	Councils
Everard's	Collections
Philpot's	Survey of Kent
Sayndy's	History of China
Wilson's	History of Great Britain
Crossel's	History of England
————	The Union of the Houses of York and Lancaster
Jones's	Antiquity of Great Britain
Burlons	description of Leichester
Delaval's	Travels

Howel's	History of London
Isaacson's	Chronology
Brughton's	Ecclesiastical History of Great Britain
Evebins [Evelin]	Discourse of Trees
Morison's	Travels
Summer's	Antiquity of Canterbury
Isaac's	Rarities of Exeter
Langhorn's	Introduction to the History of England
Ailan's	History of King Henry VII
Pitit's	ancient Right of the Commons of England
———	The History of Mary Queen of Scotland
———	The History of the Navy of Great Britain
———	The Life of Merlin
———	The History of Scanderberg
Prin's [Prynne]	new Discovery of the Prelates Tyranny
Bacon's	Natural History
Bacon	Hist[oria] Naturalis
Baconi	Hist[ory of] Hen[ry] 7th
Demosthen[es]	Oration[es] &c.
Homeri	Iliad (3 copies)
Homeri	Odysse[y] (5 copies)
Lucan	cum notis
Ashylii	Tragediæ
Terentii	Tragediæ
Hesiodi	opera cum Scholiis
Pindari	Odes
Persii	Satyr[æ]
Sophaclis	Antigone
Sophaclis	traged[iæ] cum Scholiis
Horatius	(3 copies)
Aristophanis	(3 copies)
Euripidis	Hecuba Græca
Salust	———
Martialæ	Epigram
Tascitus	———
Macrobius	———
Boetius	de Gemmis
Plutarchi	vitæ
Caesaris	Comment. (2)

Ceneca [sic]	Tragicus
Erasmi	Colloqui
Beda venerab.	de natura rerum (2)
———	Marmora Arundeliana

As another example of the variety to be found in colonial libraries, the following list of titles from a library of only thirty volumes in all is of interest.[58]

> London Despencettory
> Dixonarey
> Norwood's Trigonometry
> Gervase Markham's Gentleman Jocky
> Lambarde's Perambulation of Kent
> Morton's New England's Memorial
> Sir Matthew Hale's Contemplations
> The Effect of Warr
> 11 books on law

Some idea of Increase Mather's library may be gained from the statements as to his reading which are found in his fragmentary diary for the years 1675 and 1676.[59] The authors read, with the titles of the books when given, are listed here. It should be noted that this list contains almost no duplicates of the titles found in the lists given on pages 52 and 53 and on pages 237–242.[60]

Albaspinus	De Ritibus Ecclesiæ
Alsted	[not stated]
[Alwaerden?]	History of Severitus [Servetus?]
Autores	De Sinceritate
Bates	Vocatio
Bell	[not stated]
Boreman	"de swearing"
Bownd	"of Sabbath"

[58] Proceedings of the American Antiquarian Society, xviii. 136.
[59] Massachusetts Historical Society, Proceedings, 2d Series, xiii. 339 ff.
[60] The lack of duplication in these three different lists is typical in that the writer has found it almost invariably true that every new source of information in regard to colonial libraries has added details entirely new. Our knowledge of most of the colonial libraries is at best fragmentary.

Bridges	On Luke 17: 37
Buxtorf	Lex. Thalmud
Camel	not stated
Carter	On Hebrews 1: 1
Caryl	[not stated]
Chamberlain	State of E[urope]
Cicero	Orations
Clark	Vanity of Earthly Things
Clark	Examples
Elias Levita	[not stated]
Fenner	Alarm
Firmin	Real Christian
Franklin	Of Antichrist
Franzius	History of Brutes
Aul. Gellius	[not stated]
Goclenii	Logicæ
Goodwin	Sermons
Hall	On Timothy 3: 2
Herbert	Country Parson
Hubbard	History of Pequot War
Jerome, St.	Of Pliny
Johnson	[not stated]
Leigh	Of Colledges
May	History of War in E[ngland]
Morton	History of New England
Moxon	Of Globes
Owen	[various]
Paget	Chronography
Pareus	Orationes
Powell	[not stated]
Purchase [sic]	"of America"
Revius	de Capillitio
Reynolds	[not stated]
Rivet	[not stated]
Rutherford	"de drawing to Ct [Christ]"
Schindler	de Moseroth
Sibs	On Hosea 14
Smith, C.	Experiences
Stoughton	Of Covetousness

Twisse	[various]
Voetius	[not stated]
Ward, R.	Politick Strategy
Willisius	de Memoria

Other books are mentioned without sufficient detail for identification. A few of these items follow.

> Discourse of Witchcraft
> Help to discourse
> Cabinet of Mirth
> Autores de Conviction
> Tollis[n] of ye Jews
> de doctoribus Misnicis
> Coma Berenices
> Capell Hall
> Life of Richard 3
> History of Formosa.

The Public Libraries as well as private ones continued to grow. There are unfortunately few references to the Boston Public Library in the town-house during this period. Sir Thomas Temple, in a will drawn up and filed October 14, 1671, before he sailed for England, inserted the following clause:

> . . . . as also all my Bookes which I estimate at £150 &c in case of sd Nelsons death before he receive them then I doe give & bequeath . . . . the Bookes above sd. at the select men of Bostons dispose viz: such as are fit for the Towne Lybrary unto that; and the rest to be sold & given to the poor of this Towne.

Before he died he drew up another will in London, in which there was no mention of the Library.[61] In a will dated March 12, 1673–4, John Oxenbridge made the following bequest:

> To the Public Library in Boston or elsewhere, as my executors

[61] Suffolk Probate Files No. 697, quoted in Publications of the Colonial Society of Massachusetts, xii. 122.

and overseers shall judge best, Augustine's Works in six volumes, the Century's in three volumes; the catalogue of Oxford Library.[62]

The Boston Athenæum owns a copy of Samuel Mather's "Testimony against Idolatry and Superstition," inscribed "ffor the Publike Library at Boston, 1674."[63] On August 2, 1683, the Selectmen gave an order to David Edwards

to receaue of Elder John Wiswall & Doct[r] Elisha Cooke £34.4s. in mony for severall things he brought from England for y[e] vse of the Library, by order of Captain Brattle. . . .[64]

In 1686 the Town Records mentioned "the library room at the east end of the town house;"[63] and the same year Andros met the ministers "in the Library" at the town-house.[65] At a town meeting March 11, 1694–5, it was voted

. . . . that all Bookes or Other things belonging to the Library . . . . be demanded and Taken care of by the Selectmen.[66]

At a meeting of the Selectmen January 1, 1701–2, it was

Ordered that whereas Samuell Clough did formerly borrow the Towns Globes that he do now return them unto the Town Treasurer.[67]

In Chiswell's letter already given on pages 124 and 125 there is also a reference to this Library which would seem to indicate that Chiswell was accustomed to having many books of his sending bought by or for it:

I hope may help some of them off his hands by recommending

[62] Winsor, Memorial History of Boston, i. 501.

[63] *Ibid.*, iv. 279.

[64] Boston Record Commissioners' Reports, vii. 162, quoted in Publications of the Colonial Society of Massachusetts, xii. 124.

[65] Sewall, Diary, i. 162.

[66] Boston Record Commissioners' Reports, vii. 220, quoted in the Publications of the Colonial Society of Massachusetts, xii. 125.

[67] Boston Record Commissioners' Reports, xi. 13, quoted in the Publications of the Colonial Society of Massachusetts, xii. 126.

them to your publick Library, *especially the new ones, which can-not be there already.*[68]

The last phrase sounds as though any books but the newest might be expected to be found there.

The Harvard Library during this period received many important accessions. Under date of May 1, 1675, John Knowles wrote to John Leverett,

Alderman Ashurst hath about 50 books of history for the College from Mr. Baxter.[69]

The same year John Lightfoot bequeathed his library, containing "the Targums, Talmuds, Rabbins, Polyglot, and other valuable tracts relative to Oriental literature."[70]   In 1677 the Reverend Theophilus Gale left to it all his books, consisting chiefly of patristic and controversial theology.[71] In 1682 Sir John Maynard, sergeant-at-law, gave to the Library eight chests of books, valued at £400.[72]   The last two gifts brought in so many duplicates that the Fellows of the College ordered "that the double Books in the Colledge Library be prized & sold & yᵉ money improved for the buying other books yᵗ are wanting."[73]

There exists in the collections of the Massachusetts Historical Society a manuscript "Catalogue of such books as are double in ye Colledge Library," and with it what purports to be a record of volumes sold, with the amounts paid. The second list, containing 396 items, is more extensive than

[68] The italics are mine.

[69] North American Review, cvii. 572.   Richard Baxter, fearing that his library would be seized to pay a fine, planned to give most of it to Harvard, but learned that Sir Kenelme Digby had given them "the Fathers, Councils, and Schoolmen, and that it was history and commentators which they wanted.   Whereupon I sent them some of my commentators, and some historians, among which were Freherus', Reuberus', and Pistorius' collections."

[70] *Ibid.*, cvii. 572.

[71] *Ibid.*, cvii. 573.   Neal, History of New England, i. 202, called Gale's "a large and Valuable Collection of Books."

[72] North American Review, cvii. 573.

[73] Harvard Library, Bibliographical Contributions, lii. 10.

the "catalogue," which lists 99 in folio, 36 in quarto, and 37 in octavo and smaller. There are no dates on either. The record of sales is partly in Increase Mather's hand. It may be that the second list covers a longer period of time, including later additions of duplicates. At any rate, about 400 titles of duplicates were sold, adding to the Library's funds about £98.10.00. Among the duplicates sold were:

> Bacon's Essays (2 copies sold, one at 2s, one at 1s.)
> Bacon's Advancement of Learning
> Feltham's Resolves
> Hackluit's Voyages
> Herodotus
> Aristophanes
> Gassendi
> Keckermann
> Plutarch in English[74]

John Dunton's visit also added books to the Harvard Library, and gives us a glimpse of it through London eyes. He wrote home,

> I was invited hither [to Harvard] by Mr. Cotton[75] . . . by his means I sold many of my Books to the Colledge.[76]

Elsewhere he wrote,

> The *Library* of this *Colledge* is very considerable, being well furnish'd both with Books, and *Mathematical Instruments*.[77]

With the increased importation of books and with the growth of libraries there seems to have been an increase rather than a decrease in the borrowing and lending of

[74] Cotton Mather took advantage of this sale of duplicates to the extent of 96 titles, for which he paid £43.19.00 in installments. (Ms. list in possession of the American Antiquarian Society. See Publications of the Colonial Society of Massachusetts, xviii. 407 ff., for a photographic reproduction of this list and a catalogue of the books included.)

[75] John Cotton was Library-keeper at Harvard 1681–1690.

[76] Dunton, Letters, p. 156.

[77] Dunton, Life and Errors, p. 157. Neal, History of New England, i. 202, estimated it at between three and four thousand volumes before 1700.

books. Of this the following extracts from letters written during this time are indicative. More letters illustrating this tendency are given in the Appendix.

G. F.[78] hath sent the a booke of his by Jere: Bull, & two more now, which thou mayest communecatte to thy Counsell & officers.

Allso I remember before thy last being in England, I sent the a booke, written by Francis Howgall againest persecution, ... which booke thou loueingly accepted. . . .[79]

My last to thee was of the 29 D. 4. 72,[80] which Richard & Ester Smyth informed me they sent it to thee, so that they made noe doubt of thee safe convaience of it, with George Ffox bookes to thee, to which I shall refere thee. I haue other writings of G. F. not yet copied, which, if thou desireth, when I heare from thee, I may convaie them vnto thee; . . .[81]

May these few hasty lines salute you acceptably though only to certify the receiving of yours of the 18 of the former, & to thank you for that kindnesse, & that little volume of poetry therewith.[82]

Thinking it might be acceptable, I have sent you a verse-book; and desire you would send the other to Mr. Walley.[83]

It is evident from the details given in this chapter that the colonists did not lack for books, and that those which deserve the term literature were on their shelves in a fair proportion for the time. Evidence of the possession of still other books, and of their familiarity with and use of them, is to be found in the quotations with which they embellished their own writings.

[78] George Fox, then visiting New England.
[79] William Coddington to John Winthrop, Jr., 1672. Winthrop Papers, ii. 289.
[80] June 29, 1672. "My last" refers to the letter just quoted.
[81] William Coddington to John Winthrop, Jr. Winthrop Papers, ii. 291. The reference to copying books by hand demonstrates another method of supplementing libraries. Edward Taylor of Westfield had a considerable library of books which he had himself copied and bound.
[82] John Winthrop, Jr., to Roger Williams, January 6, 1675. Winthrop Papers, i. 306. If only he had mentioned the title!
[83] Samuel Angier to Governor Hinckley of Plymouth, January 29, 1677. Mr. Walley was preacher at Barnstable. Massachusetts Historical Society, Collections, 4th Series, v. 13. Governor Hinckley was a writer of verse.

Chapter VIII: Quotations by New England Writers.

AS a large part of the published writings of the New Englanders consisted of sermons, and as it seems to have been against their custom to use in their sermons any quotations except from Scripture or rarely from some of the Fathers, the field for quotations is somewhat limited. It is still further limited by the fact that few of the writers of narrative embellish their narratives with borrowed ornaments, either of prose or of poetry. From such books as do not belong to these two classes, from letters, and from a few narratives, the quotations to be included are taken.

Daniel Gookin, in his "Historical Collections of the Indians," Chapter IV, referred to "that seraphick prediction of holy Herbert, that excellent poet, ... which he elegantly declared in that poem: Herbert, Church Militant, 190, 191 page." He proceeds to quote twenty-four lines, from

> Religion stands on tiptoe in our land
> Ready to pass to the American strand

to

> But lends to us, shall be our desolation.

From his reference to the paging, which is the same in the fifth edition as in the first, it is evident that he had a copy of Herbert's "The Temple" before him. There are two or three errors in the quotation which he may have made in copying, but which are more likely typesetters' mistakes.

In a letter to Increase Mather, Nathaniel Morton wrote,

. . . . and in some sort comply with our Englis Poett, George Withers; (saith hee) Alas that I was borne soe late, or else soe

soone; to see soe cleare, soe bright a morne, soe darke an after-
noone.[1]

Thomas Shepard, writing to his son, then entering Harvard, in regard to his studies, echoed Bacon's essay, "Of
Studies":

Lett your studies be so ordered as to have variety of Studies
before you, that when you are weary of one book, you may take
pleasure (through this variety) in another: and for this End read
some Histories often, which (they Say) make men wise, as Poets
make witty; both which are pleasant things in the midst of more
difficult studies.[2]

The witchcraft controversies naturally called forth much
citing of authorities.   John Hale, in his "Modest Enquiry,"
referred to or quoted the following:

Bernard[3]
Baxter and R. Burton, their Histories about witches.[4]
Finch: Common Law[5]
Keeble of the Common Law[6]
St. Germans: Abridgment of Common Law
Wierus: De Præstigiis Demonum[7]

He also quoted a story by "my Lord Cook," evidently

[1] Written August 8, 1679. Mather Papers, p. 594.
[2] Publications of the Colonial Society of Massachusetts, xiv. 194. Probably
written in 1672, as Thomas Shepard, third of that name, was of the class of 1676.
Bacon's phrase is "Histories make Men Wise; Poets Witty." Shepard may have
acquired this phrase at second hand; but, as several copies of the "Essays" have
already been noted in the comparatively few libraries of which record remains,
presumably he took it from its source.
[3] Bernard, "Guide to Grand-Jury men · . . in cases of Witchcraft," 1627.
[4] Baxter, "The Certainty of the Worlds of Spirits fully evinced by unquestion-
able Histories of Apparitions and Witchcrafts," 1691. R. Burton, or R. B., was the
pseudonym of Nathaniel Crouch, publisher of London, who wrote many chapbooks. The reference may be to "The Kingdom of Darkness," 1688.
[5] Sir Henry Finch, "Treatise of Common Law," 1627, 1638, 1678; or "Sum-
mary of Common Law," 1673.
[6] Joseph Keeble wrote "Statutes," 1676, and "An Assistance to Justices of the
Peace," 1683, 1689.
[7] Johann Weyer, a Rhenish physician, 1515–1588; quoted by the Mathers, and
also by Burton in "The Anatomy of Melancholy."

Sir Edward Coke. A phrase which he used, "A dwarf upon a giants shoulders can see farther than a giant," may have been taken from Burton's "Anatomy of Melancholy," where it is found;[8] it may, however, have been a current phrase.

Robert Calef, merchant of Boston, in his attack on the Mathers which he called "More Wonders of the Invisible World" in mockery of Cotton Mather's "Wonders of the Invisible World," also showed familiarity with the literature of demonology, from which he freely quoted:

And in the Mercury for the month of February, 1695, there is this account[9] [from which he quotes]

. . . . the indians' adorations, which agrees well with what A. Ross sets forth, in his Mistag. Poetic. p. 116,[10] that . . . .

> Bernard's work on witches[11]
> Mr. Gaule's book on witches[12]
> Perkins' work on witches[13]
> Bodin[14]
> . . . . the fancies of Trithemius[15]

Calef was not content, however, with recent authors on the subject, but went back to the lives of Justin Martyr, Apollonius Tyaneus, and Julian the Apostate, and to the works of Josephus; he even quoted Ovid and Virgil. He has two quotations from Sandys' metrical translation of the "Metamorphoses": eighteen lines from Liber 7, and nine from Liber 14; and two passages from a metrical translation of Virgil's "Bucolics" which I have been unable to identify:

[8] Democritus to the Reader, p. 8, Chatto & Windus edition, 1907.
[9] P. xv. Calef's book was written in 1697.
[10] P. 129. Alexander Ross, "Mystagogus Poeticus, or the Muses Interpreter," London, 1647.
[11] See p. 138 note 3, above.
[12] John Gaule, "Select Cases of Conscience touching Witches and Witchcrafts," London, 1646.
[13] "Discourse of the Damned Art of Witchcraft," 1608.
[14] Jean Bodin, "Demonology."
[15] Johann Trithemius, 1462-1516.

two lines from Eclogue 13, and eleven lines from Eclogue 8. Although Calef complained that he was not an educated man, in contrast to the Mathers whom he was opposing, he knew both his Virgil and his Ovid, in English at least, sufficiently well to recall passages which very effectively illustrated his point that the current notions of witchcraft came from paganism and had no authority from the Bible.

The Mathers, especially Cotton, with his vast learning and a willingness to exhibit it, are very helpful to this study because they did quote so freely as to give some idea of the books with which they were familiar. Increase Mather quoted or cited (giving page or chapter reference) at least one hundred and thirty different authors, not including anonymous works quoted or cited, such as "The History of Sham Plots" or the "German Ephemerides." Besides these there are over thirty authors to whom he referred familiarly, but did not directly use. Cotton Mather quoted or cited over three hundred authors, and referred without direct use to nearly two hundred others. As it would be tedious to comment on all of these, only a few will be discussed, the rest being merely listed.

The most interesting quotation by Increase Mather is one from Burton's "Anatomy of Melancholy." Mather wrote:[16]

. . . . There is in special, a sort of melancholy madness, which is called *lycanthropia* or *lupina insania, h. e.*, when men imagine themselves to be turned into wolves or other beasts. Hippocrates relates concerning the daughters of king Prætus, that they thought themselves kine. Wierus (*de Prœstigiis Dœmonum*, 1. iii. c. 21) speaketh of one in Padua, that would not believe to the contrary but that he was a wolf; and of a Spaniard, who thought himself a bear. Euwichius (and from him Horstius) writeth of a man that was found in a barn under the hay, howling and saying he was a wolf. The foolish rusticks, who surprized him, began to flay him, that so they might see if he had not hair growing on the

16 Remarkable Providences, p. 122.

inside of his skin. Forestus has many instances to this purpose. Heurnius saith, that it is a disease frequent in Bohemia and Hungaria. No doubt but this disease gave occasion to Pliny's assertion, that some men in his time were turned into wolves, and from wolves into men again. Hence was Ovid's fable of Lycaon, and the tale of Pausanius being ten years a wolf, and then a man again. He that would see more instances, may read Austin, *de Civ. Dei.* 1·. xviii, c. 5; Burton of *Melancholly*, page 9. They that are subject unto this malady, for the most part lye hid all the day, and go abroad in the night, barking and howling at graves and in desarts. We may suppose that Nebuchadnezzar was troubled with this disease.

From Mather's brief reference to Burton in the above no one would imagine his real indebtedness to him for almost every detail in the passage. An idea of his wholesale borrowing in this instance will be obtained by a comparison of this with the parallel passage in Burton which follows:

Lycanthropia, which Avicenna calls Cucubuth, others Lupinam insaniam, or Wolf-madness, when men run howling about graves and fields in the night, and will not be persuaded but that they are wolves, or some such beasts. Ætius and Paulus call it a kind of melancholy; but I should rather refer it to madness, as most do. Some make a doubt of it whether there be any such disease. Donat ab Altomari saith, that he saw two of them in his time: Wierus tells a story of such a one at Padua 1541, that would not believe to the contrary, but that he was a wolf. He hath another instance of a Spaniard, who thought himself a bear; Forrestus confirms as much by many examples; one amongst the rest of which he was an eye-witness, at Alcmaer in Holland, a poor husbandman that still hunted about graves, and kept in churchyards, of a pale, black, ugly, and fearful look. Such belike, or little better, were King Prætus' daughters, that thought themselves kine. And Nebuchadnezzar in Daniel, as some interpreters hold, was only troubled with this kind of madness. This disease perhaps gave occasion to that bold assertion of Pliny, "some men were turned into wolves in his time, and from wolves to men again:" and to that fable of Pausanias, of a man that was ten years a wolf, and afterwards turned to his former shape: to

Ovid's tale of Lycaon, &c.   He that is desirous to hear of this disease, or more examples, let him read Austin in his 18th book *de Civitate Dei, cap.* 5. *Mizaldus, cent.* 5. 77. *Sckenkius, lib.* 1. *Hildesheim,* . . . . [names several others].   This malady, saith Avicenna, troubleth men most in February, and is now-a-days frequent in Bohemia and Hungary, according to Heurnius. Schernitzius will have it common in Livonia.   They lie hid most part all day, and go abroad in the night, barking, howling, at graves and deserts; . . . .[17]

There are one or two original items in Mather's, but nearly everything is borrowed, even to the phraseology, except the order.   Was Mather the first of the many who have borrowed from the "Anatomy" without giving due credit?

Increase Mather knew Sir Thomas Browne as well as Burton, and quoted three times from his "Pseudodoxia Epidemica,"[18] citing the page once.   He also cited Sir Kenelme Digby's "Discourse of Bodies," pp. 409, 410.[19]   Thomas Fuller he cited and quoted;[20] and of course Joseph Glanvil, whose writings were the chief stronghold of those who believed in the necessity of witch-hunting.[21]   His acceptance of the absurdities of the witchcraft delusions was not, however, due to any lack of access to or familiarity with the best scientific writings of his time.   He took illustrations from five numbers of the Philosophical Transactions of the Royal So-

[17] Pp. 88, 89, Chatto & Windus edition, 1907.

[18] "Johnston (and from him Dr. Browne in his *Vulgar Errors*) hath truly asserted the contrary." (Remarkable Providences, p. 73.)   "Dr. Browne, in his *Pseudodoxia Epidemica,* p. 63, does rationally suppose . . ." (*Ibid.*, p. 74.)   There is also a reference on p. 76.

[19] *Ibid*, p. 72.

[20] "Such persons do (as Fuller speaks) fence themselves . . ." (*Ibid.*, p. 180.) "The like is reported by Dr. Fuller, in his *Church History*," (*Ibid.*, p. 261.)   "Fuller's History of the Church p. 424." (Prayer, Early History of New England, p. 269.)

[21] He quotes or cites from the "Sadducismus Triumphatus or the Collection of Modern Relations," on pages 112, 127, 133, 149, 156, 158, 166, 170, 171, of Remarkable Providences.

ciety,[22] from two volumes of the Philosophical Conferences of the Virtuosi of France,[23] and from half a dozen volumes of the "German Ephemerides;"[24] he also quoted Robert Hooke[25] and Robert Boyle.[26] Of the latter he remarked in the Preface to "Remarkable Providences," "I have often wished that the Natural History of New-England might be written and published to the world; the rules and method described by that learned and excellent person Robert Boyle, Esq., being duely observed therein."

The list of the other books or writers made use of by Increase Mather, given in the Appendix, will show the variety of his reading, and, with the lists already given on pages 130 and 131, will throw light upon the content of his library.

The quotations by Cotton Mather are not only more in number than his father's, but have a more literary tone at times, partly because they include more poetry. He was familiar with "Paradise Lost," as is shown by three well chosen passages from that poem which he used in the "Magnalia."   Charles Francis Adams, although he quotes these passages, makes the inference that we have no positive record of any copy of Milton's poems in New England before 1720;[27] a study of Mather's treatment of the passages he quotes will, however, I think, convince the reader that there must have been at least one copy of "Paradise Lost" in New England before 1698, lying open on Cotton Mather's table as he wrote his greatest book. Speaking of the diffi-

[22] Numbers cited are for 1665, 1666, 1670, 1672, and 1676. Remarkable Providences, pp. 83, 226, 213, 216, and 219, respectively.

[23] Vols. i and ii. Remarkable Providences, pp. 212, 82.

[24] Also called the "Observations of the Imperial Academy."   The years quoted are 1670, 1671, 1675, 1679, 1687, 1689.

[25] "the late *Philosophical Collections*, published by Mr. Robert Hook, page 9."

[26] "The truly noble and honourable Robert Boyle, Esq., . . . in his book of the *Usefulness of Natural Philosophy*, p. 15."

[27] Massachusetts Historical Society, Proceedings, xlii. 154 ff. See, however, p. 123, above, and p. 181, below.

culties met by the colonists in their wars with the Indians, he wrote:[28]

    . . . . they found that they were like to make no weapons reach their enswamped adversaries, except Mr. Milton could have shown them how

> To have pluckt up the hills with all their load—
> Rocks, waters, woods—and by their shaggy tops,
> Up-lifting, bore them in their hands, therewith
> The rebel host to 've over-whelm'd.—

A comparison of this with the original, "Paradise Lost," VI, 643–647, 650–651, shows that Mather's changes are not misquotations from memory, but careful changes, evidently with the original before him, to preserve the rhythm and at the same time fit the new context.

> From their foundations, loosening to and fro,
> They plucked the seated hills, with all their load,
> Rocks, waters, woods, and, by the shaggy tops
> Uplifting, bore them in their hands.   Amaze,
> Be sure, and terror, seized the rebel host,
>
> .   .   .   .
>
> Till on those cursed engines' triple row
> They saw them whelmed, ...

   The great impression made upon Mather by the details of the contest between the rebel host and the forces of the Almighty is shown by his own statement and by the two other paraphrases on the poem:

    . . . . but we who felt ourselves assaulted by unknown numbers of *devils in flesh* on every side of us, and knew that our minute numbers employ'd in the service against them, were proportionably more to *us* than mighty *legions* are to nations that have existed as many centuries as our colonies have years in the world, can scarce forbear taking the colours in the Sixth Book of Milton to describe our story:[29]

[28] Magnalia, i. 183.
[29] *Ibid.* ii. 566.

For after this, the *Auri sacra Fames*, that "cursed hunger of lucre," in the diverse nations of Europeans here, in diverse colonies bordering upon one another, soon furnished the salvages with *tools* to destroy those that furnish'd them:

> —Tools, pregnant with infernal flame,
> Which into hollow engines, long and round,
> Thick ramm'd at the other bore, with touch of fire
> Dilated and infuriate, doth send forth
> From far with thund'ring noise among their foes
> Such implements of mischief, as to dash
> To pieces and o'erwhelm whatever stands
> Adverse.——[30]

Milton, "Paradise Lost," VI, 482–491, wrote:

> These in their dark nativity the Deep
> Shall yield us, pregnant with infernal flame;
> Which, into hollow engines long and round
> Thick-rammed, at the other bore with touch of fire
> Dilated and infuriate, shall send forth
> From far, with thundering noise, among our foes
> Such implements of mischief as shall dash
> To pieces and o'erwhelm whatever stands
> Adverse, that they shall fear we have disarmed
> The Thunderer of his only dreaded bolt.

Mather, "Magnalia," ii. 568.

> And now, *sic magnis componere parva!*   Reader,
> And now their mightiest quell'd, the battel swerved,
> With many an inrode gor'd; deformed rout
> Enter'd, and foul disorder; all the ground
> With shiver'd armour strown, and on a heap,
> Salvage and Sagamore lay overturn'd,
> And fiery, foaming blacks: what stood, recoil'd,
> O'er wearied, and with panick fear surpris'd.

"Paradise Lost," VI, 386–393.

> And now, their mightiest quelled, the battle swerved,
> With many an inroad gored; deformed rout

[30] *Ibid.*, ii. 557.

Entered, and foul disorder; all the ground
With shivered armour strown, and on a heap
Chariot and charioter lay overturned,
And fiery foaming steeds; what stood recoiled,
O'er-wearied, through the faint Satanic host,
Defensive scarce, or with pale fear surprised—

Chaucer, too, Mather evidently knew, for he hoped "that saying of old Chaucer [might] be remembred, 'To do the genteel deeds, that makes the gentleman.' "[31] Presumably this is a recollection of a passage in the "Wife of Bath's Tale."

Loke who that is most vertuous alway,
Privee and apert, and most entendeth ay
To do the gentil dedes that he can,
And tak him for the grettest gentil man.[32]

If the phrase had come to Mather as a current saying it would hardly have had Chaucer's name attached; at least it is hardly to be expected that people in general in New England would be so careful to preserve the name of a poet of whom Pope could write so slightingly, within ten years,

Now length of fame (our second life) is lost,
And bare threescore is all e'en that can boast;
Our sons their fathers' failing language see,
And such as Chaucer is, shall Dryden be.

Presumably Mather had a copy of Chaucer, or had used the Harvard Library copy.[33] He made one other reference to Chaucer, speaking of "the famous old Chaucer's motto:

[31] *Ibid.* i. 107.
[32] Chaucer, D. 1113–1116 (Skeat's Oxford edition).
[33] As the copy of Chaucer listed in the 1723 catalogue of the Harvard Library is reported as having no title page (see p. 273, below), it is probably not the Urry edition of 1721, which would hardly be so mutilated in a little more than a year, the catalogue being compiled largely in 1722; it is then either one of the Speght editions of 1598, 1602, or 1687, or some earlier edition. In any case it might easily have been in the college library for several years before the "Magnalia" was written.

Mors mihi ærumnarum requies."[34] On Chaucer's tomb in
Westminster Abbey this is given as *Ærumnarum requies
mors.*

Other quotations by Cotton Mather are from Cowley's
Latin poems,[35] Fuller's "Church History" and other writings,[36]
James Howel's "Familiar Letters,"[37] Dr. Burnet's "History of
the Reformation,"[38] Wood's "Athenæ Oxoniensis,"[39] and so
on. From Sir Richard Blackmore's "Prince Arthur," published in 1695, while the "Magnalia" was being written, he
quoted two passages, one of 26 lines.[40]   Besides these quotations he has references to "Hudibras,"[41] to Tom Tusser's lines
on the harshness of Nicholas Udall, master of Eton,[42] to Ron-
sard's comment on DuBartas,[43] to Rabelais' "Pantagruel,"[44]
and to the legend of the Pied Piper.[45] He seems, also, to have

[34] Magnalia, ii. 613.   The phrase really belongs to Sallust (Catiline, 51.20).
It is not found in any edition of Chaucer previous to Urry's of 1721.   Mather
probably became acquainted with it through the account of Chaucer's tomb given
in Cambden's "Reges, Reginæ, Nobiles, et Alij in Ecclesia Collegiata B. Petri
Westmonasterij Sepulti," London, 1606, pp. 66, 67.

[35] On the title page of the 4th Book are three lines from the "Plantarum," Lib.
5, end.

[36] In Magnalia, i. 290, he quotes from the "Church History," Cent. xvii, Book xi.
213; in Magnalia, ii. 15, from the "History of Cambridge University," in Magnalia, i. 76, from his "Comment on Ruth."

[37] Magnalia, i. 27, 35; ii. 27, 46.

[38] *Ibid.*, i. 441.

[39] *Ibid., passim.*   He sometimes vents his spleen at this anti-Puritan writer:
"as a certain *woodden* historian . . . has reported," (Magnalia, i. 321).

[40] *Ibid.*, i. 65, "Prince Arthur," Book I, 552–567; 569–579.   *Ibid.*, Title page to
Book IV, "Prince Arthur," Book II, 101–103.   See p. 198, below, for correspondence between Mather and Blackmore.

[41] Magnalia, i. 58, tells of use of Weymouth episode in *Hudibras.*

[42] *Ibid.*, i. 303, "whom now we may venture, after poor *Tom Tusser*, to call,
'the severest of men.'"

[43] *Ibid.*, ii. 28.

[44] *Ibid.*, ii. 645: "Let us now leave our friend Maule's works as a fit volume to
be an appendix unto the famous '*Tartaretus*,' and worthy of a room in Pantagruel's
library."

[45] This he might have found in Burton's "Anatomy of Melancholy" or Howel's
"Letters;" but he seems to have taken it from Richard Verstegan's "Restitution of
Decayed Intelligence in Antiquities," p. 92 (edition of 1673).   Mather speaks of
"the Transylvanian children;" there is no mention of Transylvania in either

been familiar with "Don Quixote," for he speaks of "romances of *Don Quixote* and the *Seven Champions*,"[46] and elsewhere[47] speaks of the "quixotism" of Roger Williams. It would be interesting to know whether Mather "coined" that term for himself; the "New English Dictionary" records but one use of it earlier than this, in a book or tract, "Pulpit Popery, True Popery," 1688, and quotes the next example from *The Briton*, No. 20, 1723. Certainly Cotton Mather, before the end of the century, had considerable literary background. The other books which he quoted or cited are listed in the Appendix.

In addition to all these, Cotton Mather was fond of using such phrases as "a saying of the Jews," "the Arabian proverb," "an account of a certain bishop of Rome," "the Italian proverb," "a certain proverb in Asia," "the witty epigrammatist hath told us," "as he that writes the life of holy Mr. Bains expresses it," "the author of the life of Belgic Wallæus," "the famous judge's motto," etc. In the "Magnalia"[48] occur two lines from Herbert, which, however, are not quoted by Mather, but in a prefatory epistle written by Matthew Mead of London. Presumably Mather could have quoted Herbert had he cared to, as a copy of Herbert's poems was in his father's library as early as 1664.[49]

Samuel Sewall's "Diary" and "Letter-Book" contain a few references to his reading. On his voyage to England in 1688 he carried with him a volume by Dr. Preston, Manton's "Exposition of James," and Erasmus.[50] At another time he recorded saying to Benjamin Colman, "Philomela would have

Burton or Howel, but Verstegan tells the tale in connection with his account of the Transylvanian Saxons, giving the location of the episode, however, as do the others, in Brunswick, at Hamel. Mather's memory was inaccurate here. A copy of Verstegan's book was in his father's library; see p. 53, above.

[46] Magnalia, i. 208.

[47] *Ibid.*, ii. 497.

[48] *Ibid.*, ii. 153.

[49] See p. 52, above.

[50] "my Erasmus was quite loosened out of the Binding by the breaking of the water into Cabbin." (Diary, i. 238.)

found out some words . . . .,"[51] Philomela being the *nom de plume* of Elizabeth Singer Rowe, a popular English poetess of the day.   On the cover of his journal he copied in full "An Elegie on Mrs. Alicia Lisle, which for high Treason was beheaded at Winchester, September the 2.d 1685," evidently taken from an English broadside.[52]   This is followed by letters dated 1686, and therefore was copied not long after publication.   Sewall was no doubt especially interested in this poem because one of the daughters of the unfortunate Lady Alice Lisle was living in Boston, the wife of Hezekiah Usher, and formerly wife of President Hoar of Harvard.[53] The following item shows his interest in reading, and his taste.   He was trying a case at Bristol at the time.

Rain hinder'd our setting out that day.   So after diñer at Mr. Saffin's, Not knowing better how to bestow my time, Look'd on Mr. Saffin's Books, and lit on Dr. Fullers History of the Worthies of England, and in p. 116. 117. found mention made of the Inundation at Coventry, on Friday April, 17. in the Maioralty of Henry Sewall my Father's Grandfather.   Mention is made p. 134. of W.m Dugdale's Illustrations of Warwickshire.[54]

Sewall did not need to go to Bristol to read Fuller, however, for two passages in his "Letter-Book" would indicate that he had more than one volume of Fuller in his own library, and was familiar with their contents.

I transcribe the following passage out of Dr. Fuller's Engl[ish] Worthies in London, p. 202[55] . . . .

Transcribed the passages of George Abbot Archb[ishop] out of Fuller's Ch[urch] History; knew not what better to write.[56]

[51] *Ibid.*, i. 507.
[52] *Ibid.*, ii. 8.
[53] See note 4, p. 99, above.
[54] Diary, i. 484. *Ca.* 1695.
[55] Letter-Book, i. 369.
[56] *Ibid.*, i. 374. Although Sewall wrote that "he knew not what better to write," the quotation was not a mere spacefiller but recorded a close parallel to a recent event in the life of the man to whom he was writing. Sewall knew his Fuller well enough to draw upon it for illustrations.

Other authors or books which he quoted, or to which he referred, are: Augustine's Psalms,[57] Baxter's "Glorious Kingdom of Christ Described,"[58] Calvin's "Institutions,"[59] Calamy's "Life of Baxter,"[60] Horn's "De Originibus Americanis,"[61] Hornius' "Carthaginian Dream,"[62] Pareus' "Commentaries,"[63] Thorowgood's "Jews in America,"[64] and *The London Gazette* of June 27, 1700.[65]

If the anonymous lines to Cotton Mather, written about 1700,[66]

> For *Grace* and *Act* and an Illustrious *Fame*
> Who would not look from such an *Ominous Name*,
> Where *Two Great Names* their Sanctuary take,
> And in a *Third* combined, a *Greater* make!

are, as Barrett Wendell very reasonably suggests,[67] in imitation of Dryden's lines "Under Milton's Picture"

> Three poets, in three distant ages born,
> Greece, Italy, and England, did adorn.
> The first, in loftiness of thought surpassed;
> The next, in majesty; in both, the last.
> The force of nature could no further go;
> To make a third, she joined the former two.

then we have another evidence of acquaintance with Milton's

---

[57] *Ibid.*, i. 199.

[58] *Ibid.*, ii. 202.

[59] *Ibid.*, i. 260.

[60] *Ibid.*, i. 294.   He wrote to Calamy to correct statements in the latter's abridgment of Baxter's Life.

[61] *Ibid.*, i. 23.   See Publications of the Colonial Society of Massachusetts, xiv. 167.

[62] Letter-Book, i. 289.

[63] Diary, i. 115.

[64] Letter-Book, i. 22.

[65] *Ibid.*, i. 16.

[66] Mather copied these lines in his diary on February 12, 1700, under the title *Ab Amico Satis Adulatore on Cotton Mather*, with the comment "Too gross Flattery for me to Transcribe; (tho' the Poetry be good." According to the editor of the Diary the lines are struck out in the manuscript—but in such a manner that they may still be read easily.

[67] Cotton Mather, p. 182 note.

poems, or at least with "Paradise Lost," in the 1688 edition of which these lines first appeared.

The foregoing quotations not only add many items to the book lists of the preceding chapter, but also give some idea of the familiarity of the colonists with the books which they possessed. They certainly were not as lacking in books as has been generally believed; and it seems equally true that they read and appreciated such literary books as they possessed to an extent for which they have never been given due credit.

Chapter IX: Relations with England and Other Phases of Culture.

THE close and sympathetic interest between the colonists and the government of England, as described in Chapter III, naturally came to an end at the Restoration. In its place a mutual suspicion developed, fostered on the one side by the colonists' disloyal protection of the Regicides, and on the other by the loss of colonial independence and the fear of possible religious coercion. At the same time a generation was growing up which knew not England; in fact it was almost a second generation from England, since in many cases the parents had left England when mere children. Those who had grown to maturity in England and had personal friends there were passing away; the death of John Winthrop, Jr., in 1676 broke one of the chief links that kept the best of the new world in touch with the best of the old. Social intercourse between New England and Old England seems to have reached, during the last quarter of the century, a lower ebb than at any time before or since.

It would be a mistake, however, to think of the colonies as isolated from the outside world even during this period. As has been shown in Chapter VII, the gifts of friends in England and the establishment of several booksellers made it possible for both the college and the colony to keep in touch with current thought. Settlers continued to come, too, even if in smaller groups than during the first period; and among them were occasionally men of high scholastic attainments, such as Samuel Lee,[1] who settled in Bristol, and Charles Morton[2], who settled in Charlestown. Occasionally,

[1] See p. 127, above.
[2] See p. 100, above.

too, young colonists went back to England to try their fortunes there, and not without success, as, for example, three sons of the Reverend John Higginson, of Salem. Thomas Higginson became a goldsmith in England; Francis went to live with his uncle Francis in England[3] and was educated at the University of Cambridge; and Nathaniel was first steward of Lord Wharton, and later went to the East Indies, where he succeeded Elihu Yale as Governor of Madras, and, like him, grew rich.[4] His letters, both from India and from England after his return,[5] show that he was interested in New England and had tentative plans for returning thither, as his father so earnestly urged him to do; but he never came. The Reverend Warham Mather had thoughts of going to England, for he wrote to his uncle, Increase Mather, then in London, as follows:

S[r], we expect not your return before winter. It will be profitable for me to know what advice you think it will be best for me to follow, relating to a remove for England, before that time, for it is not likely I should sell what estate I have here for the worth thereof at short warning.[6]

He did not go, however.

New Englanders continued to visit England for both business and pleasure. Increase Mather went twice as agent of Massachusetts. Of his second trip a modern historian writes:

During Andros's administration some of the prominent men of the colony, dissatisfied with the curtailment of their former privileges, determined to appeal to England for relief. Increase Mather, the influential pastor of the Old North Church, was selected to bear to the king, James II., the complaints of the colony,

---

³ See p. 65, above.

⁴ Massachusetts Historical Society, Collections, 3rd Series, vii. 196; F. B. Dexter, Publications of the New Haven Historical Society, iii. 238.

⁵ Massachusetts Historical Society, Collections, 3rd Series, vii. 198 ff. The eagerness with which his father urged him not to forget his native place is quite pathetic.

⁶ Mather Papers, p. 671. July 6, 1688.

and to obtain, if possible, a restoration of the charter. He was admirably adapted to the task, having served as agent in England only a few years before, while his pleasing address and familiarity with the men and ways of the court at Whitehall were certain to stand him in good stead in the work to be done.[7]

It is worth noting that on this errand he was well received by the courts both of James II and of William and Mary.

In 1688 Samuel Sewall, accompanied by his brother Stephen and two others, went to England on a trip which combined the pleasure of a visit to his birthplace in England with considerable buying of commodities, presumably upon commission.

Joseph Dudley went to England in 1682 as an agent of Massachusetts.[8] In 1693 he again went to England and there resided for nine years, taking an active part in English affairs, even serving in Parliament.[9] Another who spent several years in England was Benjamin Colman, who went to London in 1695. He was well received by the Dissenting clergy there, once being sent by a committee of them to preach at Cambridge, and later, after preaching at Ipswich, being chosen by the London Presbytery to take an important church at Bath, where he remained two years. He left only to accept a call to a new church in Boston.[10]

Benjamin Lynde, Harvard 1686, went to London to study for the bar at the Middle Temple. His wife accompanied him either at that time or on some later trip, for her portrait was painted in England by Sir Godfrey Kneller.[11]

During this period there is practically no evidence of any intercourse or friendship between any one in New England and the literary men of England, if such writers of religious literature as Richard Baxter be excluded.[12] Anthony à

[7] C. M. Andrews, Narratives of the Insurrections, p. 271.
[8] Kimball, Public Life of Joseph Dudley, p. 13.
[9] *Ibid*. pp. 65, 208.
[10] Turell, Life of Colman, *passim*.
[11] Massachusetts Historical Society, Proceedings, 1st Series, xvi. 396.
[12] See p. 134, above, for details of Baxter's gift to Harvard.

Wood turned to Increase Mather, when the latter was in
London, for information in regard to the Oxford graduates
who had emigrated to New England;[13] but the "Athenæ
Oxoniensis" can hardly be classed as pure literature.

In spite of all this lessening of intercourse, the colonists
continued to feel a keen interest in England and conditions
there, as their constant eagerness for gazettes and news-
letters shows;[14] and this sometimes found definite expression, as in the following passage from John Higginson's
"Attestation" to the "Magnalia."

That the little daughter of New-England in America, may bow
down herself to her mother England, in Europe, presenting this
memorial unto her; assuring her, that though by some of her
angry brethren she was forced to make a *local secession*, yet not a
separation, but hath always retained a dutiful respect to the
Church of God in England; and giving some account to her, how
graciously the Lord has dealt with herself in a *remote wilderness*,
and what she has been doing all this while; giving her thanks for
all the *supplies* she has received from her; and because she is
yet in her *minority*, she craves her farther *blessing* and *favour* as
the case may require; being glad if what is now presented to her,
may be of any use, to help forward the *union* and *agreement* of her
brethren, which would be some satisfaction to her for her unde-
sired local distance from her dear England; and finally promising
all that reverence and obedience which is due to her good *mother*,
by virtue of the *fifth* commandment.[15]

If the colonists did not go to England as much as at an
earlier period, certain elements of English life, formerly ab-
sent, were introduced, especially under Governor Andros.
A dancing-master set up in Boston,[16] and a fencing master

---

[13] Massachusetts Historical Society, Collections, 2d Series, vii. 187.
[14] See pp. 222 and 223, above.
[15] Magnalia, i. 16.   Dated 1697.
[16] Wendell, Cotton Mather, p. 44.   The first dancing master of whom there is
record was one Henry Sharlot or Sherlot, who is described both as Irish and as
French.   On September 6, 1681, the Court of Assistants decided that "Henry Sherlot a frenchman, that is newly come into this Towne as he sajth, a Dancing master
and a person very Insolent and of ill fame, that Raves and scoffes at Religion

as well.[17] Public fencing bouts were held, and a maypole was erected.[18] Just previous to this John Dunton and other booksellers had brought over plays and romances and playing cards.[19] In connection with the latter the following passage in Sewall's "Diary" is of interest.

Wednesday, June 21 [1699]. A Pack of Cards are found strawed over my fore-yard, which, tis suposed, some might throw there to mock me, in spite of [for] what I did at the Exchange Tavern last Satterday night.[20]

Boston was losing its former character of a city devoted to religion, and was becoming a worldly commercial seaport. This was felt strongly by the critical Dutch traveler, Jasper Danckaerts, who wrote of Boston in 1680:

Nevertheless you discover little difference between this and other places. Drinking and fighting occur there not less than elsewhere; and as to truth and true godliness, you must not expect more of them than of others. When we were there, four ministers' sons were learning the silversmith's trade.[21]

. . ." be ordered away. It is unfortunately not clear whether his personality or his profession was chiefly responsible for the Court's action. (Massachusetts Historical Society, Proceedings, xlix. 99 ff.)   His successors had better fortune. To meet this new evil, Increase Mather considered it necessary to prepare "An Arrow against Profane and Promiscuous Dancing. Drawn out of the Quiver of the Scriptures," published in 1684 by Joseph Brunning. (Sibley, Harvard Graduates, i. 445.)

[17] The Council granted, September 15, 1686, the following petition: "The humble petition of Richard Crisp, humbly sheweth, That whereas there are several gentlemen in this town, that are desirous your petitioner should instruct them in the use of weapons, and whereas there is a law, that forbiddeth the building of any edifice with wood, above such a bigness as the said law permits, I humbly pray . . . liberty to build a low, slight house for that purpose . . ." (Massachusetts Historical Society, Collections, 3rd Series, vii. 157.)

[18] Increase Mather recorded in his diary in 1687: (April 27.) "Sword playing was this day openly practised on a Stage in Boston & that immediately after yᵉ Lecture, so yᵗ the Devil has begun a Lecture in Boston on a Lecture-Day wh was set up for Christ . . ." (May 1.) "A May pole was set up in Charlestown." (Massachusetts Historical Society, Proceedings, 2d Series, xiii. 411.)

[19] See p. 120 ff., above.

[20] Diary, i. 498. Unfortunately there is no further report of the affair at the Exchange Tavern.

[21] Journal of Jasper Danckaerts, pp. 274, 275.

In connection with Danckaerts' last remark it must be remembered that there were nearly a score of silversmiths working at their craft in Boston before the end of the century. Many of the things which they wrought were necessary articles; but the rapid growth in their numbers toward the end of this period, as well as examples of their work which have been preserved, indicates that Boston afforded a good market for luxuries.[22] That four ministers' sons at once were turning to this lucrative work instead of preparing to follow in the footsteps of their fathers shows the tendency of the time.

The wealthy men of the first period had been those who brought fortunes with them. In the second period we find men who had made their own fortunes in the new land, such men as John Hull, silversmith and mint-master, whose wealth is a tradition with us.[23] Hezekiah Usher, bookseller, dying in 1676, left a fortune of over £15,000 for his two sons to quarrel over.[24] John Dunton speaks of the wealth acquired by John Usher[25] who succeeded his father. Wait Winthrop in Boston and Fitz-John Winthrop at New London were living in a style resembling that of the landed gentry of England, whom they were planning to imitate in the establishing of an estate practically in entail.[26] Even in Plymouth there was an increase in wealth, according to

[22] Bigelow's "Historic Silver of the Colonies and its Makers" gives interesting details of the lives of these silversmiths and contains illustrations showing the beauty of their work. His record is not complete, however, for he does not mention the Dutch silversmith, Willem Ros, from Wesel, whom Jasper Danckaerts found carrying on his trade in Boston in 1680. (Journal of Jasper Danckaerts, p. 260.)

[23] There seems to be no satisfactory estimate of his wealth, but he was unquestionably wealthy for his day. His gift to his daughter upon her marriage to Samuel Sewall is estimated at £500 ($10,000 in modern equivalent). (Hull's Diary, p. 275.)

[24] See pp. 79 and 114, above.

[25] See p. 114, above.

[26] John Winthrop, F. R. S., won his suit against the other heirs of his uncle, Fitz-John, and his father, Wait, by showing that the two brothers had planned to leave their vast holdings of land to a single heir that they might be handed down intact from generation to generation, and not to be broken up and soon dissipated by division among group after group of heirs. (Winthrop Papers, vi. *passim.*)

Governor Josiah Winslow's statement that "most men there
are freeholders, few tenants; incomes of 2000*l.* are rare
among them."[27]   They may have been few, but the interesting thing is that there were any.   Twenty-five years earlier
estates totaling one-quarter of that sum were unknown.[28]
Comprehensive lists of men of wealth and their estates seem
unnecessary here, for the very fact that so many booksellers
and silversmiths set up shop in Boston[29] is in itself evidence
that there was a considerable public which could afford the
luxuries of books and silver plate.   Even portrait painters
were beginning to cater to the vanity of the colonists.   Before
1667 the Reverend John Wilson refused to have his portrait
painted for his friends, although Edward Rawson brought
to him a "limner, with all things ready."[30]   Portraits of
Henry and Margaret Gibbs bearing the date of 1670 are
still in existence.[31]   In 1679 or 1680 Increase Mather sat for
a portrait which he sent to his brother Nathaniel, of Dublin.[32]
In 1684 Joseph Allen came from Dublin bearing letters from
Nathaniel to Increase Mather in which he was described as
skilled in "graving" and "limning."[33]   Wait Winthrop
wrote in 1691 of a man who could copy miniatures.[34]   Evidently as far as Boston and the older settlements were concerned, the pioneer days of hardship were over.

[27] Calendar of State Papers, Colonial Series, America and West Indies, 1677–
1680, p. 522, no. 1349.
[28] See pp. 28 and 29, above.
[29] See pp. 114–117 and 157, above.
[30] Magnalia, i. 320.
[31] Massachusetts Historical Society, Proceedings, 1st Series, x. 41 ff.
[32] Mather Papers, p. 28.
[33] *Ibid.*, p. 52.
[34] Winthrop Papers, iv. 500.   Under date of October 31 he wrote to Fitz-John
Winthrop, "If you could by a very carefull hand, send the litle picture of my
grandfather, put carefully up in som litle box, here is one would copy it for my
cousin Adam . . ."

Chapter X: The Production of Literature.

AS the previous chapters have shown, New England grew provincial after the middle of the century, and especially after the Restoration. This is shown most strikingly in the literature produced during this period. Literary movements in England had practically no influence across the sea. Of course the most important element in the English literature of the time, the dramatic, because of its very nature, could in no way stimulate literary activity where the drama was tabooed. Furthermore, most non-dramatic literature was written by Tories and Royalists, many of them courtiers, in whose writings New England Puritans could take little interest. It is not so easy to explain why Milton aroused no echo in New England; but it is evident to any student of the period that the chief writer of Boston, Cotton Mather, although he evidently knew "Paradise Lost" well,[1] made no attempt to imitate the grandeur of its style, preferring the elaborate conceits and puns characteristic of the style which the earliest settlers brought over with them. In England there had been great changes; in New England the literary style, like the language, tended to remain fixed. The leaders of thought in Boston were generally as conservative in their writing as in their religious thinking, looking to the past rather than to the present or the future.

Where the influence of the earlier colonial verse-writers is not evident, as in Peter Folger's "A Looking-Glass for the Times," in some of Benjamin Tompson's poems, and elsewhere, as in some of the poetry of the almanacs, the style seems either original, or else derived from ballads or hymns, the metres especially resembling those of the ballad or short

[1] See p. 143 ff., above.

or common metre hymn. There is absolutely no suggestion of contemporary English poetry of the better kind here.

Very much the same thing is true of the prose of the period. The style of Cotton Mather in the "Magnalia," written in the last decade of the seventeenth century, resembles, as does his father's style, the prose writings of such Englishmen as Robert Burton and Thomas Fuller, who belong to the earlier part of the century.[2]

It is necessary to distinguish here between literary influences and influences of a political or even intellectual nature. Unresponsive as the people of New England were to literary movements, they were in close touch not only with English politics, but with certain philosophical movements. Their interest in politics was natural, as they were personally affected by what happened in London. Their familiarity with the scientific movement of the time has been noted.[3] Their reaction to the writings of the Cambridge Platonists is more striking. The attempts of such writers as Joseph Glanvil and Henry More to prove the reality of the spiritual world culminated in "Sadducismus Triumphatus," begun by Glanvil and finished by More in 1681. Three years later Increase Mather published his "Remarkable Providences" as a contribution to the growing body of material which sought to support the teachings of Glanvil and More. Within ten years New England had reacted to the belief in demons in

[2] Cotton Mather's love of quoting Latin and Greek, and even Hebrew, is a relic of the tendency which led Lord Coke, who died in 1633, to illustrate the knotty points and subtle distinctions of the law with 300 extracts from Virgil—and then boast of his achievement. (Mullinger, Cambridge in the Seventeenth Century, p. 64, note.) Before Cotton Mather was born, Samuel Butler had ridiculed this style of writing, calling it (Hudibras, Canto I, 93–98)

> A Babylonish dialect,
> Which learned pedants much affect:
> It was a parti-colour'd dress
> Of patch'd and piebald languages;
> 'Twas English cut on Greek and Latin,
> Like fustian heretofore on satin.

[3] See above, pp. 107 ff. and 142–3.

an even more striking way, by the persecution of witches, especially at Salem. Witch-hunting did not begin in the colonies at that time, but the extent and violence of the Salem persecutions in contrast with the sporadic witchcraft cases in New England previous to 1680 would seem to be the result of a direct reaction to the Cambridge philosophers. The fact that Deodat Lawson, whose lecture at Salem Village, March 24, 1692, marked the beginning of the worst persecutions, had studied at Cambridge gave weight to his words and was largely responsible for the severity of the frenzy.

The provincialism of the period is nowhere better shown than in the growing preponderance of sermons in the publications of the local presses. In the eight years including 1682 and 1689, of the 133 books published in Boston, 56 were sermons, 39 more were of a religious nature, and of the remaining 38, 12 were almanacs, and 17 were proclamations or political pamphlets arising from the revolt against Andros in 1689.[4] The lowest ebb of American literature was reached at this time; the only poetical items are Cotton Mather's "A Poem Dedicated to the Memory of . . . . Mr. Urian Oakes" and "An Elegy on . . . . Rev. Mr. Nathanael Collins," Richard Steere's "A Monumental Memorial of Marine Mercy," and reprints of Wigglesworth's "Meat out of the Eater" and "The Day of Doom."

The dearth of literature is not relieved to any great extent, as in the first period, by publications abroad. Some colonial writings were published in England, but most of these, as Increase Mather's accounts of the Indian wars, were reprints of books already printed in New England. One book, and that undoubtedly the most important book of the period,[5] Cotton Mather's "Magnalia Christi Americana," was considered by its author sufficiently important to be sent

[4] These figures are compiled from Evans' American Bibliography, and include books printed in Cambridge.
[5] Although not published until 1702, it was written about 1697.

to England for its original publication; but this is rather the exception.

Some poetry of the period escaped publication at the time, and should be added in estimating the amount of literature produced; but this is much less in quantity than in the earlier period. Edward Taylor of Westfield filled a notebook with verse, none of which has ever been published, as the writer forbade publication. Many elegies, such as those preserved in Blake's "Annals of Dorchester" and others passed on from generation to generation in family records, waited until later times for their appearance in public. But even these are not sufficient either in amount or in merit to bring the production of this period to the level of either the earlier or the later periods.

All this does not mean that there were no writings of literary value during these years, for that would not be true. The most interesting and important of the writings of the two Mathers belong to this period: "Remarkable Providences," "The Wonders of the Invisible World," and the "Magnalia Christi Americana." To these must be added the four clever political fables which Cotton Mather wrote in defence of his father's activities as agent of the Colony.[6] Robert Calef's "More Wonders of the Invisible World" also deserves mention here for its rationality, which gives it, in contrast with the Mather witchbooks, a surprisingly modern tone. Another modern seeming book is Sewall's anti-slavery pamphlet, "The Selling of Joseph."

The poetry of the period was inferior to the prose; there was, however, some verse with poetic merit. One example of a poem which is at least natural, and not without humor, has been printed in part on page 91, Samuel Bailey's "The College Ferula." Of the conceits which marred much of the colonial poetry perhaps the most effective and fitting is the one used by Joseph Capen at the end of his elegy upon John Foster, printer and almanac maker:

[6] Printed in the Prince Society Andros Tracts, ii. 325 ff.

Thy Body which no activeness did lack
Now's laid aside like an old Almanack
But for the present only's out of date;
Twil have at length a far more active State.
Yea, though with dust thy body Soiled be,
Yet at the Resurrection we Shall See
A fair Edition & of matchless worth,
Free from Errata, new in Heav'n Set forth:
Tis but a word from God the great Creatour,
It Shall be Done when he Saith IMPRIMATUR.[7]

The concluding stanzas of Urian Oakes' lament for Thomas Shepard are worth quoting, although the greater part of this elegy exhibits the usual faults of New England poetry.

In vain we build the prophets' sepulchers,
In vain bedew their tombs with tears, when dead;

[7] "It has been thought," writes Samuel A. Green, in his study of John Foster (page 35), "that the closing lines of Capen's Elegy suggested to Franklin the quaint epitaph which he wrote for himself." The parallel is so interesting that the epitaph is given here for comparison:

The body of Benjamin Franklin, printer, (like the cover of an old book, its contents torn out, and stript of its lettering and gilding) lies here food for worms; yet the work itself shall not be lost, for it will (as he believed) appear once more in a new and more beautiful edition, corrected and amended by the author.

The parallel becomes more interesting when we carry it back a generation to Benjamin Woodbridge's elegy upon John Cotton, who died in 1652. Presumably the elegy was written soon after that date.

A living, breathing Bible; tables where
Both covenants, *at large, engraven were;*
Gospel *and law, in's heart, had each its column;*
His head an index to the sacred volume;
His very name a title-page; *and next,*
His life a commentary *on the text.*
O, what a monument of glorious worth,
When, in a new edition, *he comes forth,*
Without erratas, *may we think he'll be*
In leaves *and* covers *of eternity!*

It would be remarkable if Woodbridge's figure of speech should have recurred twice unconsciously; if it was used consciously, it forms a curious link between the seventeenth and eighteenth centuries in American literature.

In vain bewail the deaths of ministers,
Whilest prophet-killing sins are harboured.
  Those that these murtherous traitors favour, hide;
  Are with the blood of Prophets deeply dy'd.

New-England! know thy heart-plague: feel this blow;
A blow that sorely wounds both head and heart,
A blow that reaches all, both high and low,
A blow that may be felt in every part.
  Mourn that this great man's faln in Israel:
  Let it be said, "with him New-England fell!"

Farewell, dear Shepard! Thou art gone before,
Made free of Heaven, where thou shalt sing loud hymns
Of high triumphant praises ever more,
In the sweet quire of saints and seraphims.
  Lord! look on us here, clogg'd with sin and clay,
  And we, through grace, shall be as happy as they.

My dearest, inmost, bosome-friend is gone!
Gone is my sweet companion, soul's delight!
Now in an hud'ling croud I'm all alone,
And almost could bid all the world "Goodnight."
  Blest be my Rock! God lives: O let him be,
  As He is All, so All in All to me!

Whereas literary production during the first period of
colonial life was in keeping with the culture of the people,
during the second period literature lagged behind culture.
The chief reason for this, provincialism, has already been
discussed. While the culture, although not as low as it has
often been pictured, had grown somewhat provincial, the
literature had become entirely divorced from English literary
movements. The colonists did have London books; but
their ears could not catch the note of the literary activity
which centered in London. There were other reasons for
this than the width of the Atlantic. The Restoration had
in time brought about the loss of charter and privileges;
and thus began that long struggle between colonist and

crown which was to monopolize the interest and energy of the people of New England for over a century. Cotton Mather was eager to peruse any books which his father might bring from England; but he was vastly more interested in the charter which his father might bring back for the colony and indirectly for the college. Whether the ministerial party headed by himself and his father would be able to control the colony; whether the orthodox element in New England could continue to guide the college;—these matters were vastly more important than the fact that a new period in English literature was developing. Even if this had not been the case, the tremendously busy life which Cotton Mather led was enough to make careful literary work impossible. As Barrett Wendell writes,

Until one actually inspects the documents, it seems incredible that in forty-five years any single human being could have penned so many words as we thus see to have come from the hand of one of the busiest ministers, one of the most insatiable scholars and readers, and one of the most active politicians whom America has ever known.[8]

Cotton Mather himself referred to the difficulties of literary work in the face of his other activities:

. . . . I have been forced . . . .to throw by the work [the "Magnalia"] whole months together, and then resume it, but by a stolen hour or two in the day, not without some hazard of incurring the *title* which Coryat put upon his History of his Travels, *"Crudities hastily gobbled up in five months."*[9]

If I could redeem the Time, now and then to dress up sublime Thoughts in an agreeable Metre, I might in Time, have a Collection, which may prove a profitable and an acceptable Entertainment, unto the Church of God.[10]

Two extracts from his diary show his hasty manner of writing.

[8] Literary History of America, p. 47.
[9] Magnalia, i. 32.
[10] Diary, ii. 335.

The Printer, wanting something to fill the last Leaf of his Almanack, for the year, 1699, came unto mee, to furnish him. . . . .
I took my Opportunity, and wrote a few pungent Lines, concerning the Changes, which may bee coming as *a Snare upon the Earth.* . . .[11]

There is printing a new Edition of our *Psalm-book.* In every former Edition, that excellent Portion of Scripture, the 36TH CHAPTER OF ISAIAH, was in such a metre, that few of our Churches could sing it. Wherefore I this day, took a few Minutes, to turn it into another Metre, with perhaps, a smoother and sweeter Version. So tis published in the *Psalm book;* . . . [12]

As, in spite of the unfavorable circumstances under which they were composed, Cotton Mather's productions taken all in all are not without literary merit, it is interesting to surmise what he might have done in literature had he not been so distracted by other things, including the constant abuse of his health by vigils and fasts.[13] The one man in New England who had the greatest familiarity with English literature, whose mind was a veritable storehouse of learning of every kind, never gave what literary ability he may have had an opportunity to develop.

What is true of Cotton Mather is true in less degree of all New England. Life was too full of other interests to allow much energy to be devoted to literary work. During the seventies the colonists were carrying on a bitter war with the Indians, a war which cost the United Colonies over £100,000 and many lives. During the eighties public interest was absorbed by the struggle to maintain colonial rights against the encroachments of Randolph and Andros. In the last decade of the century began the struggle between the ministerial party, headed by the Mathers, and the more liberal party for the control of the government and the college.

---

[11] *Ibid.*, i. 276.　The article appeared in Tulley's Almanack for 1699.

[12] *Ibid.*, i. 300.

[13] Tyler, in his History of American Literature, ii. 76, says, " . . . it was computed that, in the course of his life, the number of his special fast-days amounted to four hundred and fifty."

The censorship still added its restraint to the other influences which retarded literary production. According to their instructions, provincial governors held complete control of the press. Before Andros came, Randolph, as secretary of the province, had appointed an official printer and had sent the following notice to the other printers:

I am com̃anded by Mr Secretary Randolph, to give you notice that you doe not proceed to print any Almanack whatever without haveing his approbation for ye same.

Yo^{rs} Ben: Bullivant

Boston: 29 Novemb^r 1686.[14]

Soon after the installation of Governor Andros the proceedings of his Council contained this entry:

The Councill being met His Ex^{ce} acquainted them that it was his Maj^{ties} express commands that the printing Presses in the Towns of Boston and Cambridge in New England should be effectuall [sic] taken care of. Upon which an order passed in Councill, that no Papers, Bookes Pamphlets &c should be printed in New England untill Licensed according to Law. . . [15]

Andros' loss of power did not end the censorship, for the House of Representatives in November, 1689, passed orders to control the press.[16] The first newspaper in America, *Publick Occurrences, both Foreign and Domestick*, was suppressed immediately upon the appearance of its first number, unlicensed, on September 25, 1690.[16] In 1695 action was brought against Thomas Maule of Salem for circulating a book of his which he had had published in New York.[16] He was acquitted by jury, but the fact that action was brought against him shows that the censorship was active.

The final reason for the low estate of literature during this period was the lack of any sympathetic support by either the reading public or any literary coterie. Enough litera-

---

[14] Duniway, Freedom of the Press in Massachusetts, p. 64.
[15] *Ibid.*, p. 65.
[16] *Ibid.*, p. 67 ff.

ture from England was available through the booksellers
for those who were interested in literature, and from the
local presses only books of purely local interest were expected, such as contemporary sermons, almanacs, and political pamphlets. It is true that "Pilgrim's Progress" was
reprinted on one of the New England presses,[17] but this was
exceptional for the period, and is counterbalanced by the
fact that such a local book as the "New England Primer"
seems to have been printed first in England.[18]

Group interest in literature as literature, or any mutual
encouragement toward the production of literature, is not
in evidence until the very end of the period. The influx
of books through the many booksellers who came to Boston
after 1685[19] could not but have some effect upon literary
production in New England; but results are not evident
until the very end of the period, and are more noticeable in
the opening years of the eighteenth century. The earliest
indication of any group interest in literature is found in the
literary friendship between Samuel Sewall and Richard
Henchman, schoolmaster, which probably began before the
year 1700, the first evidence of it being given in Henchman's
poem to Sewall under date of January 1, 1700–1. There is
more evidence of their mutual interest in poetry during the
years that follow, as will be shown in Chapter XIV.

In conclusion, then, it may be said that although this
period marks the nadir of American literature, at the end
of the period, thanks to the activities of the Boston booksellers and to renewed intercourse with England, there was
beginning a literary movement in New England which was
to develop rapidly in the opening years of the new century.

[17] Bunyan's prefatory verses to the second part of Pilgrim's Progress, published
in 1684, refer to an edition of the first part printed in New England. This was
printed in 1681 by Samuel Green for Samuel Sewall. A copy of this edition is in
the Boston Public Library.

[18] At least a New England Primer was printed in England by John Gaine in
1683. As all copies have disappeared, it is impossible to ascertain to what extent
it resembled the New England Primer printed by Benjamin Harris about 1690.
(See the letter by Worthington C. Ford in *The Nation*, January 11, 1917, p. 46.)

[19] See p. 116 ff, above.

Part III:
The New Century.
1700-1727.

Chapter XI: Education.

THE new century brought no changes into the educational work carried on at Cambridge. The growing liberality of the Harvard theology caused certain of the conservatives in the colonies to become disaffected and resulted in a contest for the control of the college in which the liberals were victorious;[1] but the contest, although it affected the political life of the community, seems to have made little if any change in the value of the instruction given to the students. The old system continued under the same men, or under men similarly trained; and it was not until the end of the period under consideration that the benefactions of Thomas Hollis, and especially the establishment by him of two professorships, one of Divinity and one of Mathematics and Natural Philosophy, gave the college a new impetus.[2]

If, during these years, no change in educational methods took place, at least increased opportunity for education was offered through the establishment of a new college in Connecticut in the very first year of the century. The "Collegiate School" at Saybrook, later moved to New Haven and re-named "Yale College," was modeled after Harvard, the founders and teachers being Harvard graduates. The young college benefited by the support of the Mathers, Judge Sewall, and others who, disliking the liberal tendencies at Harvard, turned to the younger school as the last refuge of New England orthodoxy. They enlisted the aid of their friends in England with such success that Yale soon had a fair endowment and a library which, if not as large as

[1] See Quincy, History of Harvard University, i. chaps. x–xiv.
[2] *Ibid.* i. The first gift from Hollis arrived in 1719. The Professorship of Divinity was offered in 1721, and the Professorship of Mathematics and Natural Philosophy in 1727.

Harvard's, was well chosen and contained a larger proportion of current literature.[3]

The education given in the new college seems to have been equivalent to that at Harvard. The graduates were fitted to hold high positions in the community, and two members of early classes were honored by recognition by the English Universities. Samuel Johnson, of the class of 1714, was given the honorary degree of Master of Arts in 1723 by both Cambridge and Oxford, and was made a Doctor of Divinity by the latter in 1743.[4] Jonathan Arnold, of the class of 1723, was granted the honorary Master's degree at Oxford in 1736.[5]

Outside of the formal education of the college there was a growing interest in science. Thomas and William Brattle, Cotton Mather, Paul Dudley, Thomas Robie, and the younger John Winthrop were all members or correspondents of the Royal Society, and nearly all had papers published in the Society's Transactions.[6] Others, like Dr. William Douglass,[7] were making observations and keeping in touch with contemporary science. Increasing intercourse with England, and the temporary residence in Boston of Englishmen who came over to take part in the government of the colonies, were further educational and liberalizing influences.

Thus we find in the colonies, by the end of the first century of colonial life, a large and steadily growing body of educated men. The proportion of college men has never been as great as it was during the first years of the colonies, when conditions were abnormal,[8] but it was much greater in the third period than in the second, when the college as well as the colonies showed the most provinciality, and it had de-

[3] See p. 184 ff., below.
[4] Dexter, Biographical Sketches of the Graduates of Yale College, i. 124.
[5] *Ibid.*, p. 275.
[6] See p. 108, above, and pp. 199 and 200, below.
[7] See pp. 200 and 201, below.
[8] See Chapter I, above.

veloped under more liberal surroundings.[9]   That this growth in numbers and the changing environment resulted in an increasing literary productivity will be shown below.[10]

[9] See Chapter XIII, below.
[10] See Chapter XIV, below.

Chapter XII: Books and Libraries.

DURING the early years of the new century the flow of books to New England continued. Judge Sewall constantly imported, as the records of his "Diary" and "Letter-Book" show. In 1701 he ordered

Dr. Nehemiah Grew: Cosmologia Sacra (two copies)
Dr. Holder: Time
Dr. Holder: Natural Grounds of Harmony
The Assembly Confession of Faith and Catechisms in Latin.[1]

The same year he recorded in a letter to John Love, his London agent,

I have received the Box of Books . . . . Mr. Colman has deliverd me my Dictionary . . . . I was very desirous of the new Edition of the Dictionary. But Mr. Collier has mard and not mended it by his alterations.[2]

He inquired in the same letter about a book by Sir William Petty on the greatness of London, and about another showing that London is bigger than imperial Rome was, ordering one of the first, and three or four of the second.

In 1705 he bought "the two Folios of Mr. Flavell's works for £3.10,"[3] and sent the following order to London:

Buy for me all the statutes at large made since Mr. Keeble's Edition 1684. Let them be well Bound in one or two Covers as shall be most convenient:

The Register[4]

[1] Letter-Book, i. 261.
[2] *Ibid.*, i. 259. Jeremy Collier edited the 1701 edition of "The Great Historical, Geographical, and Poetical Dictionary . . . . printed for Henry Rhodes." See p. 118, above.
[3] Diary, ii. 122.
[4] Crompton, Richard: L'Authoritie et Jurisdiction des Courts. Bracton, Henricus de: De Legibus et Consuetudinibus Angliæ. Britton, Joannes: On the Laws of England.

> Crompton[4]
> Bracton[4]
> Britton[4]
> Fleta
> Mirror[5]

as many of them as you can get in Latin or English;

> Heath's Pleadings
> Sir Edward Coke's Reports.[6]

In 1711 he "sent to Mr. Love for the Books following; viz.

> Pole's English Annotations, two Setts.
> Mr. Henry's Añotations
> Dutch Annotations.
> Cambridge Concordance;
> Preaching Bible.
> Junius and Tremellius, a fair Print to carry to Church.
> Pareus, his Adversaria on the Bible.
> Dr. Lightfoot's Works in two volumns
> Harris's Lexicon Tecnicum.
> Alcuinus;
> Tigurine Bible.
> Pauli Freheri theatrum vivorum Eruditione claror.
> Rushworth's Collections Abridgd and Improvd.
> Dr. Preston's Works.
> Ray of the Wisdom of GOD in the Creation.
> All Calvin's Comentaries.
> Dr. Owen on 6–13. of the Hebrs.
> Dr. Saunderson's Sermons.
> Stillingfleet's Origines Sacrae.
> Irenicum, Ch. Rome.
> Pearson on the Creeds[7]."

This list was sent again a few months later with the exception of the "preaching Bible," Saunderson's Sermons, and Pearson on the Creeds, and with the following addenda:

[4] See p. 174, note 4 above.
[5] Horn's Miroir des Justices.
[6] Letter-Book, i. 310.
[7] *Ibid.*, i. 411.

Supplement to the great Historical Dictionary.
Dr. Edwards his Tracts.
Two Herbert's Poems.
Mr. Watts's Hymns.
Virgil in usum Delphini. I have Ovid's Metamorphosis; if
there be anything else of Ovid in Usum Delphini, let me have it.
Dr. Arrowsmith's Armilla.
If any of the Old Books be so scarce, that they are very dear;
forbear buying them; and acquaint me with the Price.[8]

A year later he recorded

I by him presented his Excellency the Governour with Dr.
Calamy's Abridgment of Mr. Baxter's Life &c. in Two Volumes,
Cost me 30^s . . . [9]

In 1704 a Madam Rebecca Overton of London considered
Boston a sufficiently good market to send over by Mr. Anthony Young "to be by him disposed of for her Most advantage" a consignment of nearly fifty books, mostly theological.[10]
Wait Winthrop, like Sewall, was sending to London for
old books. Samuel Reade wrote to him in 1708,

Y^e person you mention that did collect those bookes hath been
dead many yeares, & none hath succeeded him in that curiosity;
ye bookes almost out of printe, & upon inquiry of severall booksellers cannot heare of but very few. . . . [11]

That Sewall and Winthrop sent to London for certain
books is not to be construed as an indication that books
were difficult to obtain in Boston. The opposite is rather
the case. New book shops were opened in addition to all
those established before 1700,[12] and these were supplemented
by auction sales of imported consignments of books, generally at some coffee-house. Catalogues of these collections

[8] *Ibid.*, ii. 10.
[9] Diary, iii. 154.
[10] Publications of the Colonial Society of Massachusetts, xiii. 291.
[11] Winthrop Papers, vi. 171.
[12] See p. 115 ff, above, and Littlefield, Early Boston Booksellers.

were printed for free distribution, and the sales were well advertised in the Boston papers. New importations for the regular book trade were also advertised. Boston evidently furnished a good market for the bookseller and sufficient opportunity for the book buyer.[13]

The most zealous and successful book collector of this period was Cotton Mather, who constantly recorded in his diary his joy at the steady growth of his library.[14] The following quotations will give an idea of some of the ways in which it grew.

. . . . I have a mighty Thirst after the Sight of Books, now and then published in *Holland:* which may upon sending you the *Titles* be transmitted with the Goods that you may send hither, and I pay here . . . . There is one *Thomas Crenius*, who had published . . . .[15]

I have had of late Years, many great and strange Accessions to my *Library* . . . . I will not have unmention'd, a Present of

[13] The following are typical advertisements:

"*Corderius Americanus* . . . . sold by Nicholas Boone . . . . As also a large parcel of choice English Books of Divinity, Poetry, History, &c. In the last Vessel from England." (*News-Letter*, October 11–18, 1708.)

"And many other New Books from England in the last Ship . . . . B. Eliot, at his shop in King Street." (*Ibid.*, March 23–30, 1713.)

"A valuable Collection of Books, consisting of Divinity, Physick, Mathematicks, History, Classicks, Belles Lettres, in Latin, English and French, to be sold by Publick Vendue or Auction, at the Crown Coffee-House in Boston . . . . Printed Catalogues may be had *gratis*." (*Ibid.*, February 6–13, 1715/6.)

"A Collection of choice Books, Ancient and Modern, in several Languages, upon most of the Arts and Sciences, few of them to be had at the Stationers, the Books very neatly Bound, to be sold by way of Auction . . . . at Mr. *Sibly's* Coffee-House . . . . King-Street, Boston." (*Ibid.*, August 20–27, 1716.)

"A Fine & Large Collection of BOOKS, lately Imported from London, is to be Exposed to Sale by RETAIL . . . . By *Samuel Gerrish* Bookseller in *Corn-Hill* near the Town-house. The Sale to begin at 10 of the Clock. The Catalogue is Printed, and may be had gratis. The Number of Books contained in it is as follows, Folios, 154. Quartos. 596. Octavos, 712." (*Boston Gazette*, September 23–30, 1723.)

[14] He frequently mentions among other favors of God or answers to prayer his "convenient study with a well-furnished Library;" "my exceedingly-well-furnished Library;" "a Library, exceeding any man's in all this land;" "my extraordinary *Library*, and the Possession of several thousands of Books." (Diary, *passim*.)

[15] Diary, ii. 421. Crenius is an error for Crusius.

Books made me this Winter, from the united Library of our three famous *Shepards;* which enriched me, not only with printed Books, which very low prized, might be counted worth more than 12 lb. but also with *Manuscripts* of each of those three worthy Men, which are vastly more valuable than all the other Books. . . . [16]

Within these Few Days, I have received packetts from *Gresham-Colledge;* by which I am sensible, That some former packetts from them hither, have unhappily miscarried. . . . . [17]

I have newly received large packetts from *Tranquebar* in the *East-Indies;* with a New Testament & some little Books of piety, printed in the *Damulic* Language & character; which are the first things that ever were printed in those parts of the world.. . . . [18]

Mather's eagerness for books resulted in the gathering of a library of probably four thousand volumes.[19]

Unfortunately no comprehensive list of the books in this greatest of colonial private libraries exists. Nearly a century ago descendants of the Mathers gave to the American Antiquarian Society such books of Cotton Mather's as were still in their possession. From this collection and from books containing Mather's autograph in various other libraries, Julius H. Tuttle of the Massachusetts Historical Society has compiled a list of books known to have been in his library.[20] The following are a few of the titles in that list:

	Collectanea Chymica: [10 tracts]
Hakluyt	Principal Navigations
Hatton	A New Treatise of Geography
Howel, Wm.	An Institution of General History

[16] Diary, i. 532.
[17] Letter to John Winthrop, July 15, 1720. Mather Papers, p. 440.
[18] Letter to John Winthrop, December 26, 1720. Mather Papers, p. 445.
[19] In 1700 it was approaching 3000. See p. 127, above. Mr. C. S. Brigham, Librarian of the American Antiquarian Society, estimates the library at 4000 volumes. (Publications of the Colonial Society of Massachusetts, xviii. 408.) W. H. Whitmore's note on page 75 of John Dunton's Letters is incorrect in ascribing to Cotton Mather the 7000–8000 volumes which composed the library of his son. See Drake: Mather's "King Philip's War," p. xxiii.
[20] Proceedings of the American Antiquarian Society, xx. 301. See also chapters VII and VIII, above.

Purchas	his Pilgrimage
Boyle, R.	6 vols. of science
Browne, T.	Religio Medici
Digby, K.	Observations upon Religio Medici
Hayward, J.	Life and raigne of King Henrie the IIII
Hayward, J.	Life and Raigne of King Edward the Sixt
Hooke, R.	Several volumes of science
Laet, Jean de	Several volumes of descriptions of countries
————	Judicial Astrologie judicially condemned
Machiavelli	Princeps
Milton	Eikonoklastes
————	Overthrow of Stage Playes, 1600
Plautus	Comœdiæ XX
Prynne	Histrio-Mastix and others
Rawlinson	New Method of . . . History and Geography
Roberts	Merchants Mappe of Commerce
Stubbes	Anatomie of Abvses
Withers	Grateful Acknowledgment of a late Trimming Regulator
Osborn, F.	Miscellany of sundry Essayes
Fletcher, G.	Israel Redux
Delamer, H.	Works

It was during the latter part of this period that the Reverend Thomas Prince began to collect his splendid library of colonial books. It is impossible to determine what books he gathered during these years; but some idea of the number may be gained from the following single item in the manuscript account-book of Daniel Henchman, bookseller, preserved, curiously enough, in the Prince Collection of the Boston Public Library.

Dec. 20, 1726.

Revd Thos Prince, Dr.

To 56 octavos 2^d hand	7.00.00
8 Quartos 5/	2.00.00
3 Folios	2.00.00

During these years the Boston Public Library both grew and suffered loss. On August 31, 1702, the Selectmen ordered "that M.[r] John Barnard jun.[r] be desired to make a Cattalogue of all the bookes belonging to the Towns Liberary and to Lodge the Same in y.[e] s.[d] Liberary."[21]   On February 28, 1704, they further ordered that "Mr. John Barnard Jun.[r] having at the request of the selectmen Set the Towne Liberary in good order he is allowed for s.[d] Service two of those bookes of w.[ch] there are in y.[e] s.[d] Liberary two of a Sort."[21]   The fire of 1711 damaged the Town-House, and Judge Sewall made the following note in his letter-book:

In our Boston Library several valuable Books were lost, as the Polyglott Bible, the London Criticks, Thuanus's History, a Manuscript in two Folios left by Capt: Reyn [Keyn] the Founder; &c.[22]

After the fire an attempt was made to recover as many as possible of the books mislaid at the time of the fire, as the following advertisement in *The Boston News-Letter* of June 8, 1713, shows.

All Persons that have in their Keeping, or can give Notice of any of the Town Library; or other things belonging to the Town-House in *Boston*, before the late Fire: are desired to Inform the Treasurer of the said Town thereof, in order to their being returned.

The first Volumn of *Pool*'s Annotations was carryed away in the late Fire in *Boston;* any Person that has it, or any other Books, carry'd away at that time, or any other Goods, are desired to bring them to the Post Office, that the true Owners may have them again.[23]

Of the Harvard Library at this time there are more records, though for a time there seem to have been few gifts. The following are from the records of meetings of the Harvard Corporation.

Voted that the Library keeper within the Space of one month

[21] Publications of the Colonial Society of Massachusetts, xii. 126.
[22] Letter-Book, i. 422.
[23] Publications of the Colonial Society of Massachusetts, xii. 128.

next coming, take an Inventory, of all Books, mathematicall Instruments, & other things of value committed to his Custody, & Give receipt for them to the praesident, to be accompted for by him at the Expiration of his Year annually, or at his leaving his place, before he receive his salary.[24]

Voted

2. That M[r] Edward Holyoke be Library keeper for this year & that Six pounds be allowd him for the said Service.

3. That fifty shillings be allowed and paid to M[r] Gookin for his taking a Catalogue of the books in the Library.[25]

Voted, that M[r.] Presid[t] and the Resid[t] Fellows agree with M[r] Brattle for what Books may be in the late Treasurers Library, they think proper for the College Library.[26]

Voted, that S[r] Welsted be Library Keeper for the Year Ensuing, and that £8 be allow'd him for that Service, and that he be directed to take Speciall Care that the Library and Books be kept in a better and more decent Condition than heretofore.[27]

On the second of February, 1721–2, Thomas Hollis, who was then just beginning to take an interest in Harvard, wrote to Benjamin Colman that he had two volumes of Milton's "Works," the new edition, to send to the college. He also asked for a catalogue of the books in the college library that he might know what to send them.[28] This letter resulted in the following actions of the Corporation of Harvard:

The worthy M[r] Hollis having Sent Over a new & fair Edi͞con of Milton's Poetical Works, directing, That if the College have Such like already, the s[d] Books are at M[r] Colmans Service either to dispose of or keep, Now M[r] Colman being desirous that the College sh[d] Have these new, fair and Well-bound Books intire, thô part of the Like be in the Library, Voted that what of Milton's Poetical Works heretofore belonged to the Library be de-

[24] Meeting of August 6, 1707. Harvard College Book IV, p. 27.
[25] Meeting of September 5, 1709. *Ibid.*, p. 36.
[26] Meeting of October 27, 1713. *Ibid.*, p. 52. The late Treasurer was Thomas Brattle, who died in 1713.
[27] Meeting of September 24, 1718. *Ibid.*, p. 63.
[28] Manuscript letter.

liver'd to the Rev[d] M[r] Colman to be disposed of as he sees meet.[29]

Upon the Intimation lately made by M[r.] Hollis, and formerly by M[r] Neal, that it may be of great Advantage to the College Library, that a Catalogue of the Books in the s[d] Library be printed and Sent abroad, Voted, that forthwith the Library-keep[r] take an exact Catalogue of the Books in the Library, and that the same be printed in Order to transmitt to friends abroad.[29]

. . . . The Treasurer is directed to pay the Printer afores[d] the Sum of £22.5[s] out of the College Treasury from [sic] printing the s[d] Catalogue containing 13½ sheets.

2. Voted, That M[r] Treasurer pay M[r] Sam[l] Gerrish the sum of £12.14[s] upon the delivery of 300 of the Printed Catalogues.

3. Voted, That M[r] Gee be paid out of the College-Treasury £20. for his Service in preparing the Catalogue . . . .

4. Voted, that One hundred of the afores[d] Catalogues be sent to England, & that 30 of them be deliver'd to M[r] Hollis. . . .[30]

This catalogue of 1723 contained about 3100 *titles*, almost equally divided among folios, quartos, and octavos (including all smaller), the library being catalogued according to size. A selected list of the literary, historical, and scientific books will be found in the Appendix, pp. 272 to 293. Reference to this list will show that Harvard had a satisfactory collection of books, including, outside the field of theology, representative works and authors in philosophy, science, and literature. It is weakest in English literature, but even there some of the best poets, such as Milton and Shakespeare, are found, and many lesser poets from Herbert to Wither. Such prose works as the seventeenth century produced are well represented from Hakluyt to Sir William Temple.

Upon the distribution of the 1723 Catalogue, interest in the Harvard Library greatly increased, especially in England under the stimulus of the interest of Thomas Hollis, himself

[29] Meeting of April 30, 1722. College Book IV, p. 75. It is unfortunate that we cannot know how long the Harvard Library had possessed part of the poetical works of Milton, or just what part it was.

[30] Meeting of December 25, 1723. College Book IV, p. 93.

the chief benefactor of the library throughout his life,[31] and of Henry Newman, at one time "Library-keeper" at Harvard, and from 1709 to 1741 agent of the College in England.[32] In 1723 Newman wrote from the Middle Temple to Henry Flint reporting that he was sending copies of the statutes of Cambridge and Oxford, the third and fourth volumes of Brandt's "History of the Reformation," and the first volume of Saurin's "Dissertation on the Old and New Testaments" as presents to the College Library.[33] In 1724 came a gift of books from Isaac Watts.[34] Gifts were also received from interested friends at home, as shown by the vote of thanks of the Corporation to Samuel Gerrish "for his bounty to College Library, he having presented to the College sundry Books to the Value of Ten pounds."[35]

The Library grew so rapidly after the publication of the 1723 Catalogue that the Corporation saw fit to order, at the meeting of June 2, 1725, the printing of three hundred supplements to the Catalogue, one hundred of which were to be sent to Thomas Hollis for distribution in England.[36] This supplement listed 61 *titles* in folio, 25 in quarto, and 80 in octavo and smaller, a good growth for less than two calendar years. A selected list of these additions will be found in the Appendix, pp. 293 to 295.

[31] Harvard College Book IV, p. 112, in the records of the Corporation reports a "Box of Books, N.º 10, from Mʳ· Hollis." See also pp. 181, 182, above.

[32] The sketch of Newman in "The Librarians of Harvard College," p. 11, states that "during the whole of his life in England, Newman was active in furthering the interests of the College in that country, and procured for it many gifts both of money and of books." An example of his work is given in a vote of the Harvard Corporation passed April 6, 1741, as follows: "That the Presᵈᵗ be desir'd to give the Thanks of the Corporation to Henry Newman of London, Esq., for the information he gives us by Dʳ Colman of some Prospect there is, of our obtaining a part of the Library of Sʳ Richard Gyles Bar. which he is about to bestow upon Dissenters, & pray him to continue his good Offices to the College, and particularly in that affair." (Harvard Library, Bibliographical Contributions, No. 52.)

[33] Massachusetts Historical Society, Collections, 1st Series, vi. 118.

[34] Harvard College Book IV, p. 97.

[35] Meeting of December 25, 1723. *Ibid.*, p. 94.

[36] Meeting of June 2, 1725. *Ibid.*, p. 102.

During these years another college library had been established in Connecticut, first at Saybrook and later at New Haven. The library of Yale began with books donated from the ministerial libraries of the colony and grew by means of gifts at home and abroad. Sir Henry Ashurst, for many years the London agent of Connecticut, wrote to Gurdon Saltonstall in 1709 offering to send "Mr Baxter's practicall volumes" if they would be acceptable to him for the young college.[37] Sir John Davie, a graduate of Harvard in 1681, and a farmer at New London when he unexpectedly succeeded to an English title and wealth, sent nearly 200 volumes to Yale in its early days.[38] In 1714 there arrived over 700 volumes sent by Jeremiah Dummer, one-fifth given by himself, the rest contributed by various English gentlemen, including Sir Richard Steele, Sir Isaac Newton, Bishop Kennett of Peterborough, Sir Edmund Andros, Francis Nicholson, Sir Richard Blackmore, Dr. John Woodward of the Royal Society, Richard Bentley, Dr. William Whiston, Edmund Halley, the astronomer, and Elihu Yale.[39] In many cases these men contributed volumes of their own works, Steele contributing, for instance, "all the Tatlers and Spectators being eleven Volumns." Besides many theological books, the collection included practically all of the important current books on medicine and philosophy, and representative works on science and in history and literature. Some idea of the books in the latter classes may be gained from the selected lists which follow:

Science

Boyle	Complete works, philosophical and moral
Wilkins	Mathematical works
Woodward	Natural History of the Earth

[37] Winthrop Papers, vi. 196.

[38] The year in which these books arrived is not known; they are recorded in Clap's catalogue before the Dummer books.

[39] The details in regard to these books are taken from President Clap's manuscript catalogue of early accessions to the library of Yale.

Locke	Upon Education
Locke	Essay on Human Understanding
Huylin	Cosmographia
————	Sea Chart of the Mediterranean
————	Guide to the Practical Gauger
————	Miscellanea Curiosa . . . . Discourses read to the Royal Society
————	Musaeum Regalis Societatis
von Helmont	Works
Newton	Principia Mathematica Naturalis Philosophiæ
Newton	Optics
Glauber	Works
Whiston	Astronomical Lectures
Whiston	Theory of the Earth
Gregory	Elements of Astronomy
Halley	Synopsis of Comets
Gassendi	Metaphisica
Hugenius	Discovery of Coelestial Worlds
Pemberton	View of Sir Isaac Newton's Philosophy

History and Literature

Raleigh	History of World
Clarendon	History of the Rebellion and Civil Wars
————	Complete History of England to the Reign of William III
Ricaut	History of the Ottoman Empire
Herbert	Memoirs of Charles I
————	Annals of Queen Anne for 1710–1711
Steele, etc.	Tatler
Steele, etc.	Spectator
Blackmore	King Arthur
Blackmore	Prince Arthur
Blackmore	Eliza
Blackmore	A Paraphrase on Job
Blackmore	Creation
Browne	Religio Medici
Browne	Vulgar Errors
Cowley	Works
Chaucer	Works and Life

Cleveland	"Works of Mr. Cleveland the poet"
Milton	Paradise Lost and all Poetical Works
Milton	Complete Collection of Prose Works
Jonson	Works
Spenser	Works
Wotton	Works
Bacon	Advancement of Learning
Bacon	Natural History
Barclai	Argenis
Buchanani	Poemata
Butler	Hudibras
Temple, Wm.	Miscellany
Glanvil	Sadducismus Triumphatus
Hale	Contemplations
Feltham	Resolves
————	The Turkish Spy
————	The Athenian Oracle
————	A Defence of Dramatic Poetry in Answer to Collier
Collier	Essays
Shaftesbury	Works

In 1718 over four hundred volumes more arrived, the gift of Elihu Yale. These added many classical books, many historical books, and some current literature. Other gifts followed, of which detail is lacking, but the library evidently continued to grow, as is indicated by the following vote of the trustees of Yale at the meeting of September 8, 1731:

Whereas there are several Books in the Library that are duplicates we resolve that one Book or Sett of each duplicate be sold by the Rector & Tutors & the money improved in purchasing of other Books that the Library at present is not furnished with.[40]

An attempt was made to interest Thomas Hollis in Yale, but the attempt failed as the following letter shows:

I have now another letter—anonimous—about Yale College— I know not the man, but supose him to be urged unto it by your

[40] Dexter, Documentary History of Yale, p. 290.

agent Dummer—I inclose it you. I have no inclination to be diverted from my projected design—if you know the Author, pray let him know so—I have told Dummer the same.[41]

The failure to interest Hollis was compensated by the interest which Bishop Berkeley took in the young college, which resulted in his gift, shortly after the close of this period, of over one thousand volumes, including the best of English literature from Shakespeare and Bacon to Pope, Gay, and Swift, with several volumes of plays—even Wycherley.[42]

Besides these public libraries, at least one semi-public library was established during the latter part of this period in connection with Franklin's *New England Courant*, the first issue of which appeared August 7, 1721. In No. 48 of the *Courant*, published July 2, 1722, is given a list of the books kept in the office of the paper for the use of writers. It includes the following:[43]

Shakespeare's Works
Virgil
Aristotle's Politicks
Hudibras
Milton
The Spectator, 8 volumes
The Guardian, 2 volumes
The Turkish Spy
The Athenian Oracle
The British Apollo
The Art of Thinking
The Art of Speaking
The Reader
The Lover
Cowley's Works
Burnet's History of the Reformation

[41] Letter of Hollis to John White, Treasurer of Harvard, July 12, 1721. From copy in the files of the Librarian of Harvard University.
[42] President Clap's manuscript catalogue.
[43] Cook, Literary Influences in Colonial Newspapers, p. 20.

Burnet's Theory of the Earth
Oldham's Works
The Tale of the Tub
St. Augustine's Works
Tillotson's Works
Dr. Bates' Works
Dr. South's Works
Mr. Flavel's Works
Mr. Charnock's Works
Many pamphlets.

Of interest in connection with the lists already given are the lists of the books which William Adams, Yale 1730, packed to carry to college with him at the beginning of his Freshman and Sophomore years:

Acc^t of Books y^t William Adams put up to carry to College, Nov 5. 1726.

Elisha Coles Dictionary,
A Latin Grammar,
A Greek   "
Tully's Offices,
    "   Orations,
Virgil's Works,
Horace,
English Virgil,
Greek Testament,
Latin   "
Catechisms, and Confessio Fidei,
Latin Bible,
Septuagint,
Florilegium Phraseωn,
Phraseologia Anglolatina,
Pasor's Lexicon,
Lucius Florus,
An English Bible,
A Call to Backsliders,
English Exercises,
Ovid de Tristibus,
Corderius' Colloquies,

Terence,
Ramus,
Mr. Willard's Penitent Prodigal,
An English Dictionary,
Observations on the Present State of Turkey,
The Strong Helper,
The Everlasting Gospel,
The life of Mr. Edmund French,
The Songs of the Redeemed,
Nomenclator, Singing Book,
    Catechism,
Some of his father's Sermons.[44]

The next year he carried the following, October 23:[45]

Locke of the Human Understanding,
Locke of Education,
Hebrew Bible, with Greek Testament at the end,
Hebrew Grammar,
Amesii Medulla Theologiæ,
Burgersdicii Logica,
Buxtorf's Lexicon,
Clark's Formulæ,
Allin's Alarm,
Mr. Coleman of Mirth,
Mr. Williams' Redeemed Captive,
Flemming's Rod or Sword,
Mr. Penhallow's Hist: of ye Indian War,
Mr. Flavel's Divine Conduct, or Mystery of Providence.
Kennet's Roman Antiquities,
Gordon's Geographical Grammar,
Hist. of ye House of Orange.
Pope's Homer, Vol. 2.
Homer's Iliad,
Dugard's Rhetorick,
Grotius, De jure Belli et Pacis,
Sanderson, De Conscientiâ,
    "   De juramento.

[44] Massachusetts Historical Society, Collections, 4th Series, i. 43.
[45] *Ibid.*, p. 44.

With all the growth of libraries and the means to acquire books, the old custom of borrowing and lending continued, and those who lived near the booksellers sent gifts of books to those who were at a distance. As in the early days of the colonies, the name of Winthrop is most prominent in this exchange of books; but this may be partly because we have more records of the Winthrops than of any other family. Wait Winthrop wrote to his son,

I want Buckstone's Lexicon for one of the words . . . [46]

Again he wrote,

I likewise send an Almanack and the Importance of Duncark, which is worth reading if you go through; it is M[r] Lechmers[47] brothers, and must be sent again, and then you may haue more.[48]

John Winthrop wrote to Cotton Mather,

I thank you heartily for yo[r] very agreeable and entertaining communications from y[e] Royall Society, and especially for y[e] sight of D[r] Woodwards *Naturalis Historia Telluris*.[49]

Cotton Mather wrote to him January 11, 1718–9,

I have begun with sending you, that peece of my dear S[r] *Richard*,[50] which will prepare you for the rest.[51]

November 30 of the same year he wrote,

When shall S[r] *Richard* return! some of my Neighbours dun me for him.[52]

Again the next February he wrote,

My dear,—Hast thou not yett with thee one of S[r] *Richards* volumes, His "*Essayes*," in prose? Examine thy Library.[53]

[46] Winthrop Papers, vi. 225. Dated October, 1710.
[47] This is probably the Thomas Lechmere who married Wait Winthrop's only daughter, Anne, in 1709.
[48] Winthrop Papers, vi. 280. October 28, 1713.
[49] *Ibid.*, p. 332. November 5, 1716. Dr. Woodward's book was published in 1714.
[50] This is Sir Richard Blackmore. See p. 198, below.
[51] Mather Papers, p. 433.
[52] *Ibid.*, p. 435.
[53] *Ibid.*, p. 437.

In spite of Winthrop's tardiness in returning books, Mather continued to send them:

I hope, you have received the packetts which I sent you a few weeks ago: Both a Number of COHELETH;[54] And also D[r] *Woodward's* pamphletts.[55]

As a borrower Mather wrote to Thomas Prince, April 16, 1718, to ask,

. . . . if you'l favour me, by this Bearer, with the Book of Poetry, you bought the last week at your Booksellers.[56]

Samuel Sewall, writing to John Williams, of Deerfield, added,

Inclosed the Non-Conformists Letter, this weeks News-Letter, Half Duz. Mr. Hobart's verses, with the occasion; They are chiefly hortatory, and therefore I might honestly print them.[57]

Many similar quotations might be given as further evidence of this custom, but it seems unnecessary to add more than the following statement of Cotton Mather's which shows how far the practice was carried:

Seldome any *new Book* of Consequence finds the way from beyond-Sea, to these Parts of *America*, but I bestow the Perusal upon it.[58]

In the meantime the popular distribution[59] of books, pamphlets, and broadsides had increased, for Mather recorded in his diary, in 1713,

I am informed. that the Minds and Manners of many People about the Countrey are much corrupted, by foolish Songs and Ballads, which the Hawkers and Pedlars carry into all parts of the Countrey. By way of Antidote, I would procure poetical Com-

---

[54] Coheleth: A Soul upon Recollection. Written by a Fellow of the Royal Society. Cotton Mather. 1720.
[55] Mather Papers, p. 442.
[56] Proceedings of the American Antiquarian Society, xx. 295.
[57] Letter-Book, ii. 8.
[58] Diary, i. 548.
[59] See p. 126, above.

posures full of Piety, and such as may have a Tendency to advance Truth and Goodness, to be published, and scattered into all Corners of the Land. There may be an Extract of some, from the excellent *Watts's* Hymns.[60]

When, in the latter part of that year, the Assembly passed laws restricting pedlars,[61] Mather feared lest its provisions might interfere with his plan, for he noted in his diary:

I must also assist the Booksellers, in addressing the Assembly, that their late Act against Pedlers, may not hinder their Hawkers from carrying Books of Piety about the Countrey.[62]

From the last sentence of the above it would seem that the booksellers made regular use of such hawkers in extending their business; this may have been the case for many years, for Mather planned to have books of piety so distributed as early as 1683.[63] Of course it cannot be presumed that these hawkers carried much or, perhaps, any real literature, their stock being made up chiefly of broadside ballads, chapbooks, and almanacs; but if there were so many pedlars selling so many questionable books that a law was necessary to regulate them, evidently there was a public demand for interesting narrative in either prose or verse, if not for real poetry. Most of their ballads and chapbooks were probably imported from England, but such homemade productions as Wigglesworth's "The Day of Doom," "The New England Primer," and Cotton Mather's "Life of Sir William Phipps" would be among the best sellers.

If James Gray, the only book hawker of whom there seems to be any extant record, may be considered typical, these pedlars found their business profitable. Upon his death the following notice appeared in *The Boston News-Letter* of April 9–16, 1705:

On Thursday last Dyed at Boston, James Gray, That used to

[60] Diary, ii. 242.
[61] Province Laws, i. 720.   Published November 14, 1713.
[62] Diary, ii. 283.
[63] See p. 126, above.

go up and down the Country Selling of Books, who left some considerable Estate behind him, and 'tis confidently affirmed that he
made a Will, which he left in some honest persons hand, with some
other Papers, which have not yet been found: And any person in
Town or Country who have said Will or Papers, are desired to
bring them unto the Office of Probates in Boston.

Judge Sewall was sufficiently interested in either the man
or the case to make a note of the amount of the estate in
the margin of his copy of the *News-Letter*.   Edward Brom-
field and Paul Dudley were appointed administrators of the
estate.   According to their final accounting, the value of the
estate was £712.11.3, of which £699.06. was in cash, eight
bags of coin of all kinds and denominations being listed in
the inventory.[64]   "James Gray, Bookseller *als*. Pedler," as
he is entitled in the Probate Record, had evidently found
the country folk of New England ready and eager to purchase
his books.

Other information in regard to books owned or read during
these years is found in quotations from or references to them.
Samuel Sewall, for instance, recorded in his diary,

. . . set out [from Bristol] . . . . for Narraganset. Din'd at
Bright's: while Diñer was getting ready I read in Ben Johnson,
a Folio . . . [65]

From the folio he copied some dozen lines into his diary.
At other times he recorded:

I gave the President and him the reading of Mr. Sewell's
Answer to the Bp. Salisbury's new preface. . . .[66] Gave each of
them Maroll's Martyrdom, Marbled.[67]

Inclosed . . . . Dr. Edwards's Answer to Sacheverell.[68]

Inclosed Mr. Prior's Epitaph (which Gov[r] Saltonstall had not
seen before):

[64] Suffolk Probate Records, xvi. 289 and 620, 621.
[65] Diary, ii. 167.
[66] *Ibid.*, ii. 391.
[67] *Ibid.*, ii. 391. This was published in 1712.
[68] Letter-Book, i. 398.

"Monarchs, and Heraulds, by your leave
"Here ly the bones of Matthew Prior;
"The Son of Adam and of Eve:
"Let Bourbon, or Nassau, goe higher!"[69]

This last quotation is very interesting because it seems to have reached New England before it was published in England. Austin Dobson writes,[70] "This epitaph does not appear to have been published during Prior's lifetime." Prior died in September, 1721, and Sewall quoted the poem January 15, 1721–2. It was probably first published in "A New Collection of Poems," 1725. It may have circulated in manuscript or even by word of mouth; in either case its reaching America so soon would indicate that some of the colonists were in close touch with English letters. This is also indicated by the following "good device" jotted down by Cotton Mather in August, 1713:

Perhaps, by sending some agreeable Things, to the Author of, *The Spectator*, and, *The Guardian*, there may be brought forward some Services to the best Interests in the Nation.[71]

Anything he might have sent would probably have been too late for publication, as *The Guardian* ceased with the issue of September 22, 1713; on the other hand, as it began publication May 28, 1713, Mather was not slow to realize its value. At the end of his printed sermon or "essay," "A New Year Well Begun," which bears the date of January 1, 1718–9, Mather added *New-Years-Day*, "From Sir Richard Blackmore's Collection of Poems, Printed at London, Anno 1718." Still another example of colonial interest in English literature is the item published in *The New England Courant* No. 22, January 1, 1722, "a noble Duke is about to erect a Monument in Westminster Abby to the Memory of Milton, the Poet."[72]

[69] *Ibid.*, ii. 142.
[70] Selected Poems of Matthew Prior, p. 233.
[71] Diary, ii. 227.
[72] Albert Matthews in *The Nation*, December 24, 1908. (Vol. 87, p. 624.)

That James Franklin was interested in Milton as a poet is shown by the presence of a copy of Milton in the *Courant* library,[73] and by his twice quoting from "Paradise Lost," once with the introductory remark, "Hear how the lofty *Milton* sings of this in his own inimitable Strain."[74]

Another who was interested in Milton was the Reverend Thomas Buckingham of Hartford, who carried with him on the expedition against Crown Point in 1711, along with a Bible and Psalm-book, "Milton on Comus," as he called it in his journal.[75]

Speaking of the reprinting of "George Barnwell" in *The New England Weekly Journal*, beginning February 14, 1732, Miss Cook remarks:[76]

One of the most noteworthy realistic tragedies of the eighteenth century was thus reprinted in the Puritan stronghold of America, within a surprisingly short time of its first appearance.[77] This fact seems to have escaped observation until now. Probably a stray copy of the play had found its way into Kneeland's bookshop. We cannot suppose that it had a place in the Prince or Byles libraries! Evidently Boston readers were rather more liberal in their tastes than we have been accustomed to think.

If we recall the interest in contemporary literature which has been shown in this chapter, as well as the possibility that John Dunton sold plays and romances in Boston nearly fifty years earlier,[78] it will not seem so strange that such a play as "George Barnwell," with its sturdy Puritan morality, should be reprinted in Boston. On the contrary, such reprinting is just what we might expect when we take into consideration the evidences of the growing liberality of life in Boston which will be presented in the next chapter, as well as the constantly increasing accessibility and appre-

[73] See p. 187, above.
[74] Massachusetts Historical Society, Proceedings, xlii. 164.
[75] The Journals of Madam Knight, and Rev. Mr. Buckingham, p. 106.
[76] Literary Influences in Colonial Newspapers, p. 55.
[77] The play was produced in 1730, two years earlier.
[78] See p. 120, above.

ciation of books and literature of all kinds during the last forty, and especially the last twenty, years of the first century of colonial life.   At the close of its first century New England was in touch with and responding to the literary movements of England.[79]

[79] See Chapter xiv, below.

Chapter XIII: Other Phases of Culture.

IN the opening years of the new century there seems to
have been a revival of intercourse between New Englanders and representative men in England. Joseph
Dudley, who returned to Boston in 1702 as Governor, after
a nine years' residence in England,[1] had during those years
become a close friend of Sir Richard Steele, who was private
secretary to Lord Cutts, Governor of the Isle of Wight,
when Dudley was Lieutenant-Governor. The following extract from a letter written by Steele to Dudley shows their
intimacy.

S^r,— I have your kind raillery of the 4th and shall not pretend
to answer it: you may excuse my not doing that in your observation of the losse of my brains, ...[2]

Benjamin Colman's four years in England[3] gave him the
opportunity to form many friendships which he continued
by correspondence. Among his correspondents were Thomas
Hollis, Isaac Watts, Daniel Neal,[4] Edward Calamy, Bishop
White Kennett of Peterborough,[5] Sir Richard Blackmore[6]
and Mrs. Elizabeth Singer Rowe ("Philomela").[7]

Cotton Mather established a correspondence with men

[1] See p. 152, above.

[2] Massachusetts Historical Society, Proceedings, 2d Series, iii. 201. The letter
bears the date of June 25, 1700.

[3] See p. 152, above.

[4] Colman contributed much material to Neal's History of New England. (Turell,
Life of Colman, p. 150.)

[5] Jeremiah Dummer wrote to Colman from England, January 15, 1714, "I
pray your acceptance of the prints inclosed. . . . . I have committed to captain
Willard, a book presented you by your good friend the dean [later the bishop]
of Peterborough." Massachusetts Historical Society, Collections, 1st Series, v.
199.

[6] Blackmore sent him copies of his poems. (Turell, Life of Colman, p. 150.)

[7] *Ibid., passim.* See p. 149, above.

not only in England but on the Continent. On May 23, 1711, he made the following entry in his diary:[8]

Having some epistolar Conversation with Mr. *De Foe*, I would in my Letters unto him, excite him to apply himself unto the work of collecting and publishing an History of the Persecutions which the Dissenters have undergone from the Ch[urch] of E[ngland].

In September of the same year he named Sir Richard Blackmore among the "eminent Persons beyond-sea" who "take notice of me, and such as I myself never have written unto, send me their Letters and their Presents."[9]   In December he recorded an idea:

I would write unto Sir *Richard Blackmore*, my Desires, that His incomparable Pen may make its furthest Efforts, in paying an Homage to our admirable JESUS; in celebrating His Beauties, before which those of the whole Creation languish and vanish; in uttering the awakened Songs of His Love to the Children of Men; in describing the illustrious Exemple of all Goodness, which He has given us; in asserting His Government over the Works of God; and Painting out the Grandeurs wherein He shall come to raise the Dead and judge the World, and the Delights of the new Heavens and the new Earth, which shall succeed the Resurrection.[10]

Mather also corresponded with Dr. Franckius, in Lower Saxony,[11] with Anthony W. Boehm of Halle, who had written to him in regard to a copy of the "Magnalia" which had come into his hands,[12] and with certain other professors at the University of Halle.[13]

In 1713 Mather's paper on "Curiosa Americana" was read before the Royal Society and he was proposed for membership. Soon after he was elected, but his name did not appear

[8] Diary, ii. 74.
[9] *Ibid.*, ii. 105.
[10] *Ibid.*, ii. 141.
[11] *Ibid.*, ii. 74.
[12] *Ibid.*, ii. 411.
[13] *Ibid.*, ii. 150.

upon the rolls of the society for a decade because at the time members had to qualify in person, which he was unable to do as he did not visit England. In 1723 arrangements were made whereby his name appeared upon the rolls as a regular member.[14]

William Brattle was elected a Fellow of the Royal Society March 11, 1714.[15] Paul Dudley, many of whose articles were published in the Transactions of the Society, was elected a Fellow on November 2, 1721.[15] Dr. Zabdiel Boylston, who was the first in America to experiment with inoculation for smallpox, was invited by Sir Hans Sloane, the court physician, to visit London. He received flattering attention from the scientists of England, being elected a Fellow of the Royal Society, before which he read a paper on the subject of inoculation. This paper was published in London in the year 1726, being dedicated by permission to the Princess of Wales.[16]

John Winthrop, son of Wait Winthrop, generally referred to as John Winthrop, F.R.S., to distinguish him from the other John Winthrops, also corresponded with the members of the Royal Society. He wrote to Cotton Mather in April, 1721,

W^t is become of the Doct^r at Gresham?[17] I am making an other sett of rarieties & curiositys for the Royall Society, wch I am thinking to present wth my owne hands.

In 1726 he did go to England, and there became an active member of the Royal Society, the 40th volume of the So-

[14] Publications of the Colonial Society of Massachusetts, xiv. 81 ff. Criticism has often been directed against Mather for using the initials F.R.S. after his name many years before 1723. As he had been officially notified of his election in 1713, and as No. 339 of the Philosophical Transactions, issued in 1714, gave him this title, such criticism is unjust.

[15] Publications of the Colonial Society of Massachusetts, xiv. 291.

[16] Green, History of Medicine in Massachusetts, p. 67.

[17] Winthrop Papers, vi. 399 note. The Doctor referred to is presumably Dr. John Woodward, Secretary of the Royal Society, who continued to reside at Gresham College, London, after the Royal Society moved to other quarters.

ciety's Transactions being dedicated to him.[18]   Winthrop enjoyed English life so much that he never returned to New England.

Thomas Robie, Harvard 1708, later a tutor and Fellow of the Corporation, had several papers on mathematical and physical subjects published in the Transactions of the Royal Society, but does not seem to have been a member.[19]   He died in 1729 at the age of forty-one; had he lived longer he might have been chosen a Fellow.   Dr. William Douglass, a Scotch physician (best known perhaps because of his strong opposition to the practice of inoculation and its sponsor, Cotton Mather,) accepted Robie's observations of eclipses, latitude, longitude, etc.[20]

Others than Winthrop went to England to reside during this period.   Henry Newman, Harvard 1687, went about 1707.   For a time he lived in the family of the Duke of Somerset, in what capacity is not known, and later acted as the agent of Harvard College, from 1709 to 1741, and also as agent of New Hampshire.[21]   Jeremiah Dummer, Harvard 1699, after studying at Utrecht,[22] settled in England, where he acted for a time as the agent of Connecticut.[23]

While such Americans living in England formed a bond between the old and the new, other links were formed by the Governors sent out from England and their trains, and by those who still turned to the new world to better their fortunes.   The latter included such men as Dr. William Douglass, who, in spite of his very conservative attitude toward smallpox inoculation, was interested in science.   In a letter to Dr. Cadwallader Colden of New York he sent a complete report of the weather for the year past—that is, as complete as he could keep it with "no other instru-

[18] *Ibid.*, iv. 571 note.
[19] Librarians of Harvard College, p. 16.
[20] Massachusetts Historical Society, Collections, 4th Series, ii. 185.
[21] See p. 183, above.
[22] See p. 104, above.
[23] Winthrop Papers, vi. *passim.*

ments than the naked eye, pen, ink, and paper, I know of no Thermometer nor Barometer in this place."[24] He added that there was a "good Quadrant and Telescope in the College about four miles from this," whereby he hoped to take observations of the sun, study eclipses, and so on. Some time after this he was one of the organizers of the Boston Medical Society.[25]

Another who came in search of a fortune was Thomas Lechmere, younger son of Edmund Lechmere, Esq., and grandson of Sir Nicholas Lechmere, a distinguished judge. Thomas Lechmere's older brother, Nicholas, became the Attorney-General of England and was raised to the peerage as Lord Lechmere in 1721. Lechmere brought with him money with which to trade, and soon added to it by marriage with Anne Winthrop, sister of John Winthrop, F.R.S.[26]

Of wealth and luxury in New England at this time one illustration will perhaps be sufficient. The expenditure at the time of the funeral of Fitz-John Winthrop, in 1707, amounted to over £600, the modern equivalent for which would be somewhat over $10,000.00. The single item of sugar for the burnt wine was £2.09.06, or about $50.00![27]

There are evidences that the "worldliness" noticed in the second period[28] was increasing. In 1714 Samuel Sewall found it necessary to write to Isaac Addington:

There is a Rumor, as if some design'd to have a Play acted in

[24] Massachusetts Historical Society, Collections, 4th Series, ii. 165. Letter dated Feb. 20, 1720–1. In connection with the lack of such instruments it must be remembered that the Fahrenheit thermometer had been invented only in 1714, and that the barometer, although devised earlier, was but slowly coming into use. There had been a barometer in Boston many years before this, for in the inventory of the estate of John Foster, the printer, occurs the item "wether glasses," which was the seventeenth century term for barometer. The inventory was taken in 1681. (Green, John Foster, p. 52.)

[25] This was formed about 1735; it published some papers. Massachusetts Historical Society, Collections, 4th Series, ii. 188.

[26] Winthrop Papers, vi. 367 note.

[27] Ibid., v. 412. When Mrs. Katherine Eyre married Wait Winthrop in 1707, the inventory of her property totaled £5,328.12.2. (Winthrop Papers, vi. 158–9.)

[28] See p. 156 ff., above.

the Council-Chamber, next Monday; which much surprises me: And as much as in me lyes, I do forbid it. The Romans were very fond of their Plays: but I never heard they were so far set upon them, as to turn their Senat-House into a Play-House. Our Town-House was built at great Cost and Charge, for the sake of very serious and important Business; . . . . Let it not be abused with Dances, or other Scenical divertisements . . . . Ovid himself offers invincible Arguments against publick Plays.[29]

The next year Wait Winthrop, writing to his son John, mentioned the fact that "Molle . . . . is well and brisk, and goes to dancing."[30] *The Boston News-Letter* for August 22–29, 1715, published the following notice:

This is to give Notice that at Cambridge on Wednesday the 21st day of September next, will be Run for, a Twenty Pound Plate, by any Horse, Mare or Gelding not exceeding Fourteen and an half hands high, carrying 11 Stone Weight, and any Person or Persons shall be welcome to Run his Horse &c, entering the same with Mr. *Pattoun* at the Green Dragon in Boston, any of the six days preceding the Day of Runing, & paying Twenty Shillings Entrance.[31]

For Tuesday night, January 7, 1717–8, Judge Sewall recorded, "The Gov[r] has a Ball at his own House that lasts to 3 in the Morn."[32] Such items show the tendency of the time, as do also the growing popularity of the taverns and coffee-houses, the increase in numbers and wealth of the silversmiths, and the laments of such men as Cotton Mather over the degeneracy from the better days of old.

These years saw also the establishment and development of the newspaper upon English models. A single issue of a paper called *Publick Occurrences* had appeared before the end of the previous century, but the paper was promptly suppressed by the authorities. On Monday, April 24, 1704,

[29] Letter-Book, ii. 29.   Sewall quotes passages from Ovid to illustrate.
[30] Winthrop Papers, vi. 310.
[31] A notice of another horse race at Cambridge is reprinted in Publications of the Colonial Society of Massachusetts, xiv. 408.
[32] Diary, iii. 158.   Samuel Shute was governor at this time.

appeared the first number of *The Boston News-Letter*, published by John Campbell, postmaster. When William Brooker succeeded Campbell as postmaster, one of his first acts was to establish a new weekly, *The Boston Gazette*, begun December 21, 1719. These were poor enough as newspapers, printing little but news items taken from London papers whenever the latter were accessible, and at other times filling in with local news, reports of speeches in provincial legislatures, or anything available.[33]

James Franklin was the printer of Brooker's *Gazette*. After forty numbers Brooker sold the paper to Philip Musgrave, who succeeded him as postmaster. When Musgrave employed Samuel Kneeland as printer instead of Franklin, the latter, "encouraged by a number of respectable characters, who were desirous of having a paper of a different cast from those then published . . . . began the publication, at his own risk, of a third newspaper, entitled, *The New England Courant*."[34] This paper was not founded just to furnish news; its purpose was to provide readable essays on the order of those which had made the *Spectator* and its successors popular. Franklin had served his apprenticeship in London previous to the year 1717, when he set up his press in Boston, and thus had come in touch with the English journalism and literature of the day. The nature of the articles published in the *Courant* must be left until the next chapter for discussion. The point that should be emphasized here, as the last evidence of the culture reached at this time in New England, is the fact that Franklin felt that there was sufficient interest in literature, as apart from news, in the neighborhood of Boston, to warrant the establishment of a paper without news, and in competition with two established newspapers. The success of his paper proved that he was right. Thus we find within a year after

[33] For details in regard to colonial newspapers see Elizabeth C. Cook's "Literary Influences in Colonial Newspapers," from which much of the material in these paragraphs is taken.

[34] Thomas, History of Printing, i. 110.

the close of the first century of New England, if we reckon
from the founding of Plymouth, and several years before
the end of the first century of Boston's existence, a deliberate
and recognized literary organ which reflected the growing
literary culture of the colonists, even if it did not, as we
shall see, accurately mirror contemporary literary taste.

Chapter XIV: The Production of Literature.

THE literary movement which was beginning in and around Boston at the end of the seventeenth century[1] developed more rapidly after the new century opened. The central figure in this movement was Samuel Sewall, who, although he has no fame as a writer of poetry,[2] wrote considerable verse, both Latin and English. His Latin verses were sufficiently well known in Boston in the first year of the century to call forth a burlesque.[3] Sewall was less interested in English poetry,[4] and yet some of his verses in English are not without merit. His penchant was epigrammatic verse, the following lines on the death of Tom Child, the painter, being perhaps the best example of his art.

> Tom Child had often painted Death,
> But never to the Life, before:
> Doing it now, he's out of Breath;
> He paints it once, and paints no more.[5]

Others who were interested with Sewall in the writing of poetry were Richard Henchman, Nicholas Noyes, Nehemiah Hobart, Experience Mayhew, and a Mr. Bayly. It is not

---

[1] See p. 168, above.

[2] He is not mentioned as a writer of poetry by such historians of American poetry as Moses Coit Tyler and William B. Otis, or in the Cambridge History of American Literature. This is true also of the literary friends of Sewall mentioned in the text (see above), with the exception of Noyes.

[3] Sewall recorded in his diary, May 29, 1701, "This day a Burlesqe comes out upon Hull-street, in a Travestie construing my Latin verses." (Diary, ii. 35.)

[4] In one of his letters to Richard Henchman, Sewall wrote, "It is convenient to sing the Downfall of Babylon, in verses that will stand." As the accompanying verses are in Latin, it is evident that Sewall chose that rather than English for work which he considered important and desired to have endure. (Letter-Book, i. 318.)

[5] Diary, ii. 170. November 10, 1706. The verses are prefaced by the statement, "This morning Tom Child, the Painter, died."

possible to determine whether these men ever came together as a group for mutual encouragement in literary work; but it is evident that Sewall kept in touch with the literary work which all of them were doing, encouraged them, and both criticized their verses and sent his own to them for criticism.[6] This group did not produce any body of good verse, because none of its members had any real talent for poetry; but that they made the effort to produce, and that they encouraged each other's efforts, shows that literary culture in New England had reached the creative stage.

There were still many things to handicap literary development. The most important of these was the lack of suitable means of publishing short or occasional poems, such as these men usually wrote. If we may judge by the poems that have survived, or of which we have record, no one of these men produced enough for a volume of poems. The newspapers of Boston printed practically no poetry until after 1720.[7] Therefore the only means of publication was the

[6] Sewall's Verses upon the New Century, bearing the date of January 1, 1700–01, brought immediate response from Henchman in a long and effusive poem in praise of Sewall, dated January 2, 1700–01. To Henchman, Sewall wrote, February 24, 1703–04, "Sir,—I send home your Verses with Thanks. There are many good strokes in them: but in my mind, the English excell. I think—*dominantur undiq[u]e fraudes*, does not well end a verse; the last syllable in [*Dominantur*] is short by Rule." (Letter-Book, i. 293.) He wrote to Henchman in 1705, "It is convenient to sing the Downfall of Babylon, in verses that will stand: let me therefore have your Examination and censure of the following Distich . . . . " (Letter-Book, i. 318.) At about the same time he wrote to Nicholas Noyes, "Sir, —How am I ready to sink down into ingratitude on a sudden, and unawares! My Brother in a Letter had raised my Expectation of receiving a distich or 2 from you; and the disapointment puts me out of Tune." [He adds an apposite quotation from Ovid.] (Letter-Book, i. 315.) On March 27, 1712, Nehemiah Hobart addressed a Latin poem of thirty-seven lines to Sewall, who sent to Hobart in acknowledgement of the compliment a copy of Virgil: "I give him' Virgil on account of the Poem he has gratify'd me with." (Diary, ii. 346.) This was soon turned into English verse by Henchman. (Letter-Book, i. 314 note 2, which gives both Latin and English versions.) Evidence of his interest in the poetry of Bayly and Mayhew is given in note 8 on page 207, below.

[7] A very few times the *News-Letter* reprinted from English papers articles which included lines of verse. One four line Latin epigram by Sewall, published in the *News-Letter* in 1705, is the only original poem which I have been able to find in

broadside, and in this form some of the verses of these men appeared. Other poems that circulated did so in manuscript. Sewall seems to have been as interested in the circulation of these poems as in their production, and therefore in a double sense was the center of this literary movement.[8]

One poem by Richard Henchman may indicate the existence of literary patronage in Boston at this time. This poem, entitled "Vox Oppressi,"[9] was addressed to the Lady

the papers before 1720, and we have Sewall's testimony (Diary, ii. 149) that it was with difficulty that he persuaded John Campbell to print it.

[8] The following quotations show Sewall's custom of enclosing poetry in his letters. It should be noted that some of the poems were evidently printed as broadsides. "This day I made this Distich . . . . [omitted]. Gave them and two more to Mr. Phips at Charlestown." (Diary, ii. 140. October, 1705.) "In my Letter I inclosed a News-Letter, two Copies of Mr. Bayly's Verses, Babylon is fallen." (Letter-Book, i. 351. August, 1707.) "Writ . . . . to Mr. Moodey . . . . [enclosed] this day's News-Letter; Two Setts of Verses; Libels, and proceeding thereupon. Vindicated Glascow. Sent p Capt. Lyon to whom I gave Mr. Danforth, and Mayhew's Verses." (Letter-Book, i. 408. December, 1710.) "To Sir Charles Hobby . . . . inclosing . . . . 2 of Mr. Mayhew's Poems on daughter Gerrish." (Letter-Book, i. 412. 1711. Sewall's daughter, Mrs. Gerrish, died in 1710.) "To Mr. Joseph Lord . . . . Sent him . . . . One Consolations, Frenches Verses, My verses on the Taking of Port-Royal. 4. Mr. Mayhew's verses; 1 Mr. Danforth on Daughter Gerrishes Death." (Letter-Book, i. 408. February, 1710–11.) "I visit Mr. Wadsworth . . . . Give a verse to him and to Mr. Pemberton." (Diary, ii. 359. August, 1712.) "Left the Gov[r] two of Mr. Hobart's verses . . . . Gave Mr. Colman one of Mr. Hobart's verses." (Diary, ii. 360–1. August, 1712. These would seem to be printed copies of the Latin poem to Sewall to which reference has been made on page 206, note 6.) "Writ to Mr. Williams of Derefield, inclosed . . . my Verses on Merrimak River finish'd yesterday." (Diary, iii. 240. January 16, 1719–20.) "Inclosed *Merrimak* dry'd up, with the occasion of it . . . . Inclosed 6. of Mr. Hobart's printed verses." (To Timothy Woodbridge, February 1, 1719–20. Letter-Book, ii. 104.) "Merrymak is printed off, about 300. I give Sam. Mather two of them." (Diary, iii. 279. February, 1720–21. This poem is printed in the Proceedings of the Massachusetts Historical Society, 2d Series, ix. 8.) "Sent . . . . Mr. Hobart's Verses—*Nocte viator.*" (To Edward Taylor, February 16, 1719–20. Letter-Book, ii. 105.) "Mr. Prince and I go next the Relations. I gave him Merrimack; he desired me to give him copies of all my performances." (Diary, iii. 283. March 7, 1720–21.) "Having only one *Renatus* by me, I have inclos'd it, & a copy or two of Judge Lynde's verses." (To John Winthrop, January 8, 1725–6. Winthrop Papers, vi. 422.)

[9] Preserved in manuscript in the Boston Public Library.

Phipps, the wealthy widow of the former governor to express the poet's gratitude for a gift of money. As further evidence is lacking, it is impossible to say whether the gift was to encourage Henchman's poetical efforts, or to reward him for some poem in Lady Phipps' honor or in honor of her husband, or merely charity; but the tone of the poem seems to be that of poet to patron.

Outside of the group of Sewall's friends there were several who were writing verse, some for their own amusement, others for publication. Of the first class, the most interesting is Sarah Kemble Knight, whose journal of her trip from Boston to New York in 1704 owes much of its charm to the rhymes which furnished her a means to express privately the feelings which she could not express in public.[10] Her satirical humor is matched by that of other poets of the day, of varying merit as poets, but deliberately satirical.[11] Such

---

[10] "But I could get no sleep, because of the Clamor of some of the Town tope-ers in next Room, ... I set my Candle on a Chest by the bed side, and setting [sic] up, fell to my old way of composing my Resentments, in the following manner:

> I ask thy Aid, O Potent Rum!
> To Charm these wrangling Topers Dum.
> Thou hast their Giddy Brains possest—
> The man confounded wth the Beast—
> And I, poor I, can get no rest.
> Intoxicate them with thy fumes:
> O still their Tongues till morning comes!"
>
> (The Journal of Madam Knight, p. 38.)

Being refused accommodation at the house of a Mr. Devill, she wrote the following warning to other travelers:

> "May all that dread the cruel feind of night
> Keep on, and not at this curs't Mansion light.
> 'Tis Hell; 'tis Hell! and Devills here do dwell:
> Here dwells the Devill—surely this's Hell.
> Nothing but Wants: a drop to cool yo'r Tongue
> Cant be procur'd these cruel Feinds among.
> Plenty of horrid Grins and looks sevear,
> Hunger and thirst, But pitty's bannish'd here—
> The Right hand keep, if Hell on Earth you fear!
>
> (Ibid., p. 40.)

[11] Sewall recorded in his Letter-Book (i. 255) a satire upon "The Gospel Order Revived" (an answer by Benjamin Colman and his friends to Increase

satire may reflect the growth of English satirical poetry during the latter part of the seventeenth century and at the opening of the eighteenth. John Danforth, who had written some verses for his own almanacs at an earlier date, printed a poem a page in length at the end of his published lecture Mather's "The Order of the Gospel") which was being circulated at Plymouth (March 1701). Part of the poem follows:

. . . .

> *The old strait Gate is now out of Date,*
> *The street it must be broad;*
> *And the Bridge must be wood, thô not half so good*
> *As firm Stone in the Road.*

. . . .

> *Saints Cotton & Hooker, o look down, & look here*
> *Where's Platform, Way & the Keys?*
> *O Torey what story of Brattle Church Twattle,*
> *To have things as they please*

> *Our Merchants cum Mico do stand Sacro Vico;*
> *Our Churches turn genteel:*
> *Parsons grow trim and trigg with wealth wine & wigg*
> *And their crowns are coverd with meal.*

A better satire is John Banister's on Cotton Mather's degree of Doctor of Divinity from Glasgow University, also found in Sewall's Letter-Book (i. 407. November, 1710), Increase Mather having loaned him a copy of it.

ON C. Mᵣˢ DIPLOMA.

> *The mad enthusiast, thirsting after fame,*
> *By endless volum'ns* [sic] *thought to raise a name.*
> *With undigested trash he throngs the Press;*
> *Thus striving to be greater, he's the less,*
> *But he, in spight of infamy, writes on,*
> *And draws new Cullies in to be undone.*
> *Warm'd with paternal vanity, he trȳs*
> *For new Suscriptions, while the Embryo* lyes*
> *Neglected—Parkhurst† says, Satis fecisti,*
> *My belly's full of your Magnalia Christi.*
> *Your crude Divinity, and History*
> *Will not with a censorious age agree.*

* His 2 volumus [*sic*]—Sewall's note. The reference is undoubtedly to Mather's Biblia Americana, which Mather several times vainly endeavored to publish by subscription. It is still in existence—unprinted.

† Parkhurst was the London bookseller who published the Magnalia.

"The Right Christian Temper in every Condition."[12]   Cotton Mather wrote several poems, found in his diary and elsewhere, most of which show more poetical feeling and expression than do the poems which he published in the "Magnalia."[13]   Samuel Wigglesworth, son of the author of "The Day of Doom," wrote one long poem, "A Funeral Song,"[14] which, in spite of its title, in no way resembles the elegies of the earlier periods, but on the contrary shows

> *Daz'd with the stol'n title of his Sire‡*
> *To be a Doctor he is all on fire;*
> *Would after him, the Sacrilege commit*
> *But that the Keeper's care doth him affright.§*
> *To Britain's northern Clime in haste he sends,*
> *And begs an Independent boon from Presbyterian friends;*
> *Rather than be without, he'd beg it of the Fiends.*
> *Facetious George brought him this Libertie*
> *To write C. Mather first, and then D. D.*

Another satire, less poetical but very bold, appeared in 1717.   To quote Sewall, ". . . . a virulent Libel was starch'd on upon the Three Doors of the Meeting House [the New South], containing the following Words;

> ### TO ALL TRUE-HEARTED CHRISTIANS.
> *Good people, within this House, this very day,*
> *A Canting Crew will meet to fast, and pray.*
> *Just as the miser fasts with greedy mind, to spare;*
> *So the glutton fasts, to eat a greater share.*
> *But the sower-headed Presbyterians fast to seem more holy,*
> *And their Canting Ministers to punish sinfull foley."*

(Diary, iii. 116.)

Still another satirical poem, which has disappeared, is mentioned in Thomas' list for 1714 (History of Printing, ii. 372) under the title "Origin of the Whalebone petticoat."   A Satyr (In Verse).   Boston, August 2d, 1714.

‡ Increase Mather's degree of Doctor of Divinity had been conferred upon him through his own influence at a time when it is questionable whether Harvard had the right to confer such a degree.   His enemies criticized him for accepting it.

§ Leverett—Sewall's note.   President Leverett belonged to the party unfriendly to the Mathers.

[12] Published at Boston, 1702.   He also wrote a poem upon the death of Elder Hopestill, of Dorchester, in 1719.   See Memoirs of Roger Clap, p. v.

[13] See his Diary, i. 450; ii. 138, 786; and Kettell, Specimens of American Poetry, i. 14.

[14] Printed in full in the New England Historical and Genealogical Register, iv. 89, and in part in Tyler, History of American Literature, ii. 36 ff.

greater poetical imagination than do his father's poems. In 1713 Richard Steere of Connecticut and Long Island brought out at Boston a ninety-page volume of verse under the title of "The Daniel Catcher."[15]

The last named volume deserves especial attention, not for the fifty-three page biblical poem in rhymed couplets, of the familiar colonial type, from which the volume gets its title, but for three of the shorter poems included in the volume. The first of these is a nineteen page poem in blank verse. The blank verse is not very good, but unique in the colonial poetry of the period, and unusual in any English poetry of the time, there being practically no non-dramatic blank verse from Milton to Thompson. The second, a poem on the visit of the angels to Bethlehem at the birth of the Saviour, is interesting for its echo of Milton's "Hymn" in "On the Morning of Christ's Nativity." The theme is the same, although treated differently, and the metre resembles Milton's in its regular stanza form with the Alexandrine at the end of each stanza; it differs in having an added line instead of the longer third and sixth lines of Milton's. The resemblance is not remarkable, but it is difficult to believe that the writer was not influenced, even if not inspired, by Milton. If so, this is the first colonial poem which shows such influence. The third poem deserves quotation here as showing more poetic feeling than most of the contemporary poetry, and even more as an instance of an appreciation of nature at a time when sincere appreciation of nature was practically unknown in English poetry on either side of the ocean.

ON A SEASTORM NIGH THE COAST.

All round the Horizon black Clouds appear
        A Storm is near:
Darkness Eclipseth the Sereener Sky,
        The Winds are high,

[15] Printed in full in Littlefield, Early Massachusetts Press, ii. This was his second volume of verse. His first, A Monumental Memorial of Marine Mercy, was published in Boston, 1684.

Making the Surface of the Ocean Show
Like mountains Lofty, and like Vallies Low.

The weighty Seas are rowled from the Deeps
        In mighty heaps,
And from the Rocks Foundations do arise
        To Kiss the Skies:
Wave after Wave in Hills each other Crowds,
As if the Deeps resolv'd to Storm the Clouds.

How did the Surging Billows Fome and Rore
        Against the Shore
Threatning to bring the Land under their power
        And it Devour:
Those Liquid Mountains on the Clifts were hurld
As to a Chaos they would shake the World.

The Earth did Interpose the Prince of Light
        Twas Sable nigh[t]
All Darkness was but when the Lightnings fly
        And Light the Sky,
Night, Thunder, Lightning, Rain, & *raging* Wind,
To make a Storm had all their forces joyn'd.

Such verse writers as these were responsible for the increased interest in literature during the early years of the
century, and prepared the way for the even greater activity
to follow when the influence of *The Spectator* and similar
papers and of Pope and his contemporaries should be felt
in New England.   That the colonists so soon reacted to the
literary movements in England may have been because of
the work of these people, poor as it was in itself.   As early
as 1714 Cotton Mather was ready to attempt essays of the
Spectator type;[16] and as soon as a vehicle was provided in
The New England Courant there were many who were eager
to contribute.[17]   The essays in the *Courant* were the work

[16] See p. 194, above.

[17] An indication of the eagerness to contribute either to the *Courant*, or, for the
more conservative, to the *News-Letter* or *Gazette*, is shown by the fact that one of

of a group of men sufficiently organized so that John Campbell, publisher of *The Boston News-Letter*, disgruntled at the
success of a new rival, and perhaps offended by the atheistic
or deistic tone of the essays, gave them the name by which
they have ever since been known, the Hell-Fire Club, that
being the name of a London atheist club of unsavory repute.
Isaiah Thomas speaks of the group as "a society of gentlemen."[18]   The essays in the *Courant* were quickly answered
by essays in the *News-Letter* and *Gazette;* and for several
years public questions of the day, such as inoculation, were
debated.   Several months after the *Courant* ceased publication in 1726, *The New England Weekly Journal* was begun.
This, like the *Courant*, was the organ of a group of men
whose purposes were definitely literary.   This group included such young writers as Mather Byles, Thomas Prince,
Judge Danforth,[19] and probably Matthew Adams, formerly
associated with the *Courant*.[20]   The name "Proteus Echo"
was assumed for the editor, as "Old Janus" had been used
in the *Courant*, both in obvious imitation of the *Spectator*.
Both journals printed verse as well as prose, and both frequently lightened the work of their writers by reprinting
from English periodicals.[21]   The chief poet of the *Journal*
was Mather Byles, whose style bears witness to his admira-
tion of Pope's poetry.[21]

Another illustration of the colonial response to English
literary movements, as well as an illustration of increasing
interest in the production of literature, is found in a manu-

the several verse contributions which Sewall sent to the *News-Letter* was an adap-
tation of a poem which he had written in 1676.   It was published in the *News-
Letter* for March 28, 1723, having waited nearly fifty years for a suitable medium
for publication.   It was evidently recalled by Sewall when he was seeking material
to contribute.   (Diary, i. 27; iii. 320 note.)

[18] History of Printing, ii. 31.

[19] *Ibid.*, ii. 41, 42.

[20] Massachusetts Historical Society, Collections, v. 211 note.

[21] Cook, Literary Influences in Colonial Newspapers, Chapters I and II, where
much detail is given.

script volume recently acquired by the Harvard Library.[22] This volume, in the handwriting of Ebenezer Turell, contains thirteen numbers of a student periodical, modeled after the *Spectator*, which evidently circulated in manuscript. The periodical is called *The Telltale*, and most of its papers are signed by Telltale. One paper gives an account of the "Telltale alias Spy Club—wch consists of these Six members: Telltale, Blablonge, Sharpsights, Courage, Intelligence, Quick." Verse is found in one of the papers. Of this volume Mr. Lane writes, "It is the earliest college production of the kind of which I have any information." That Harvard preceded any English college in attempting periodical litera- ture is striking evidence of the awakening to literary activity in New England in the first quarter of the eighteenth century.

There are other indications of the literary tendency of the time. In 1724 T. Fleet published "The Indictment and Tryal of Sir Richard Rum," a clever temperance tract with literary merit. In 1725 Nathaniel Ames began his "Alma- nac," which differed from the earlier almanacs both in its use of the best English poetry (whereas earlier almanacs printed third rate original verse), and in its blending of wit and wisdom in effective phrases, wherein Ames anticipated Franklin's "Poor Richard." From now on the almanac yearly carried real literature into every home.

It must be admitted that most of the literature produced during this period is unsatisfactory. The imitations of the *Spectator* do not measure up to their model. The imitators of Pope may have caught the trick of his verse, but they lack both his brilliant wit and his poetic power. That the colo- nists did not succeed in their attempts is much less important, however, than the fact that they made the effort, and that at the end of the first century of colonization the effort was a general one, not limited to a few ministers or to the edu-

22 This volume is described in detail in a paper by William C. Lane, Librarian of Harvard, read before the Colonial Society of Massachusetts. (Publications of the Colonial Society of Massachusetts, xii. 220.)

cated class. The leaders in the movement to establish literary journalism had been James Franklin, whose education had been merely that of a printer's apprentice, and Matthew Adams, whom Benjamin Franklin describes as "an ingenious tradesman."[23]   Benjamin Franklin himself was only a self-educated printer's apprentice, and a mere boy as well, yet he also came under the influence of the *Spectator* and attempted essays with such success that the Dogood papers, begun in the *Courant* early in 1722, when Franklin was hardly sixteen, were among the most literary essays which that periodical published.   Unquestionably we owe the writings of the greatest American writer of the eighteenth century to the literary movement which developed in New England and centered in Boston about the year 1720, as if to commemorate the one-hundredth anniversary of the establishment of English civilization in New England.

[23] Autobiography, p. 22.

Appendix.

THE *Appendix had not been completed by the author and as it stands now does not include, by any means, all of the material which he had gathered for possible publication in this volume. Owing to lack of space the editor has omitted the catalogues of libraries belonging to William Bradford, Thomas Dudley, Samuel Eaton, Cotton Mather, Increase Mather, Thomas Prince, Miles Standish, William Tyng, John Winthrop, Jr. These lists may be found in Mr. Wright's manuscript at the Yale University Library.*

Appendix.

Items Illustrating the Movement of Books to and among New Englanders.

HERE is the Young Clerks Guide, with the Banquet of Jests.[1]
Nov. 30. I was at Boston, bought Diodati's Annotations.[2]

Also I have desired & obtained of Major Bradford, a Booke in folio written by his father, which I shall send by the first opportunity by water; if I cannot send it by land. The Journall of Plimouth beginnings[3] I could send you, but I thinke it needs not, for you told me some passages in it; whence I conclude you have that booke. Major Bradford hath another printed Booke, which he thinks would well contribute to you. Its title is Good Newes from P. in N: E:[4] But he cannot finde it.[5] [A postscript reports it found.]

I can only tell you that I have sent yo[r] book (this being the first since I wrote to you last) & returne you a thousand thancks for y[e] use of y[e] same.[6]

Mr. Shove was this day at my house; as he passed along to Barnstable, (for your booke he thankes you) . . . .

Yours I received & the bookes, 7 of those which came first are sold at Bridgewater; I will endeavour to sell as fast as I can.[8]

[1] Thomas Johnson of London to Marmaduke Johnson, the printer, April 23, 1663. Littlefield, Early Massachusetts Press, i. 225.

[2] Diary of Rev. William Adams of Dedham, 1670. Massachusetts Historical Society, Collections, 4th Series, i. 15.

[3] The *Journall* is probably the so-called *Mourt's Relation*. The "Booke in folio" is Bradford's famous History of Plymouth. Mather is borrowing these as material for his own history of New England.

[4] Good News from New England, 1624, by Edward Winslow.

[5] John Cotton to Increase Mather, from Plymouth, November 24, 1676. Mather Papers, p. 229.

[6] Giles Sylvester, Jr., of South-ton, to Fitz-John Winthrop, March 9, 1677. Massachusetts Historical Society, Proceedings, 2d Series, iv. 286. In another letter (August 19, 1677) he refers to a book, evidently on heraldry, by Gwillim, which he has had and returned.

[7] John Cotton to Increase Mather, June 25, 1677. Mather Papers, p. 239.

[8] John Cotton to Increase Mather, October 20, 1677. *Ibid.*, p. 239. The books referred to are probably Mather's account of the troubles with the Indians (1677),

If you have Gorsius works by you, doe so much as send out a discours which is as I remember about a quarter or 3 part of the book in containing Exhortations to young people . . . .[9]

Tell him wee thanke him heartily for our Almanacks.[10]

I perceive you have come in the way of sundry pieces of the *Virtuosi*.[11] . . . . I would earnestly entreat you, out of a pitty to a famished man, to send me such treatises historical or philosophical as you have by you, especially that concerning the designes of a French Government in England. I shall carefully return you. And as a pledge of my care, at last I now send you your Hudson. I have kept it long . . . . I did some years agone see papers of weekly edition after the manner of the Gazets, under the name of Philosophical Observations by John[12] Oldenburgh, Felow of the Society. Those of them that I saw contained relations and passages exceeding worthy the knowledge.[13] . . . I have latly seen a smal treatise in verse, such as it is, not over Heliconian, yet honest, printed at Boston, against the Quakers, by one B. K. whose name I cannot unridle. . . . .[14]

I also haueing lately rec[d] from M[r] Whiteing's hand another booke & token of respect, viz: *Diatriba de Signo ffilii Hominis:* I know not what further returne to make, but thanks, &c., unlesse to adde some Apology for my owne indesert of a Lattin booke, being growne so rusty in that *lingua*, with wishing it might be reprinted in English for the benefit of N: E: Towards the charge whereof I shall willingly be a subscriber; haueing had a tast of what you so printed about the Calling of the Jewes; which I borrowed & red, tho: I haue it not by me now:[15]

Yours I received, what sent by Capt. Selleck to myself & freinds, M[r] Wakeman & M[r] Chauncey, of your own & M[r]

[9] Joseph Eliot to Increase Mather. 1678. *Ibid.*, p. 377.

[10] John Cotton to Increase Mather, March 12, 1679. *Ibid.*, p. 251.

[11] Probably the Philosophical Conferences of the Virtuosi of France.

[12] Really Henry Oldenburg.

[13] Joseph Eliot of Guilford, Conn., to Increase Mather, July 17, 1678. Mather Papers, p. 376. He goes on to urge Mather to send for these collections, not knowing that the Mathers had many volumes of them. See p. 143, below.

[14] B. K. was Benjamin Keach, an English Non-Conformist, whose "The Grand Impostor Discovered: or, the Quakers Doctrine weighed in the Ballance and found wanting" was printed in Boston by John Foster, 1678.

[15] William Leete of Guilford to Increase Mather, July 5, 1682. Mather Papers, pp. 621–623.

Hookes good labo[rs]. What was belonging to me I kindly accept; & what to others, I have conveyed according to your mind.[16]

I unfeynedly thank you for your kindnes to my wife,—sending her one of your last books . . . .[17]

Yours I have received, with that further expression of your love to me, the book of Remarkable Providences,[18] for which I thank you . . . . The booke you sent me last before this was Mr. Torrey his sermon, with your epistle before it. I received three of them; one for Mr. Hanford, one for Mr. Chauncey, ... & the other to myself . . . .[19]

I Received the Booke you sent, which is profitable & of very good use, for which I return you hearty thankes . . . .[20]

Mr. Saltonstall hath a printed book in vindication of the Protestants, and Captain Thomas hath many printed pieces of news. Could I obtain them, I would soon transmit them to your honor.[21]

S[r], I return you many thanks, as for the many good books which you have sent me, so I giue many thanks to you & to good M[r] Willard . . . . for this booke.[22]

Yours of the 2[d] of this instant I received, & with it your good booke upon occasion of the sore persecution of the Saints in France . . . .[23]

Mr. Willard here, I returned Alsop of Scandal.[24]

To the Rev[nd] & his estemed ffriend M[r] Increase Mather, at his house in Boston, in New England, these, together with a booke.

[16] John Bishop of Stamford, Conn., to Increase Mather, August 3, 1682. Mather Papers, p. 309. Mr. Wakeman was pastor at Fairfield, and Mr. Chauncey at Stratford.

[17] John Higginson to Increase Mather, February 5, 1683. Mather Papers, p. 283.

[18] By Increase Mather, published 1684.

[19] John Bishop to Increase Mather, June 10, 1684. Mather Papers, p. 312. Mr. Hanford, or Hunford, was pastor at Norwalk.

[20] Solomon Stoddard of Northampton to Increase Mather. Mather Papers, p. 586. Undated; probably about 1680.

[21] John Cotton to Governor Hinckley, January 13, 1681. Massachusetts Historical Society, Collections, 4th Series, v. 57.

[22] Thomas Cobbet of Ipswich to Increase Mather, December 13, 1681. Mather Papers, p. 292.

[23] Thomas Cobbet of Ipswich to Increase Mather, May 18, 1682. Mather Papers, p. 293.

[24] Sewall, Diary, i. 109. About 1685.

. . . . Be pleased to lend the litle book to my brother to [peruse] if he desires it.[25]

I received your letter in winter, with an almanack and some verses, for all which I thank you.[26]

I received the verses & Almanacks you sent . . . .[27]

I take the freedom to present thee with a Book.[28]

S[r], I dare beg no more books, but if you have any newes . . . .[29]

Cous. Greenleaf sups with Mother. I give him the Catechise, Day of Doom, &c bound together in a good Cover . . . .[30]

[Mr. Noyce] greatly desires to see Potter on the number 666. It lyes on my study Table. I should bee glad if you would bee pleased to send it by M[r] Grafton.[31]

I must again desire of you to send mee a Book, viz. my Ames' Medulla. It stands in my second shelfe. . . . . Dr. Swinnerton desires to read that volume of the Transactions that treats of Volatile Alcalies. The Book, as I remember, had on it, before the Title, those words *Laudanum Helmontii Junioris*, written by yourselfe. It is about the 100th N[o]. M[r] Higginson earnestly desires to see Knoxes History of the Island Ceylon (which lyes on my Father's Table) and Taverniers Travels. Now as for the former of them, If you will send it you will oblige him. Butt as for the latter, it being so Choice a Book and so well bound, that I should bee almost sorry to have it exposed to any Damages. Butt if you will send it, I'le take what Care I can about it.[32]

There is also som gazetts in the pocket.[33]

[25] Ichabod Chauncy of Bristol, England, to Increase Mather, February 17, 1681–2. Mather Papers, pp. 617–619.

[26] Joseph Eliot to Increase Mather, 1683. *Ibid.*, p. 378.

[27] Simon Bradstreet of Medford to Increase Mather, 1683. *Ibid.*, p. 479.

[28] William Penn of Pennsylvania to Governor Hinckley, 1683. Massachusetts Historical Society, Collections, 2d Series, vii. 185, 186.

[29] Timothy Woodbridge of Hartford to Cotton Mather, April 14, 1684. Mather Papers, p. 639.

[30] Sewall's Diary, i. 223. August 14, 1688.

[31] Nathaniel Mather to his brother Cotton, August, 1688, from Salem, whither he had gone for medical treatment at the home of Dr. Swinerton. He died there in October. Mr. Noyes (Noyce) was one of the Salem preachers. Mather Papers, p. 672.

[32] Nathaniel Mather to his brother Cotton, August 31, 1688. Mather Papers, p. 673. Mr. Higginson was a preacher in Salem.

[33] Wait Winthrop to Fitz-John Winthrop, July 7, 1682. Winthrop Papers, iv. 427.

Pray send or bring 50 ℔ of very fine salt peter; and Glaubers Works translated, and reprinted since the first edition in English.[34] I haue som of his works in Latin, but not halfe, I think.[35]

Pray send ye Gazets, &c., to Mr Saltonstall, & then to Hartford.[36]

Send me by the next post a little booke bound called the Devout Soul's dayly Exercise, in prayers, ... etc: by R. P: D. D. for a friend, as also the verses made about the queenes death.[37]

If you haue not Mr Josh. Moodyes Artillery Election Sermon, June, 1674, I would advise your Honour as a Christian & good souldier to give a look vpon my Annalls of God's Blessing of N. E. in ye yeare 1674, where you'l finde som passages of it recorded. I suppose if you haue never seen those my scripts Mr Cotton Mather may accommodate your Honour wth y^m. Those my Chronilogicall Decads haue rings or loops by wch they may be fastened together or hang'd vp, to preserve from mice or rats.[38]

For ye gent^m of the Council at Hartford I have sent a Gazet, wch I desire you to returne.[39]

I carried home to Mr. Pierpont 2 books, and borrowed Ward on Mathew.[40]

The Obligations under which you lay me are many and lasting. And these Books, with which you last favoured me, have heaped *Pelion* upon *Ossa*.

For so many fatt Birds, I now return you a Feather; and I pray you to Accept one of the Enclosed, and convey the other.[41]

[34] The same to the same, then in London. November 1, 1694. *Ibid.*, iv. 503.

[35] The same to the same, October 28, 1695. *Ibid.*, iv. 511.

[36] Fitz-John Winthrop, then in London, to Wait Winthrop, July 13, 1695. *Ibid.*, iv. 325.

[37] John Tulley of Saybrook to Mr. Harris, the printer, of Boston, July 17, 1695. He also orders a London "Ephemeris," complaining that the Boston one sent him is poorer than he himself can work out unaided. Massachusetts Historical Society, Proceedings, i. 76.

[38] Samuel Stow of Middletown to Wait Winthrop, 1696. Winthrop Papers, vi. 35. The last sentence may explain the disappearance of many valued colonial books!

[39] Fitz-John Winthrop to the Council at Hartford, February 15, 1700. Winthrop Papers, iv. 374.

[40] Diary of Rev. Joseph Green of Danvers, April 10, 1700. Historical Collections of Essex Institute.

[41] Cotton Mather to Major Stephen Sewall, October 15, 1701. New England Historical and Genealogical Register, xxiv. 110.

Send me Psalmanaazaar again in a month. I think that is time enough,—if not, six weeks.[42]

A Certain Person has Lent Fuller's Holy War, his name is on the Frontice Leaf of it: Whosoever has borrowed the said Book, or into whose hands it may come, are desired to return it unto John Campbell . . . . that the true Owner may have it again.[43]

Stolen or Lost in September last, out of Samuel Dogger of Marshfield his Sloop then in Boston, the first part of Purchasses Pilgrims a History in Folio . . . . [44]

A Certain Person some time since, Lent *Dryden's* Virgil in Folio with Cuts, but has forgot to whom . . . . [45]

A Valuable Collection of Books & Pamphlets, Consisting of Divinity, History, Classicks, Physick, Poetry, Mathematicks, &c., in several Languages: To be sold by Public Vendue or Auction at the House of Mr. *Rowland Dyke* at the Sign of the Royal Exchange in King-Street, Boston: Beginning on Tuesday the 29th Instant . . . . Printed Catalogues may be had gratis.[46]

The Books and other Things of Mr. *Edward Weaver*, Deceas'd, is to be Sold on Thursday the 28th of this Instant February . . . . at the Crown Coffee house in King Street.[47]

Invoice.

BOOKS sent to John Usher of Boston without order by Robert Boulter of London.[48]

12 Terrences
38 Bonds horrace
13 erasmus Colloquies

[42] Cotton Mather to Major Stephen Sewall, May 2, 1706. New England Historical and Genealogical Register, xxiv. 111.
[43] Advertisement in the Boston News-Letter, September 2–9, 1706.
[44] *Ibid.*, December 30–January 6, 1706–7.
[45] *Ibid.*, March 12–19, 1715–6.
[46] *Ibid.*, May 7–14, 1716.
[47] *Ibid.*, February 18–25, 1717.
[48] Sent about 1682. Ford, Boston Book Market, pp. 12, 88–107. The collection was valued at £75.2.9.

13 dyers worcks
22 apples of Gould
 3 Calamys ark
 6 meads almost a Christian
10 foxes end of tyme
 3 faramond
 4 brooks ark
 9 norwoods epitomy
15 bybles
12 Cocker Cockers tutours
 4 Glasson of law
 2 last part of the english rogue
22 turky skins
 2 parismus
 1 destruction of troy
 1 Valentyn and orson
 4 Goulmans dictionarys
15 dugarts Rhetorique
10 Complete modelist
 4 Johnson arithmatick
 4 ovid metamorphosis
 4 esops in english
 2 burroughs on matthew
 5 Carmicheal on mortification
 5 mitchells sermons
 8 alleins allarm
 3 remains [of Joseph Alleine]
 2 lyfe and death [of Joseph Alleine]
 5 sincere Convert
 9 sound beleevers
 1 owen on the sperit
 1 ———— on the hebrews
 4 person of Christ
16 boatswains art
 2 felthams resolves
 1 Cooks marrow [of chirurgery]
 8 Cotton on the Covenant
 3 queens Closet
 4 winchester phrasis

16 Cap of gray haires
2 rarlerys remains
2 Clelias
13 sellers navigation
12 seamans Companion
6 brooks remedies
9 argalus and parthenia
1 Assemblys annotations
7 Clarks tutours
2 Compleat Clark
6 burrougs Contentment
2 Collins on providence
2 Everards workes
6 Baxters Call
6 Doctrin of the byble
10 Wills Commonwealth
2 reynolds on Murther
1 pembrooks arcadia
3 Colliers divinity
2 Flavell on providence
3 touchstones [by John Flavell]
12 smiths narrative
12 Clarks formula
24 testaments
6 senecas
3 Doolitles Catechis
2 Coles soveranity
3 Januas works
5 Culpepers dispensatory
6 phisitian
2 perfect politician
6 ashwoods trade
3 rythers plat [for mariners]
1 baxter of Concord
1 tanners art of physick
2 temples miscellanea
6 pearse of death
3 douting Christian
2 Vertuous woman

4 help to discours
18 flavell on the sacrement
24 vincents Catechis
6 alleins Catt
6 leis Catt
6 Janewais life
4 Johnsons Deus Nobiscum
3 watsons Contentment
6 pooles nullity [of the Romish Faith]
12 ——— Dialogues
100 testaments
1 Bacons works
1 Cloud witnesses
1 phillips dictionary
1 Caesars Commentary
2 leighs Caesars
6 wise masters
2 Erastus
2 Vnlucky Citicen
2 Rich Cabinet
1 Senecas moralls
9 Gentle Craft
1 Cambdens Elizabeth
1 Miltons history
6 Guy of Warwick
6 Reynard fox
3 war with the Jews
1 Parys Narative
12 dr Faustus
6 tom reading
6 [Tom A] Lincolns
12 Joviall Garland
12 Crown Garland
6 Jack Newberry
4 absolute accoumpt
6 Garland of delight
6 fortunatus
6 royall arbours
8 S[c]oggins jests

6 history of Joseph
6 Devill & Dives
6 Booke of knowledg
4 Mandevills travells
6 wise masters
3 wakemans tryalls
2 Langhams
3 dugdalls
12 Processions
4 pack cards

Invoice.

BOOKS delivered by Richard Chiswell of London to Mr. John Ive, September 5, 1683, for shipment to New England.[49]

For Mr. Wise

1 Poolls Critticks 5 vol.
1 Carryl on Job.   2 vol.
1 Hacklutes Uoyages
1 Mori Utopia
1 Zanchii Opera 2 vol
1 Boltons Instructions
1 Greenhill on Ezekiel Compl in 3 vol
1 Culpepers English Physitian
1 Wilson's Christian Dictionary
4 Markhams Works
2 Sure Guide to Justices
8 Allens Allarme
3 Bridges Remaines
7 Gouges Young mans guide with word to Sts and Sinners and Xtian Housholder
12 Doz of White Clasps
10 Hodders Arithmetick
5 Janeways Heauen on Earth

[49] *Ibid.*, pp. 108–120. Value about £50.

1 Uenns Military Discipline
3 Barriffs Military Discipline
4 Little peace Maker
4 Baxters family book
20 Flauells Saint Indeed
20 ——— Token for Mourners
10 ——— on the Sacrement
8 ——— Touchstone
5 ——— on Providence
10 ——— Seamans Compas
4 ——— Husbandry
20 ——— 2 Treatises
20 Baxters Call
10 ——— Now or Neuer
5 Brooks String of Perles
6 ——— Apples of gold
4 ——— Ark for Gods Noah
1 Baxters Saints Rest
10 Brooks Mute Xtian
12 Ayres Copy books
1 Flauells Fountaine Life
12 Cockers Tutor to Writing and Arithmetick
30 Strongs Spelling book
6 Uernons Compting house
1 Felthams Resolues
20 Fox of Time
10 Dyers workes
10 Norwoods Epittomy
10 Oxford Bibles
50 Oxford Testaments
4 Skins of Blew Turkey Leather
7 Janeways Life
6 Julian
6 Allens Remaines
5 ——— Life.
7 Accademy Compliments

For Mr. Mather

3 Chamberlins Geography

1 Haworth of Consumption
1 Bens Sermons.
1 Baxters how to doe good to many.
1 Womans Aduocate
1 Miracles no uiolat. Laws Nature.
1 Shaftsburys Life
2 London gilt.

For Mr. Shepard

1 Mordens Geography
1 Piety the best Rule of Orthodoxie
1 Poeticall History
1 Owen on the Hebrews.
2 ———— of the Person of Christ
2 ———— on the 130th psalme
10 Burtons Wonderful Prodogies
20 Doolittle on the Sacriment 1st p[art]
15 ———— on the Lds Sufferings
50 New England psalms
50 Idem
30 History of Dr. Faustus
1 Teats Map of the Wilderness Sin
Terme cattallouge No. 11. 12

.   .   .   .   .   .

7 Accademy Compliments, another sorte.

.   .   .   .   .   .

The order not mentioning which Accademy of Compliments you
    would haue, both sorts are sentt.
Hookers doubting Christian ⎫
Allens Rebuke   ⎬ out of print and not to be had
Owen of Comunion   ⎭
Burtons Wares of England ⎫
———— Amicable Curiositys ⎬ out of print and doing againe.
Eltons Military Discipline—uery scarce and sold for 12*s.*
Moxons Monthly Exercises—Not to be had compl.

Invoice.

BOOKS sold by Richard Chiswell of London to Mr. John Ive for John Usher of Boston, March 3, 1683–4.[50]

  3 Virtuous Woman found.
  2 Erle of Rochesters Poems.
 30 Hoolls Corderius.
  6 Greek Testaments.
  3 Rauerius Practice of Physick.
  6 Sellers Epittomie of Astronomical Systems.
  4 Miltons Paradise Lost.
 40 Strongs Spelling booke.
  5 Sheppards Sincere Conuert.
 50 New England Psalmes.
  1 Bible 4° Oxon with Common prayer and Apockchryphia.
100 Sententiae Pueriles.
 50 Latine Catos.
 40 Ouid de Tristibus.
  6 Meads Almost Christian.
 12 Erasmus Colloquies Latin.
  6 Lestranges Erasmus in English.
  1 Baker's Chronicle.
  3 Doz. Brass Compasses largest sorte
  3 Wilsons Christian Dictionary.
 20 Foxes End of Time.
  8 Pounds of Vermillion with Box.
  1 Dutch Annotations in 2 Vol.
  2 Supplement to the Morning Exercise.
  1 Pembrooks Arcadia.
  1 Keebles Statutes last Edit.
  2 Queuedos Visions Compl. both parts.
  3 Cambridge Concordance.
 30 Nomen Claturas
 10 Dugards Rhetorick.
 10 Smiths Rhetorick.
  4 Ames Cases of Contience in Lat.
 10 Hookers Doubting Christian.
  1 Gutberleths Physick.

[50] *Ibid.*, pp. 121–132. The entire collection was valued at £61.5.6.

10 Lattine Testaments.
18 Greek Grammars.
 3 Wollebeus Compendium in Lat.
30 Token for Children Compl.
 2 Burroughs Gospel worship.
12 Norwoods Epittomy.
12 Gouges Youngmans Guide with Safe way of Thriueing.
12 ———— Directions.
 3 Accademy of Compliments.
 5 Janeways Life.
 6 Nuga Uenales.
 3 Cotton on the Couenant.
12 Warr with the Deuill.
 2 Burroughs Gospel worship.
 3 Present State of England.   Comp. all parts
 4 Jure Maritimo.
 2 Clarks Liues of the Fathers.
 2 Sturmies Mariners Magazine.
18 Dr. Faustus. 1st and 2d pt.
18 Calamys Godlymans Arke
 6 Brookes Arke.
 6 Wilds Poems.
 6 Argulus and Parthenia.
 3 Tanners Art of Physick.
 4 Littletons Dictionary.
 2 Gassendus Astronimy.
12 Sturmies Epistles.
 2 Bythner on the Psalmes.
 2 Leusdens Hol. Bible.
 6 Oxford Grammars.
 5 Oxford Jests.
13 Rami Logica.
16 Culpepers English Physitian.
16 ———— Dispensatorys.
 4 Dauenports Saints Anchorhold
 2 Zouche Jurisdiction of Courts of Admiralty.
10 Englishmens Liberties.
 1 Hebrew Bible of Mannasseth Ben Israel
 1 ———— Idem of Uenice Edition.

1 —— Idem of Plantins Edition.
Terme Catalogue No. 13. 14

1. All the books are sent that could be procured.
2. Some few are raised by reason of the scarcity.

Invoice.

BOOKS sold by Richard Chiswell of London to Mr. John Ive for John Usher of Boston, May 29, 1684.[51]

  2 Bibles 24 Ruled Turkey gilt back
30 Greek Grammers
  3 Bythner on the Psalms
  6 SincereConvert
10 Flauel on the Sacriment
10 Cattechise
  2 Cambridge Concordance
  2 Sellers Practical Nauigation
  2 Wilsons Christian Dictionary
  5 Clarks Tutor
  4 Burroughs Gospel Remission
  4 State of England in 2 vol both parts
  3 Markhams way to get wealth
  2 Eltons Military Discipline
  6 Oxon Bibles large
  5 Hesiod
  2 Blounts Law Dictionary
  2 Daltons Iustice
50 Lattine Grammers.
50 Construing books
20 Smiths Great Assize
  2 History of Parismus
20 Gentle Craft
10 Gentlemans Jockey
  5 Uernons Compting House.
  2 Flauels Fountaine of Life
  2 —— Method of Peace.

[51] *Ibid.*, pp. 133–139. Value, £25.6.10.

7 ——— Treaty of Sufferings.
3 Norwoods Doctrine of Triangles.
6 ——— Epittomy.
8 Gellibrands Epittomy.
2 Erly Religion a Sermon.
1 Showers Ser[mon] at Mrs. Ann Barnardiston funl.
1 Dorringtons Ser[mon] of the Right use of an Estate.
1 Demaris Pearses Remaines.
1 Memoires of the Fam. of the Stuarts.
2 Wonders of the Femall world.
1 Her and His.
10 Second Part of the Pilgrims Progress.
2 Two Journeys to Jerusalem
200 Pare of Clasps for writeing books
2 London Bully 1st and 2d p[art]
3 A Ramble to Hackney.
1 Popes Life.
2 Informers Doome.
2 Melius Inquirendum.
2 Sherlocismus Eneruatus.
3 Uenus in the Cloyster.
2 Womans Aduocate.

London Gilt is out of print and not to be had.

Invoice.

BOOKS sold by Richard Chiswell to Mr. John Ive for John Usher, April 13, 1685.[52]

1 Goodwins Works in 2 vol.
1 Rogers on Peter
1 ——— Parable of the Prodigal
20 Smith's Great Assize
20 Flauels Compas
15 ——— Token for Mourners
30 ——— Saint Indeed
10 Erasmus Colloquies 8° English Lestrange

[52] *Ibid.*, pp. 140–151.   Value, £61.19.01/2.

20 Doolittle on the Sacrament
15 Hookers Doubting Christian
100 Hoolls Sententia
60 ———— Cases
30 Fox of Time
20 Baxters Call
10 ———— Now or Neuer
22 Farnabys Ouid
12 Hoolls Terrence
6 Booke of Rates
30 Warr with the Deuill
4 Duty of Man
12 Aristotle's Problems
8 Hebrew Psalters
30 Token for Children Complt.
10 Flauel on the Sacrament
2 Norton's Orthodox Euangelist
3 Office of Executors
30 Lillys Rules
10 Calamys Godlymans Arke
12 Lattine Justins
18 Tullys Offices
1 Dutch Annotations in 2 vol
10 Gollibrands Epittomy
6 Woollebius Compend: Lat.
4 Lattine Bible
8 Flauels Touchstone
8 Winchester Phrases
2 Glissons Common Law Epitomized
8 Jure Maritimo.
2 Eltons Millitary Discipline.
3 Barriffs Millit. Discipline with Horse.
40 Marriners New Kallender
4 Ittallian Conuert
1 Dells Sermons.
2 Terms of the Law
3 Daltons Justice
2 Keebles Statutes.
2 Cooks Reports Engl.

3 Blounts Law Dictionary.
1 Sheppards Grand Abridgement
1 Hobbarts Reports.
3 Culpepers English Physitian.
3 ———— Dispensatory.
5 Midwifery per Culpeper.
10 Greek Gramers
20 New England Psalmes
3 Miltons Logick.
2 Wingates Arithmattick.
2 Records Arithmattick.
4 Johnsons Arithmattick.
3 Hodders Arithmattick.
10 Strongs Spelling book.
6 History of Dr. Faustus.
2 Rochesters Life.
2 Owen on the 3d p[ar]t [of Hebrews]
12 Lattine Terrence.
3 Amesii Medulla.
3 ———— de Conscientia.
3 Littletons Dictionary.
2 Pulton of the Common Pleas Engls.
5 Sheppards Sure Guide.
10 Wonderful Prodogies.
20 Accidencies.
10 Dugards Rhetorick.
15 Nomen Claturas.
6 Bonds Horrace.
3 Greek Testaments
20 Protestant Tutors.
3 Clarkes Phrases.
2 Poolls Annotations on the Bible in English.
6 Siluanus his Theocritus.
1 ———— Lucian.
1 ———— Isocratis.
1 ———— Essopi Fabula.
1 ———— Plutarck.
Term Cattalouge No. 15. 16. 17. 18.

. . . . The 4 books of Syluanus are sent as a present to the Chief

Schoolmaster in New England being a New Praxis upon some Greek Authors which is well entertained in our Schooles here and much used.

Book References in Increase Mather's Writings.

A.   Books Cited or Quoted.[53]

Author	Title
———————	The History of Sham Plotts
———————	Acta Eruditorum, Leipsic
Adam, Melchior	Vita Melancthonis
Adam, Melchior	Vita Myconii
Agricola, Georg	
Agrippa, C.	de Occulta Philosophia
Agrippa, C.	The Vanity of Sciences
Alting	Loci Communes
Ambrose	Treatise of Angels
Ames	Cases of Conscience
Augustine	de Civitate Dei
Avicenna	
Balduinus	Cases of Conscience
Baldusius	In 2 Corinthians
Bartholinus	
Baxter, R.	Book about Witchcrafts
Baxter, R.	Church History
Beard	Theater of Gods Judgements
Bernard	66 Sermones in Cantica
Bernard	A Guide to Grand Jurymen in Cases of Witchcraft
Beza	Life of Calvin
Beza	Commentaries

[53] These are in addition to those mentioned in Chapter VIII. Where no title is given, the reference in Mather was to the author only.

Binsfield	de Confessionibus sagarum
Bodin	Dæmonomania
Boissardus	de Secretis Mag.
Bootius	de Gemmis
Bovet	Pandemonium
Brockmand	Theol. de Angelis
Bromhall	History of Apparitions
———	The Bucuneers of America
Burnet	Life of Rochester
Burroughs	On Matthew 11, 28
Burton	Miracles of Nature[54]
Burton	Prodigies of Mercies
Burton	History of Dæmons
Cambden	Britannia
Camerarius	Horæ Subsecivæ
Camerarius	Centuriæ Quattuor Symbolorum
Cardano	de Rerum Varietate
Cardano	de Subtilitate
Casaubon	Of Spirits
Childrey	Britannia Baconica
Chiverius	Historiarum totius Mundi Epitome
Chytræus	
Clark, Samuel	Examples
Clark, Samuel	Lives of English Worthies
Clark, Samuel	Martyrology
Clark, William	Natural History of Nitre
Cooper, Thomas	Mystery of Witchcraft
Cotta	The Tryal of Witchcraft
Darrel	Seven Possessed Persons in Lancashire
Delrio	Disquis. Magicarum
Dubravius	Historia Bohemiæ
Eusebius	in Vita Constantii
Fernelius	de Abditis Rerum Causis
Forestus	
Gaul	Select Cases of Conscience concerning Witches and Witch-craft
Gerhard	Loci Communes
Gesner	

[54] See note 4, p. 138, above.

Gnaccius	Compend. Malefic.
Godelmannus	de Lamiis
Goodwin	Doctrine of Saints Perseverance
Gorges, F.	Narration
Goulartius	Select History
Hale, Matthew	The Account of Tryals of Witches at Bury, Suffolk
Hall, Bishop	Autobiography
Hall, Bishop	"Psalm 82"
Heinsius	in Matthew viii, 16
Hemming	de Superstitione Magica
Henkelius	de Obsessis
————	History of Lapland
Holder	"book about the natural production of letters"[55]
Honsdorsius	Historical Theater
Horace	Various
Horneck, A.	History of the Witches in Sweden
Horstius	Inst. Med.
Javellus	Medicinæ Compendium
King James	Discourse of Witchcraft
Janeway	Remarkable Sea Deliverances
Johnston	Thaumatograph
Josephus	History of Wars with the Jews
Josephus	Antiquities
Jovius, P.	History
deLaet, J.	Description of America
deLaet, J.	de Gemmis
Lavater	de Spectris
Lecus	Compend. Hist.
Lemnius	
Lewiston	Of Fulfilling the Scriptures
Malderus	de Magia
Mandelslo	Travels
Martinii	Lexicon Philologico-Etymologicum
Martyr, P.	Commentary of 1 Samuel
Mede	Works

[55] This book was a treatise on lip-reading; a very modern seeming book for the company it is in!

Mede	Discourse on John x, 20
Melanchthon	Consilia
Menna	de Purgatione Vulgari
Merden	Geographia Physica
Meurerius	Comment. Meteorolog.
Meurtius	Athenæ Batavæ
Morland	Hist. Waldenses
Munster	Notes on Leviticus xvii
Owen	Work of the Spirit in Prayer
Pensingius	de Pulvere Sympathetico
Perkins	Discourse of Witchcraft
Polydore, Vergil	
Pontano, G.	
Porta, Bapt.	
Proclus	de Sacrificio et Magia
Rainolds	de Libris Apocryphis
Remigius	
Ricaut	History of the Present State of the Ottoman Empire
Roberts	Narrative of Witches in Suffolk
Rulandus	
Schotten	Physic. Curios.
Selden	de Diis Syriis
Sennertus	Practica Medicinæ
Sennertus	Med. Precl.
Sinclare, G.	Satan's Visible World Discovered
Smetius	Miscellanies
Socrate	History
Spotswood	History of Scotland
Sprenger	Malleo Malleficarum
Sympson	Ecclesiastical History
de Thou	Historiarum sui Temporis
Thyræus	de Obsessis
Thyræus	de Apparitionibus Spirituum
Thyræus	Disput. de Dæmoniacis
laTorr	Disputationes
Tostatus	in Matthew 8
Vairus de Fascino	
Valerius Maximus	

Verstegan	Antiquities
Voetius	de Emergumenis
Voetius	de Spectris
Voetius	de Operationibus Dæmonum
Voetius	de Magia
Voetius	Disputat. Select.
Wanly	Of the Wonders of the Worldous, 1680
Webster	Book of Witchcraft
————	Weekly Memorials for the Ingeni
White	Relation
Wierus	de Præstigiis Dæmonum
Willet	Commentaries
Wm. of Malmsbury	Lib. ii
Zacchias, P.	Questionibus Medicis
Zanchy	Epistol. 2
Zuinger	Theatrum Vit. Human.

B.   Books Referred to Without Quotation or Citation.

Bannosius	Life of Ramus
Burgensis	
Cabeus	On the Loadstone
Caussin	Holy Court
Chassalion	Histories of the Judgements of God
Codronchus	
Conring	
Cornelius à Lapide	
Cumanus	Lucerna Inquisitorium
Epiphanius	
Freherus, Paulus	Theatrum Vivorum Eruditione Claru
Gassendi	Essays
Gennadius	
Gilbert	De Magnete
Hakluyt	Voyages
Henningus Witten	Memoria Theologorum nostri seculi
Isidore	
Jerome	
Kepler	On the Loadstone
Kircher	On the Loadstone
Kommannus	

Linschoten	Voyages
Mendozo	
Molianus	
Pomponatius	
Prochorus	
Schopfius	Academia Christi
Serrarius	
Spineus	
Sulpitius Severus	In Vita Martini
Verheiden	Elogia Theologorum
Ward	On the Loadstone
Windet	

Book References in Cotton Mather's Writings.

A.   Books Cited or Quoted.[56]

Aben Ezra	
Acosta, J.	History of the Indies
Adam, Mel.	Lives
Ady, T.	Perfect Discovery of Witches
Agapetus	
Agathius	
Algazel	
Alphonsus of Arragon	
Alsted, J. H.	
Altenburg	
Ambrose	
Amyraldus	
Angellius	
Anselm	
Antiochus Syracusanus	

[56] These are in addition to those mentioned in Chapter VIII.   A few quotations which really belong to the third period (after 1700) are included here in order to give a complete list of Mather's borrowings.

Antoninus

———

               Aphor. Polit.

Aquinas
Aristotle
Arnobius
Arrianus
Arrowsmith
Athanasius   Life of Antonius
Athenæus
Augustine   Several
Avril   Travels
Baily, R.
Baker, R.
Bartholinus
Barton, W.   (quotes a hymn)
Basil
Bates, W.
Baxter, R.   Several
Bede   Ecclesiastical History of England
Bellarmine
Bernard
Beroaldus
Besoldus   Axiomatæ Philosophiæ Christianæ
Bethel, S.   The Interest of Euroipe
Beverly
Beverovicius
Beza   Life of Calvin, Psalms
Blackerby
Blahoslius   History of Johannes Cronu
Boccalini
Bodin
Bolsecus   Life of Calvin, etc.
Borellus
Brahe, Tycho
Bradwardine
Brownrig
Bucer   Scripta Anglicana and others
Bucholtzer
Bullinger

Burnett	History of his Times
Burroughs, J.	
R. B.[urton]	History of Dæmons
Calamy	Sermon on Earl of Warwick, etc.
Calvin	
Camerarius	
Canus. Melch.	
Carthagena	
Carthusian	
Caryl	
Casaubon	
Cassianus	
Castel	
Cato	
Chamier	
Chemnitius	
Chrysostom	De Deo Orando and others
Cicero	De Natura Rerum
Cicero	Orat. pro Plancio, De Senectute, & others
Clark, S.	Examples, etc.
Claude	
Claudian	
Clemens Alexandrinus	
Clemens Romanus	
Cocceius	
Colerus	
Contzen	
Coryat	
Cranmer	
Cranzius	
Crespin	Histoire des Martyrs
Cudworth	Intellectual System
Curtius	History of Alexander the Great
Cyprian	
Demosthenes	
Denys, N.	Description of Coasts of North America
Diodorus Siculus	History
Dionysius Halic.	
Eccles, S.	The Quaker's Challenge

Ephemerides Medico-physicæ

Epiphanius	
Erasmus	Epistolæ, and other works
Eusebius	
Eutyches	History of Nicene Synod
Festus	de Verborum Significatione
Firmin	The Real Christian
Fisher the Quaker	Pamphlets
Flavel	
Fox, George	Great Mystery
Fox, J.	Book of Martyrs, Acts and Monuments
Fuller, Nich.	
Fuller, T.	Church History
Gaule, J.	Select Cases . . . . Touching Witches
Gerhard	Meditationes Sacræ, etc.
Gerson	
Gesner	
Gildas	
Glanvil	Collections of Sundry Trials
Gregory the Great	
Gregory Nazienzen	
Gregory of Nyssa	
Grotius, H.	
Grynæus	
Guitton	
Gulielmus Parisiensis	
Gustavus Adolphus	
Hale, Matthew	Tryal of Witches
Hall, J.	
Heinsius	
Helvicus	Epitaph
Helwigius	
Hemming, N.	Admonitio de Superstitionibus Magicis
Hesychias	
Heylin	
Holland	
Homer	Iliad
Horace	Various
Horneck	

Hornius	
Hottinger	
Hoyl, J.	
Ignatius	Various
Inghiramius	
Isidore	
Isocrates	
Jermyn	
Jerome	
Josephus	
Junius	
Jurieu	Traite de L'Unite de L'Eglise
Justin	
Justin Martyr	
Keeble	Common Law
Kimchi, Rabbi	
Lactantius	
LeClerk	
Leigh	Critica Sacra
Libingus	
Lipsius	
Livy	
Lucian	
Lucretius	
Ludovicus Molinæus	
Lupichius	
Luther	Various
Lysimachus	
Machiavelli	
Madgeburgensian Centu-riators	
Maimonides	
Manethon	
Marbeck	Concordance
Martin of Tours	
Martyr, Peter	Commonplaces, etc.
Maurier	
Mede, J.	
Melanchthon	

Mersennus	
Mohammed	Alcoran
More, Henry	Glanvil's Sadducismus, etc.
Morland	History of Waldenses
Murtadi	Egyptian History
Musculus	(verse)
Musonius	
Myconius	
Newton	
Nieremberg	
Norton	Answer to the Sylloge Quæstionum
Oecolampadius	
Origen	Various
Osiander	
Ovid	Metamorphoses
Owen, J.	Various
Panormitan	
Parker	
Parliamentary	Speeches
Patin	Travels
Penn	
Perkins	Witchcraft, etc.
Philo Judaeus	
Philostratus	
Philpot	
Photius	
Plato	
Plautus	Amphitruo, etc.
Pliny	
Plot, R.	Natural History of Oxfordshire
Plutarch	
Pœdianus	
Poiret	L'Œconomy Divine[57]
Polybius	
Polycarp	
Polydore Vergil	
Porphyrius	
Portugal, King of	Translation of Psalm

[57] English translation not published until 1773; therefore read in the original.

Posidonius   Life of Augustine
Potts, T.   Discoverie of Witches in Lancashire
Powel, V.
Prudentius
Purchas   Pilgrims
Quercetanus
———
                               Quest. et Resp.
Quintilian
Raleigh
Ramus
Randolph, N.   Letters
Rivet, A.
Rodiginus
Romanus
———
                               Roman Law, XII Tables of
Row
Ruffinus
Rushworth   Collections, 1629
Rushworth   Collections, 1640
Rycaut   History of Turks
Ryther   A Plot for Mariners
Sadoletus
Salmasius
Salomon, Rabbi
Salvian
Sanbert
Sarracius
Saumer
Scaliger
Scribonius   Physiologia Sagarum
Seneca
Sigonius
Simeon Metaphrast
Sobinus
Soulinge
Stenius
Strabo
Streitbergerus
Stupius

Suidas
Symmachus
Symons, E.   Discourse, 1637
Synesius
————   The Taanith
Tacitus
————   The Talmud
Tertullian   Apology, etc.
Theodoret
Theophylact
deThou
Tillotson   On Family Worship
Tolner
Turretin
VanHeer   Observations
Vegetius
Vincent   True Touchstone
Virgil   Various
Voetius
Vossius
Waller, W.   Meditations
Weinrichius
Wendover
Whitaker
Widerus
Wierus   de Præstigiis Dæmonum
Wigandus
Wilkinson   Conciones Sex ad Academicos Oxon.
Wotton
Zanchy
Zeira, Rabbi
Zepperus

B.   Books Referred to without Quotation or Citation.

Abericus
Alting
Ames, William   Medulla Theologiæ, etc.
Archilochus
Archimelus

————	Life of J. Angier
Arndt	Verus Christianismus
Bacon	Advancement of Learning
Baldwin	
Bannosius	Life of Ramus
Baronius	
Barrow, I.	
Basnagian	
Bekker	
Bennet	Concordance
Bernard	Guide to Grandjurymen
Bilson	
Binsfield	
Blondel	
Bochart	Curiosities
Boehm	Recapitulation, etc.
Bolton	Sermons
Bovet	
Boyle	
Brombal	
Bucan	
Burnett	Essay on Scripture Prophecies
Cambden	
Carbilius	Æneidomastix
Castalio	Sacred Dialogues
Cochlæus	
Cole, T.	Discourse of Regeneration
Corbet	Self-Employment
Corinna	
Cornelius à Lapide	
Cotton	Concordance
Davenport, C.	
Defoe	The Storm
Delrio	
Descartes	
Didymus	
Dietericus	Antiquitates Biblicæ
Diodati	
Dorney	Divine Contemplations

Dorotheus	Collections
Downham	Concordance
Edwards	Preacher
Empress Eudocia	Poems
Eunapius	
Fabius	Life of Beza
Faustinus	
Fenner	Treatise on Impenitency
Ficinus, Marcil.	Several
Florus, Luc.	
Franke	Manuductio, etc.
Gassendi	
Genebard	
Gennes	Relation of Voyage
Godefridus de Valle	De Arte Nihil Credendi
Gualteb	
Guicciardine	
Hardy	Guide to Heaven
Hevelius	Selenography
Herennius	
Herodian	
Herodotus	
Hilary	
Hildersham	
Hobbes	
Hooker, R.	
Hornius	De Origine Gentium Americanarum
Hortensius	
Hospinian	
Howe, J.	On Blessedness of Righteousness
Irenæus	
Janeway	Treatises; Token for Children
	The Oxford Jests; Cambridge Jests
Juvian	
La Placette	La Morale Chrétienne Abregée
Laertius	
Langius	Medecina Mentis
Leontius	
Lightfoot	Curiosities

Lubbertus	
Lukins	Interest in Spirit of Prayer
Lycophron	
Lyra	
Maccovius	
Macrobius	
Marot, C.	Psalms in Metre
Marshall	Gospel Mystery of Sanctification
————	Mass-books
Mathesius	
Meddendorpius	
Mendoza	
Nathans, Rabbi	Concordance
Neal	History of New England
Neander	
Norcott	
Oldmixon	English Empire in America
Oppian	
Pagius	
Palladius	Dialogus de Vita Chrysostomi
Pamphilia	
Pancirollus	Res Deperditæ
Paterculus	
Peter Crinitus	
Pezelius	
Pictet, B.	Saintes Conversationes
Platerus	
Pocock	
Pole, M.	Annotations
Posselius	
Ravanellus	
Reynolds	
Ricciolus	Almagestum Novum
Roswitha	Chronicles
Rowe, J.	Saints' Temptation
Saleius	
Sallust	
Sandford	De Descensu Christi
Sarocchia	

Schlusselbergius
Schurman
Scribanius, C.
Selden
Servius
————   The Seven Champions
Simeon Metaph.
Simplicius Verinus
Sleidan
Socrates
Spencer   Discourse Concerning Prodigies
Stapelton   De Tribus Thomis
Stegmannus   Studii Pietatis Icon; De Vero Chris-
                tianismo

Strato
Suetonius
Swinnock   Discourses
Theophylact
Thucydides
Torniellus
Tympius
Usher   Body of Divinity
Victor
Wallis
Weigel
Whiston   Apostolical Constitutions
White   The Power of Godliness
Wickens
Wilkins
Wise, J.   Vindication
Witten   Memoriæ Theologorum
Woodward   Natural History of the Earth
Xenophon   Hellenica
Xenophon   Cyropædia
Zosimus
Zuinglius

Inventory of the Library of William Brewster.[58]

2 little chatachismes
1 Lambeth on the Will of man [by François Lambert.]
1 morrall discourse
Discouery of Spanish Inquisition [by Gonsalvius Montanus.]
Johnson on 18th Math. [by Francis Johnson.]
Remaynes of Brittaine [by Wm. Camden.]
Description of New England [by John Smith.]
Nova Testamenti Malarato [by Avg. Marloratus.]
Tromelius & Junius Biblia Sacra [by I. Tremellius and F. Junius.]
Beza noua testament, lat. & gre.
Centuria Selecta
Calvin duodecim pphet [Prælectiones in Dvodecim Prophetas]
Clauis Scriptura flacio Illirico [by Flacius Illyricus.]
Peter Martyr Com[mentarii]. prior ad Corinthos
Musculus ad Isaiam & Romanos [by Wolfgang Moesel.]
Regneri prandinī
Œcolumnadī in Ieremia [by J. Œcolampadius.]
Crisostm, Mattias & Ioannes [by J. Chrysostom.]
Musculus Psalmos David [by W. Moesel.]
Calvī at Daniel [Calvin: Prælectiones in Librum Prophetiarum
    Danielis.]
Calvī on Isā [Calvin: Commentarii in Isaiam.]
Musculus ambos Epist ad Corinthos [by W. Moesel.]
Molleri ad Psalmos
Lanaterus Esequeh [L. Lavaterus: Ecclesiastes Salomonis.]
Zanchī ad Ephe[sios]
Syntagma amudo polo Syntagmatis Theologia Christian [Aman-
    dus Polanus: Syntagma Theologiæ.]
Sulteti Isaiam [Abraham Scultetus: Annotata in Proph. Esaiam.]

[58] Massachusetts Historical Society, Proceedings, 2d Series, v. 37 ff. Explanatory notes in brackets are condensed from Dr. H. M. Dexter's.

Purei Hoseam [David Pareus: In Hoseam.]
Gualterin Deluerin, nou. testa. [Rodolph Gualther: Archetypi
    Homiliarum in quatuor Evang, etc.]
Psalm Pagnii [S. Pagnini.]
Pareus in Genosa [in Genesin Mosis.]
Piscator in Nova Testament
Pareus ad Romanos
Pareus ad Priorem Corinthis
Caluin Eze[chielis] vigint prima
Tabula Analytice Stephano
Cartwright harm[oni]ā 4 Euangl
Pascillia Hemnigm [N. Hemmingius: Postilla Evangeliorum.]
De Vera Ies. Chr. Religione [P. Duplessis-Mornay: De veritate
    Religionis Christianæ liber.]
Erasmus in Marcin [Marcum]
Parkerius politica Eccle [R. Parker: De Politeia Eccle-
    siastica Christi.]
Piscator in Genesñ
Kykermano Systema Phisica [Bart. Keckerman.]
Beza Confess. Christ
Rollock in Dany [R. Rollici: In Librum Danielis Prophetæ.]
Dauen in priō Juni [L. Danæus: Commentarium in priorem ad
    Ioannem Epistolam.]
Thom Thomaseus Dix [Dictionarium, etc.]
Bastwick Apologeticus [1636]
Machauelii princeps
Elenchus papistice Bastwick [J. Bastwick: Elenchus Religionis
    Papisticae. 1633.]
Rollock at Psalmos
Rainoldi de Romana Eccles
Caluin in Josua
Syntagma Vigandus [Jo. Wigandus: Syntagma..]
Epistola Apologetica
Paraphrasa Erasmus in Luke
Latina Grammatica
Hebrew gramat
Camden Brittan [Britannia]
Rollock ad Romanos Ephes[ios]
Dictio. Triglott

Buxtorff Lexicon
Cartwright prouerbīa
Iunii ad Ecclām Dei [F. Iunius: Ecclesiastici . . . .]
Tyrocinia [J. Prideaux: Tyrocinium ad syllogismum . . . .]
Poemata Heringii [Fr. Herring: In fœlicissimum . . . . Iacobi
   primi, Angliæ . . . . Regis, etc. Poema Gratulatorium.]
Ad Reverend. patres Eccles. Anglican [Remonstrance ag^t y^e.
   treat^t of Puritans. 1625.]
Amesii contra Grevin. Co. [against Nic. Grevinchovius.]
Hypomneses [Prideaux: Hypomnemata Logica, Rhetorica, etc.?]
Antichristus prognostica
Harmonia Evangelia [by M. Chemnitius and Polycarpus Lyserus.]
1 English bible lattin letter
1 English bible
A new Testament
Mr. Ainsworths Psalms in prose & meter
1 new testament
Major Coment new testament [J. Mayor: A Commentarie . . . .]
Hexapla vpon Daniell [by A. Willet.]
2 volumes of Mr. Perkins
Mr. Hernes works [?Samuel Hieron 1624.]
Babingtons works [by Gervase Babington.]
Cartwright against Remisc [A Confutation of the Rhemists
   translation . . . .]
Byfield on Coloss
Dodoner Herball [by Rembert Dodoens.]
Mr Rogers on Judges [by Richard Rogers.]
Mr Richardson on ye state of Eur[ope]. [by Gabriel Richardson.
   1627.]
Knights Concord[ance] [by Wm. Knight.]
Calvin on Isay
Willet on Romans
Greusames works [Richard Greenham?]
Bodens Comon weale [by Jean Bodin.]
Willet on the 1st Samuel
Surveyor by Ratbone [Aaron Rathbone: The Surveyor. . . . .]
Willit on Genesis
Seneca Workes
Wilcocks on Psalmes [T. Wilcox.]

Cottons Concordance 2 volumes [1631.]
Scholastical discourse about the crosse [by R. Parker.]
Taylor upon Tytus
Hill upon Life Euer[lasting].
Wilsons Dixonor [Thos. Wilson: A Christian Dictionary. . .]
Waimes Christiā Synagogue [by Jo. Weemes.]
Gibbines question & disputacons [by Nich. Gibbens.]
Caluin Harmon Evan[gelists].
Defence of Synod of Dort by Robin [by Jo. Robinson.]
Messelina [?Nath. Richards: The Tragedy of Messalina, 1640.]
Downams Warfare 2 pt [J. Downame: The Christian Warfare.]
Barlow on 2 Tymothy [1625.]
Cartwright agst Whitgift 2 pt
Jackson ag^s. Misbeliefe [1625.]
Granger on Eccl[esiastes]. [1621.]
Brightman on Reuel[ation].
Birdag Anti [?Tho. Beard: Antichrist the Pope of Rome. 1625.]
Byfield on 1 Peter [1623.]
Weymes on Image of God in Man [J. Weemes. 1627.]
Parr on Romans [1631].
Robinsons Observacons [J. Robinson. 1625.]
Right way to go to worke [1622.].
Byfields sermons on 1 Peter
Dod on Commandm^{ts}
Mayor on Catholick Epistles [Jo. Mayer. 1627.]
Taylor parable on the Sower [Tho. Taylor. 1621.]
Narme of Chr. Strarr. [W. Narne: Christs Starre . . . . 1625.]
Morley of truth of religion [by P. de Mornay.]
Attersons badges of Christianity
Downam Consolatrix [Jo. Downame: Consolations]
Elton on 7 Romans
A declaracon of Quintill. question
Byfeild on 3 of Peter [1637.]
7 p^{r}bleames against Antechrist [G. S.: Sacræ Heptades, or seaven
    problems concerning Antichrist. 1626.]
Dike upon Repent
Sibbs Soules Comfort [1625.]
Passions of the mynd
5 bookes of Sermons stichet together

Constitucons & Cannons of bb. of Cant.
Wittenhall discovery of abuses [Th. Whetenhall.]
Rollock on Thessal[onians]
Heauen opened by Coop [by Wm. Cowper.]
Treasury of Smiles [Rob. Cawdrey: A Treasurie or Store-House
    of Similies.]
Downefall of Popery [by Th. Bell.]
Saints by calling by Wilson
Udal on Lamentacons
Dyocean Tryall [P. Baynes: The Diocesans Tryall.]
Sparks ag[st] Albin [Tho. Sparke: An Answere to J. de Albines
    notable Discourse against heresies.]
Wottons defence of Perkins Refor[med] Catholicke
Brinslow on Ezech [Ezekiel] [by J. Brinsley. 1622.]
Defence of Ministers reasons [by S. Hieron.]
Downam ag[st] Bath & Wells [G. Downame: A Defence of the
    Sermon preached at the Consecration of the L. Bishop of
    Bath and Welles . . . .]
A discourse of troubles Chu. of Amster[dam]. [by G. Johnson.]
Mr. Smyths 3 treatises
Discourse of Equivocation [by H. Mason. 1634.]
Mr. Smyths paroliles [Jo. Smyth: Paralleles, Censvres, etc.]
A peticon for reformacōn
A primer of Chr. Relig.
A discourse of variance betweene pope & Venet. [Chr. Potter:
    A Sermon . . . . added an Advertisement touching . . . .
    the quarrels of Pope Paul 5, with the Venetians. 1629.]
Broughton on Lament[ations].
Perkins on Sat[ans].   Sophist[rie]
A discourse of Adoracōn of Reliq[us]
A trew mark of Catholike Church [by T. Beza.]
A quodlibet to bewarr of preise
Iustifycacon of Sepācon [by J. Robinson.]
Storke answere to Campion [W. Charke: An Answere to . . . .
    a Jesuite (E. Campian) . . . .]
Dike on the heart
Perkins on 11 Hebrewes
Bayne on Ephes[ians]. [1643.]
Dike on repent[ance]. & ch[rists]. temtations

Bolton on true happynes

Downam agst Beller [G. Downame: A Treatise . . . . against
    all the objections of R. Bellarmine . . . .]

Wotton on 1 Iohn

Gouge Armor of God

Plea for Infants [by R. Clyfton.]

Rollock on effectual calling

Calling of Iews by Finish [by H^{y} Finch. 1621.]

Prin Antearminescence [Wm. Prynne: Anti-Arminianisme. 1630.]

Discouery by Barrow [H^{y} Barrowe: A Brief Discouerie of the
    false Church.]

Ainsworths defence of Scripture

Admonition to Parli^{nt} [by J. Field & T. Wilcox.]

Refutacon to Gifford [by H. Barrowe & J. Greenwood.]

Perth Assembly [by J. Forbes.]

Treatise of Ministery of England [by F. Johnson.]

Cassander Anglicañs [by J. Sprint.]

Downam's warfarr. [Probably another of the four parts of The
    Christian Warfare]

The meane of mourneing [by Th. Playfere.]

Hackhill History of Judges [?Geo. Hakewill: Scutum Regium,
    Id est, adversus omnes regicidas, etc.]

Sweeds Intelligencer [The Swedish Intelligencer. 1632.]

Comunion of Saints [by H. Ainsworth.]

Abridgment of Ministers of Lincolne

Jacob Attestation [H. Jacob: An Attestation . . . . that the
    Church government ought to bee . . . .]

Modest Defence [of the Petition for Reformation]

Exposicon of Canticles

Whitgifte answere to a libell

A reply to a libell

Dupless of a Chur [P. Duplessis-Mornay: A notable Treatise of
    the Church . . . .]

Perkins on Iude

Downams 4 treatises

Deareing on Hebrews

A Collection of Englands Deliũanc^{s} [G. Carleton: A Thankfull
    Remembrance of Gods Mercy, In an Historicall Collection

of the . . . . Deliverances of the Church and State of England
. . . . 1627.]

1000 notable things [by Th. Lupton.]

Riches of elder ages

tymes turne coat [Turncoat of the Times. A Ballad. 1635.]

A continuacon of adventur of Don Sebastian [? J. Teixera: The
strangest adventure . . . . A discourse concerning . . . .
the King of Portugall Dom Sebastian . . . . *or* E. Allde:
The Battell of Barbarie, between Sebastian King of Portugall, and Abdelmelec King of Morocco . . . . As . . . . plaid
by the Lord High Admerall his seruants.]

Surveyor Dialougs [Jo. Norden: The Surveyors Dialogue.]

Apology Chur. of England ag^{ts} Brownists [by J. Hall.]

Kings declaracon about Parlia^{ts}

Scyrge of Drunkerds [W. Hornby: The Scourge of Drunken-
nes.
(In verse.)   1619.]

Syons Plea [A. Leighton: An Appeal to the Parliament. 1628.]

Elton of Comandmts

Treatise of Chr. Religion [by Jo. Ball. 1620.]

A battaile of Palatinate

Treatise 122 Psalm [by Robt. Harrison. 1618.]

Concordance of yeares [by Ar. Hopton.]

Cesars Tryumphs

A dialogue concerning Ceremonies [by Saml. Gardiner.]

Essayes about a prisoner [Geffray Mynshul: Essayes and Characters of a Prison and Prisoners. 1618.]

Politike diseases

Exposicon of Liturgie [by Jo. Boys.]

Magnifycent Entertaynement of King Iames [by Th. Decker.]

Essex practise of treason [by Fr. Bacon.]

Prosopeia [?Prosopopœia, or a Conference . . . . between the
Pope, the Emperor, and the King of Spaine. (a satire, in
verse). *or* Prosopopoia, or Mother Hubberds Tale (in verse)
by Ed. Spenser.]

Withers motto [by Geo. Wither. 1621.]

Standish for woods [Ar. Standish: New Directions . . . . for the
increasing of Timber and Fire-wood. 1615.]

A recantacon of a Brownist [by P. Fairlambe.]

A supply to German History [? A suplement to the sixth part of the German History. 1634.]

Of the use of silk worms [by O. de Serres.]

Newes from Verginia [by R. Rich. A poem. 1610.]

News from Palatinate [1622.]

Hacklett [R. Haklyt: The principall Navigations . . . .]

Byfeild on the oracles of God [1620.]

Gods monarchy Deuells Kingdome [by I. Anwick.]

New shreds of old share

Discharg of 5 imputations [by Tho. Morton. 1633.]

Dauids Musick [by R. Allison.]

Horne sheild of the Rightous [by Rob. Horn. 1625.]

Ruine of Rome [by A. Dent. 1633.]

Downame on 15 Psalm

Pisca Evangelica [W. Symonds: Pisgah Evangelica.]

Virell on Lords prayer [by P. Viret.]

Answere to Cartwright

Broughton on Gods Diuinitie

Bayne tryall of Christ[ians] [e]state

Wheatley on Gods husbandry [by Wm. Whately. 1622.]

Exposicon on Reuelac

Perkins Reformed Catholik

Johnsons & Withers works [Rich. Johnson: The Golden Garland of Princely pleasures and delicate Delights. 1620. Geo. Wither: The Workes of . . . . 1620.]

10 sermons of the supper [by J. Dod & R. Cleaver. 1634.]

Ciuill Conuersacon Gnahzo [by Stef. Guazzo.]

Smyths plea for Infants

Bacons p~ficiency in Learning [F. Bacon: Advancement of Learning.]

Arguments agst seinge

Theologicks

Eming on Iames [by N. Hemming.]

Catholike Judg.

The spirituall watch [T. Gataker. 1619.]

reasons for reformacon of Chur. of Eng^{l} [by H. Jacob.]

A looking glass agst Prelates [by W. Prynne. 1636.]

A sermon of Bishop of London

Resolucon for kneeling [by D. Lindesay. 1619.]

2 Exact discouery of Romish doctrine [by T. Morton.]

Warr was a blessing [?D. Digges: Foure paradoxes . . . . of
the worthinesse of warre and warriors.]

Midland souldier [?M. Parker: The Maunding Soldier . . . .
(a ballad.) 1629.]

Humillitie Christians life [?D. Cawdrey: Humilitie, the Saints
liverie . . . . 1624]

Church Deliūance

Coment on Ecclesiastic [? by J. Granger. 1621.]

Prerogative of Parli^{nts} [by Sir W. Raleigh. 1628.]

Temple on 20 Psalm

Abbott sermon

Soules Implantacon [by Tho. Hooker. 1637.]

A treatise of Stage pleas [by J. Rainolds: Th' overthrow of
Stage-Playes.]

Apologue of Brownists [by F. Johnson & H. Ainsworth.]

State Mistery of Iesuits

Dike Schoole of affliccon

Sibbs Comfort [Rich. Sibbes: The Saints Comfort. 1638.]

Taylor on 32 psalm

Parable of the Vine by Rogers [N. Rogers: The Wild Vine. 1632.]

Apologeticall reply by Damfort [by J. Davenport. 1636.]

divers books sticht together[59]

Broughton of Lamentacons

A good wyfe [R. Brathwait: The Description of a Good Wife.
(verse.) 1619.]

Northbrook against Images

The tryall of truth by Chibbald [1622.]

The paterne of true prayer

Household gouerment

Blackwells answers

Aristotles probleames

Symers Indictment [W. Ward: A Synners Indictament.]

---

[59] Identified by Dexter as a book which he owned containing: L. Chaderton:
A Godly Sermon vpon . . . . 12. chapter of . . . . Romanes. A True, Modest,
and just Defence of the Petition for Reformation. J. Robinson: The Peoples
Plea for the exercise of Prophesie. R. Harrison: A Little Treatise vpon . . . .
122 Psalm. T. Dighton: Certain Reasons . . . . against Conformitie . . . .
T. Dighton: The Second Part of a Plain discourse . . . . W. Euring: An
Answer to the Ten Covnter Demands . . . .

Iohnsons psalmes in meeter

Mores discovery

A Sermon

Refutacon of tolleracon

Aphorismes of State [by the Colledge of Cardinalls. 1624.]

Of Union betweene England & Scotland [by Sir W. Cornwallis.]

Tales of Popes custome house [?W. Crashaw: Mittimus to the Ivbile at Rome: or the rates of the popes cvstome-hovse. 1625.]

Of Pope Ioane [by A. Cooke.]

A dialogue betweene a gent & a preist

Against kneeling

Perkins on fayth

Bacons Apologye [by Sir F. Bacon.]

A History of Mary Glouer [by J. Swan.]

A bundle of smale books & papers

Defyance of death [by Wm. Cowper.]

A Christians apparelling [by R. Jenison. 1625.]

Perkins on repentance

Essays by Cornwallis [Sir Wm.]

Spirituall stedfastnes [by J. Barlow. 1632.]

A manuell [? J. Usher: Immanuel. 1638.]

A breiffe of bible [by Henoch Clapham; in verse.]

Jacob on 2^d Comand^{nt}

A pill to purge popery

Withers

Cathologue of nobillyty of England [by R. Brooke. 1619.]

English Votaryes [by J. Bale.]

Sibbs Yea & Amen [1638.]

Sermons by Rollock

Kinges Bath [by Tho. Taylor: . . . . a Treatise on Matt. iii. 1620.]

Great Assise by Smyth [1625.]

Martin on Easter [?? N. Marten: The seventh voyage . . . . into East India . . . . 1625.]

Smyth on 6th of Hosea.

Discription of World [by G. Abbot. 1620.]

Cantelus Cannon of Masse [P. Viret: The Cauteles, Canon, and Ceremonies of the . . . . Masse.]

Gods mc̃y & Jurasā misery
Silū Watch bell [by T. Tymme.]
7 Sermons by W. B. [Ms. sermons by W. Brewster.]
Burton agst Cholmely [H. Burton: Babel no Bethel . . . . 1629.]
Sibbs Saints p^{r}viledges [1638.]
Sibbs Riches of mercy [1638.]
Regla Vite [Th. Taylor: Regula Vitæ. 1635.]
Pilgrimes p^{r}fession [by T. Taylor. 1622.]
Sermon at Pauls crosse
Nature & grace [Iohn Prime: A Treatise of . . . .]
Perkins of Predestinacon
Spirituall trumpett
Vox Regis [by Tho. Scott. 1623.]
Barrowes platforme
Exposicon of Lords prayer
Comon weale of England [by Sir Tho. Smith.]
Right way of peace [? R. Bruce: The Way to true Peace . . . .]
4th pt of true watch [J. Brinsley: The True Watch and Rule of
      Life: fourth Part . . . . 1624.]
Iohnson on Psalmes
Byfield paterne of [1627.]
Duke promises
A help to memorye [and discourse. 1621. (Partly in verse).]
p. posicons by Iohn Sprint
The morality of law
Cases of Conscience by Per[kins]
Discouery of famyly of love [by Io. Rogers.]
Sermon of repentance
Sermon at Paules Crosse
Sibbs spirituall maxims [1637.]
Memorable conceits [of Divers Noble and famous personages]
God & the Kinge [by R. Mockett.]
Smyth on Riddle of Nebuchudnez.
Estey on Comand^{nts} & 51st Psalm
Christians dayly walk [by Hy. Scudder. 1620.]
Exposicon of 11 & 12 Reuelacon [?by Th. Taylor. 1633.]
Treatise of English medicines [by T. Bedford. 1615.]
A dialogue of desiderias [Same as Barrowes platforme.]
A supplycacon to the King [? by H. Jacobs. 1609.]

Abba father [by Elnat. Parr. 1618.]
Abrahams tryall discourse [? by J. Calvin.]
Jacobbs ladder [by Hy. Smith.]
Perkins of Imagina[tions]
Burton Christī question
A toyle for 2 legged foxes [by J. Baxter.]
A cordiall for comfort [by Wm. Chibald. 1625.]
Zacheus conuersion [by Jo. Wilson. 1631.]
Spirituall touchstone [1621.]
Dearmies advantage
Englands summons [by Tho. Sutton.]
Burton wooing his Church
Goulden key [openinge the locke to Eternal Happynes.]
A remedy against famine & warr [by Jo. Udall.]
Treatise against popery [? by Tho. Stoughton.]
Treatise of Gods religion

Books Bequeathed to Harvard College by John Harvard.[60]

Ambrosij Dixionariū.
Antonius & Gralerus in Senecā.
Abernethyes physick for the soule.
Analysis Apocalypseōs.
Anglorū prælia.
Aquinatis Opa. Conclusiones.
Aynsworts workes. [Henry Ainsworth: Annotations upon the
    five bookes of Moses, the booke of the Psalms, and the Song
    of Songs, or Canticles.]
Amesij Theologiæ Medulla. De Consc: In Epistolas Petrj. contra
    Armin: Bellarminus Enervatus.

[60] Harvard Library, Bibliographical Contributions, No. 27, p. 7 ff. Explanations
in brackets are from the same source. It should be noted that under one name
several titles are sometimes given, often run together as one title. [This list
has been revised from "Catalogue of John Harvard's Library" by Alfred C.
Potter, Publications of the Colonial Society of Massachusetts, xxi. 190-230.
Ed.]

Augustinj meditationes. Opa.

Alstedij Physica Harmonia. Compendiū Thelogiæ.

Apeius in Nov. Testam[t].

Anatomy Arminianisme [by Pierre Du Moulin].

Anchorani porta linguarum.

Actus Synodi Nationalis.

Acta Synodalia.

Aschamj Epistolæ.

Arraingm[t] of the whole Creature.

Alicalj Emblemata.

Æsopi fabulæ.

Ægidius in Arist. Philos. & Metaph.

Academia Gallica.

Βασίλικον δῶρον.

Bezæ Test. N. cū Annotat. Test. Græc. Lat. In Epist. ad Galat:.
    Ephe.

Baynes on Collos:. Ephes.

Bethneri Gram̄: Hebræa.

Berchetj Catechismus.

Buxtorfi. Dixionar. Hebr:. Gram̄: hebr:.

Beton displaying of ye popish Masse.

Bellarmin. de fælicitate sanctorū. In Psalm. In 1[a] & 2[a] Epist: ad
    Thessalon. Conciones.

Bolton in 4 volumnes.

Ball on faith.

Bastingius on Palatines Catechisme.

Brerewood on the Sabbath.

Bacons advancem[t]. Essayes.

Bannes in Arist: de Gen: & Corrup.

Bovilij Adagia.

Bedæ Axiomata Philosophica.

Brentius de parabolis.

Beards theatre of Gods judgm[ts].

Brerewoods Tractatus Logicus.

Brentij Pericopæ &c.

Bullingerus in Isaj.

Biblia Tremelij & Junij.

Bucani Institutiones.

Bradshewes p[r]paration for the Sacram[t].

Broughton on the revelat: on Eccles. Positions on the Bible. On
   Daniel. texts of Script. chronol. pamphlets.

Baylyes directions for health.

Calvinus in Pent & Joshuā. Sermons vpon Job in English. p^rlec-
   tiones in Ezechiel. Institut. Religio. Christ. Tomus 4us opū
   Theologicorū. Harmonia. In Prophetas min: Homilia in
   Samuelem. In Epistolas Paulj. In Psalm.

Camararij meditationes histor.

Corradj Casus Consc.

Church his God & man. Good mans treasure.

Camdens remaines.

Cleonardi. [Entry almost illegible; trimmed off by binder.]

Chysostinj homilia. [Chrysostom.]

Castanej Distinctiones.

Calliopæia [or, a rich store-house of . . . . phrases].

Chrystopolitanj opa.

Christianity.

Cornerj Psalteriū Lat:.

Curiel in Epist. Thomæ.

Chareus in Epist.

Cornelius de artibus & Scientijs. In Eccles:. Prophetas majores,
   & minores, in Pent. in Epist: Paulj. in Acta. In Prov. in 7 vol.

Clavis græc: Linguæ.

Comentariū in Horatiū in Fol.

Coment: in 4 Euangel. & Acta Apost. On the Prov.

Cottons concordance.

Coment in Arist. Phys. de anima.

Cartwright in Eccles. & Prov.

Collection of statutes.

Conradus in Apocalyp.

Carlton ag^st Pelag. & Armin.

Chytreus in Apocal. in Levit. in Genes. Numer. in Deut. Ester.
   Judices in 6 Tom.

Characciolus his life.

Catin. Phrases.

Danej opa Theolog. Questiones. de salutaribus dej donis. in Math.
   his comon Ethicks.

Dickson on hebr.

Dictionariū Anglic. Historicū. Geograp. Poëticū. Lat. Græc.

Dounā his warfare.
Davenantius in Epist. ad Collos.
Duns Scotus in 8 Libros Arist. Phys.
Dove on the Cant.
Dike on the hart. his mischeife of Scandalls.
Death subdued.
Elton on the Comandm^{ts}.
Epictetj Enchyridion.
Eustachij Philosophia.
Euphoranius.
Erasmj Colloquia.
Elegant Phrases.
Garden of Eloquence.
Exon his meditations.
Essayes morall & Theol.
Francklin ὀρθοτονίας lib.   [Tractatus de tonis in lingua græcanica.]
Funebres Conciones 15.
Fabritius in Hoseā.
Felthoms resolues.
Fuebernes lapidua Pasmaliensis.
Fayus in Epist. ad Timoth.
Feuardensius in Epist. ad Philemonem.
Gualterus in Marcū.
Golij Ethicæ.
Griners in Dan.
Goodwins Aggravation of sin.
Household Phys:
Haxions prælections.
The honest man.
Hunnius in Joh: Evangel.
Hindersham of fasting. On the Psal. on John 4. 2 Tom. [Hilder-
     sam.]
Hieronus in Haddanū in Isai.
Horatius cū Stephanj notis.
Hemmingius in 84 Psalm. in Epist. ad Collos:.
Homers workes in English. [Chapman's translation.]
History of the Church.
Haylins Geography.
H [One title trimmed off.]

Hutton agst Comon prayer booke.
Henshaws meditations.
Jackej Instit. Philos:
Juvenalis.
Isocratis Orat: Græc & Latin.
Judic: Synodi Nationalis.
Keckermannj Philos. Disput.
Keckermanj contemplat. de loco. et de terræ-motu.
Lutherus in Genesin. Tomus 1us, 2us, 3us, 4us, 5us, 6us, 7us.
Luke Angl.
Loscij Annotationes Scolasticæ.
Lightfoots Miscelanes.
Lucanus.
Lewes right vse of pmises.
Lexicon Græco Lat:.
Lemnius medicus de complexione.
Londons complaint. [By Benjamin Spenser.]
Lamentations.
Lord Verul: Nat: History.
Livellj Vita & in Harding.
Leigh on ye pmises.
Lumberds Justice.
Lycosthenjs Apophthegmata. Similia.
Loscij Questiones.
Laurentij opa.
Mollerus in Psalmos.
Marloratj Thesaurus Scripturæ.
Musculus in Psalmos. Matthæū.
Mollinæus contra Arminios.
Marlotj Thesaurus Scripturæ.
Magirj Physica. Anthropologia.
Maxes Sermons.
Melanchj Logica.
Minshej Dictionariū.
A Manuduction to Divinity.
Martinij Gram: Hebr.
Micomius in Marcū.
Montanj in Psal. Prov^r Comt. & Hebr.
Moses Vayled.

N. Test. Catholicj Expositio Eccles:
Nichols mirrour for Magistrates.
N. Test. Lat.
Nonæ Novemb. æternitatj consecratæ.
Natales Comes. in 29 Tomis.
Osiandri Psalm.
Philosophers Banquet.   [By Sir Michael Scott.]
Pfaltsgraues Church.
Polanj Syntagma Theologiæ.   De Legendo cū fructu.
Piscator 17 Tomis.
Pelagius redivivus Prin.
Plin. Nat. Hist.
Plutarchj Vitæ Angl. Moralia Angl.   [North's Plutarch.]
Philippi Homil: in Jonam.
Pike his worthy worthy comunicant.
Pareus de doctrina X^{iana}.
Phochenius.   [Sebastian Pfochen.]
Plautus.
Porcensis orationes.
Pet. Martyr, in Epist. ad Rom.   Loci Comunes.
Piccolominej Philos.
Patresius de Regin. & reg: Institutione.
Persij Satyræ.
Politianj Epist.
Passoris Lexicon. Græc. Lat.
Pellegronj Sylva.   [Simon Pelegromius: Synonymorum sylva.]
Poetarū flores.
Pars Workes.
Pembles workes. de origine formarū.
Preston on ye Attributes.   4 Sermons.
Physick for ye Soule.
Pavenij Ethicæ.   [Francesco Pavone: Summa ethicæ.]
Quirbj coment: in Psalmos & Prophetas.
Quarles Poems.
Reinolds Vanity of ye Creature.   Conference wth ye hart.
Rogers on Luke ye 15.
Rami Græca Gram: Lat.   Logica cū Talæj Rhetorica, Molinej Log.
        vno volum:
Robinsons Essayes.

Royardus in Epist: Domin.
Rogers, his Divinity. On Loue.
Roxanæ Tragedia.
Reinoldi Liber de Idololatria.
Stola in Lucā.
Scultetj opa.
Schriblerj metaphoræ.
Schickardi gram. hæb.
Sibbs fountaine sealed.
Spongia contra Jesuit. Goloniū cū alijs opibus vno vol. compressis.
Sphinx Philosophy.
Speeds clowde of wittnesses.
Scalliger de subtilitate.
Scheibleri philosoph. compend.
Sebati Phys:
Setonj Dialectica.
Sarcerj Postilla.
Soules præparation.
Schenblerj sententiæ.
Salustius.
Smiths Logicke.
Scarfij Symphonia.
Saluthij Schola.
Sceiblerj Synopsis Philos.
Saints Legacyes.
Test. N. Græc.
Tossanj Diction. Hebr.
Terentius.
Touchstone of truth.
Thrapuntij rhetorica.
Thesaurus poeticus.
Textoris Epitheta. Epist.
Test. [Trimmed off.]
Twissus de gratia, potestate & Providentia.
Taylour on Titus. on Revel. 12.
Trunesse on X^{an} religion.
Turnerj Orationes.
Terus in Exod. Num. Deut. Josh. Jud.
Thesaurus linguæ rom: & Brittanicæ in fol.

Thomæ Aquinatis opa.
Tullij opa in 2 Tomis. de officijs.
Tyme well spent.
Treasury of God.
Vorsius de Deo.
Vdalls Heb^r Gram:.
Valerius Max:.
Vocatio Judæorū.
Warwicks Meditations.
Wall on Acts 18. V^s 28.
Withers.
Weames 4th Vol. of ye Image of God in man. on the Lawes morall, ceremoniall, Judiciall.
Willsons X^{an} Dictionary.
Watsonj animæ Gaudia. [Amintæ gaudia. A poem.]
Whakly his new birth. [William Whately: The new birth, or a treatise of regeneration.]
Wygandus de psec. piorū exilijs.
Wandelinj Contemplatio Phys. Tom 3.
Wardes Sermons.
Zanchij Opa.

Selected Titles from the 1723 Catalogue of the Harvard Library.

Folio

Aristophanis	Comædiæ
Bacon	History of the Reign of K. Henry VII
Bacon	Instauratio Magna
Bacon	Natural History
Bacon	9 Books of the Advancement of Learning
Browne, Sir T.	Pseudodoxia Epidemica
Brahe, Tychonis	Historia Cælestis
Bertii	Theatri Geographiæ Veteris
Bullialdi	Astronomia Philolaica

Baudoin	Mythologie
Bochas	Tragedies translated into Englishe by John Lidgate, Monk of Burye
Burnet, Tho.	Theory of the Earth
Clarendon	History of the Rebellion
Chaucer	Works [title page missing]
Chapman, Geo.	English Homer
Cambden	Britannia
Cambden	History of Q. Elizabeth
Clark, Sam.	Lives of sundry eminent Persons
Collier, Jer.	Great Historical and Chronological Dictionary, and Supplement to same.
Cowley, Abrah.	Works
Danyel	Collection of the History of England
Demosthenes	Orationes
Dalton	Country Justice
Eadmeri	Historia Novorum
Euclid	Elements translated by H. Billingsley
Euripidis	Tragediæ
Fuller, Tho.	Church History of Britain
Fuller, Tho.	Pisgah sight of Palestine
Fuller, Tho.	History of the Holy War
Fuller, Tho.	Holy and Profane State
Fougasses, Tho. de	General History of Venice
Godwini	Rerum Anglican. Hen. 8. Edvar 6. et Maria regantibus Annales
Guicciardines	History of the Wars of Italy, English'd by Fenton
Guicciardi.	La Description de tous les pais bas
Grymestone	Imperial History
	Godfrey of Bollogn [sic] or the Recovery of Jerusalem
Gassendi	Operum omnium, 6 vols.
Gassendi	Astronomia
Galeni	Opera
Gerhard	Herbal
Grew	Catalogue and Description of the Rarities of the Royal Society
Guillims	Display of Heraldry

Hackluit	Voyages
Hyde, Tho.	Catalogus Librorum impressorum Biblio-thecæ Bodleianæ in Academia Oxoniensi
Heylin	Cosmography
Hugo	Seige [*sic*] of Breda
Holingshed	Chronicle of England, Scotland, Ireland
	History of K. Charles
Harrington	Common-wealth of Oceana
Harris	Collection of Voyages & Travels
Hendy	Historia Mundi, or Mercator's Atlas recti-fied
Hormi	Geographia vetus Sacra et Profana
Hevellii	Machinæ Cœlestis
Hevellii	Cometographia
Hevellii	Selenographia
Hayes	Treatise of Fluxions
Hugenii	Horologium oscillatorum
Hill	Account of the Ottoman Empire
Harris	Lexicon Technicum
Herbert, Lord	Life of K. Henry VIII
Herbert, Lord	Compleat History of England
Hondius	Atlas
Howel	Institution of the General History of World
Josephus	Antiquities and Wars of the Jews, English'd by Lodge
Jonstoni	Hist. Naturalis de Piscibus, de Insectis, de Serpent., etc.
	Introductorium Astronomicum
Huygen	Itinerario, Voyage ofte Schipvært
Kircheri	Œdipus Ægyptiacus
Kircheri	De Arte magnetica opus tripart
	A Kalendar of the Statutes of England
Keeble	Statutes at large, 1684
Kersey	Algebra
Keckermann	Operum omnium
Lessii	Opuscula
Lessii	De Justitia et Jure
Liceti	De Intellectu
Liceti	De spontaneo viventium ortu

	The Lighting Colomne or Sea-Mirror
	Logarithmical Arithmetick
Longomontani	Astronomia Danica
Matchiavel	Florentine History
Montanus	Atlas Japannensis, English'd by Ogilby
Munsteri, Seb.	Cosmographiæ
Majoris, Joh.	Opera in Artes quas liberales vocant
More, Henry	Philosophical Writings
More, Henry	Operum omnium
Minshei	Ductor in Linguas
Minshei	Spanish and English Dictionary
Montaigne	Essays, London 1613
	Massachusett-Law-Book
Newton	Trigonometry
Ortelii	Theatrum Orbis Terrarum
	Ortus Sanitatis
Petiti	Leges Atticæ
Prideauxii	Marmora Oxoniensia; ex Arundelianis, etc.
Plutarch	North's Translation
Prynne	History of K. John, K. Henry 3. & K. Ed. 1.
Prynne	Canterbury's Doom
Purchase	Pilgrimes
Pulton	Collection of Statutes
Piccolominei	Universa Philosophia de moribus
Plinii	Historiæ Mundi
Plinii	Natural History, translated by Holland
Ptolomæi	Liber Geographiæ cum Tabulis
Pappi Alexandrini	Mathematicæ Collectiones, cum interpretatione et illustratione F. Commandini
Parkinson	Theatre of Plants
Parkinson	Garden of Flowers
Perrault	Treatise of the 5 Orders of Columns in Architecture
Riccioli	Chronologia Reformata
Riccioli	Astronomia Reformata
Riccioli	Almagestum Novum
Riccioli	Geograph. et Hydrograph. Reformatæ
Rushworth	Historical Collections 1618–1629
Richardson	State of Europe

Raleigh	History of World
Roberts	Map of Commerce
Rudolphinæ	Tabulæ, ex Editione Joan. Kepleri
Ricettario	Medicinale Fiorentino
Riolanus	Surest Guide to Physick and Surgery, English'd by Culpeper
A Soto	De Justitia et Jure Libri
De Serres	History of France, translated by Grymeston
Stuckii	Antiquitatum Convivialium
Schedel	De Historiis Ætatum Mundi ac Descriptione Urbium Collect.
Speed	History of Great Britain
	Statutes at large from the 35 of Q. Elizabeth to 4 of K. Charles
	Statutes at Large from Magna Charta to the 29th of Queen Elizabeth
Sandys, G.	His Travels
Socinatis	Quæstiones Metaphysicales
Seldeni	Liber de Successionibus in bona defuncti ad Leges Hebræorum
Seldeni	de Jure natural. et **Gentium** juxta Disciplinam Hebræorum
Scaligeri	Opus de Emendatione Temporum
Stephani, Carol	Dictionarium Historic. Geograph. Poetic.
Stapylton	English Juvenal
Suarez	Metaphysicarum Disputationum
Scharpii	Methodus Philosophiæ Peripateticæ
Spelmanni	Archæologus
Seller, J.	Sea Atlas
Seller, J.	Atlas Terrestris
Speed	Prospect of the most famous parts of the World
Schotii	Cursus Mathematicus
Sempilii Craigbataei	de Disciplinis Mathematicis
Sylvatici	Opus Pandectarum Medicinæ
Strype	Memorials of A.Bp. Cranmer
	Dr. Sacheverel's Tryal
Spotswood	History of the Church of Scotland
Thuani	Historiarum Sui Temporis

Tacqueti	Opera Mathematica
Tarvernier	Travels
Usserii	Annales
Virgilii, Poly.	Historiæ Anglicæ
Vincentio	Opus Geometricum Quadraturæ Circuli et Sectionum Coni
Victae	Opera Mathematica
Wing	Astronomia Brittanica
Wallis	Treatise of Algebra
Wirtzung	General Practice of Physic in English
Willis	Remaining Physical Works
Xenophon	Opera omnia
Xenophon	History of the Ascent of Cyrus English'd by Bingham
	Yearbook under K. Henry V. and K. Henry VI. From the 40 to the 50 of Edw. III.
	Young Students Library by the Athenian Society, 1692
Zuingeri	Theatri Humanæ Vitæ
Zabarella	Comment. in Aristot. Libros Physicorum
Zabarella	Opera Logica
Zabarella	De Rebus naturalibus
Zabarella	Comment. in Aristot. Libros de animâ

Quarto

Althusii	Politica
Alphonsinæ	Tabulæ, edente Paschasio Hamellio
Anderson	Of the Genuine use of the Gunne
	Acta Eruditorum Publicata Lipsiæ, from 1682 to 1698 inc.
	Ibid., Supplements for 1692 and 1696
Balduini	Tractat. de Casibus Conscientiæ
Butler	History of Bees
Boetii, Anselm	Gemmarum et Lapidum Historia
	Brittain's Busse, with a Discovery of Newfoundland and a Discovery of Trade
Boyle	Philosophical Essays
Boyle	Tracts of the Admirable Rarefaction of the Air, &c.

Boyle	Experiments Physico-Mechanical touching the Air
Boyle	Natural Philosophy
Boyle	Of forms & Qualities
Bannes	Quæstiones et Comment. in Duos Lib. Aristot. de Generatione et Corruptione
Brathwait	English Gentleman
Brerewoodi	Tractatus quidam Logici
Buridani	Quæstiones in 10 Libros Ethicorum Arist.
Balfourii	Comment. in Organum Logicum Aristot.
Balfourii	In Aristotelis Philosophiam
Brinsly	Ludus literarius; or the Grammar School
Brahe, Tychon	Astronomiæ instauratæ
Brahe, Tycho	Operum omnium
Brahe, Tycho	De Mundi Ætherei recentioribus Phænomenis
Bariffe	Military Discipline
Barrow	Lectionis Opticæ et Geomet.
Barrow	Illustrat. in opera Archimedis, in Libros Conicorum Apollonii & in Spherica Theodosii
Brown's & Wottons	Mirror & Rules of Architecture
Branker	Introduction to Algebra
Bond	Longitude found
Blackborrow	Longitude not found
Binning	Light to the Art of Gunnery
Balloni	Conciliorum medicinalium
DuBartas	Poems
Cawdry	Storehouse of Similies
Cambden	Remains
Cambden	Britannia
Cambden	Britannia abridged
Cominoei	De Rebus Gestis Ludov. XI. Galliarum Regis
Contareno	Common-Wealth and Government of Venice
Contareno	Commentaries concerning Religion and the Common-Wealth of France
Carew	Survey of Cornwal
Camerarii	Meditationes Historicæ

Champlain	Voyages de la nouvelle France
Cognet	Politick Discourses of Truth & Lying
Cartesii	Meditationes de Primâ Philosophiâ
Cartesii	Principia Philosophiæ
Cartesii	Epistolæ Lat.
Cavallerii	Directorium Generale Uranometricum
Carpenter	Geography
Campanellæ	Medicinalium
Carpi	Anatomia
Cartesii	Geometria
Calovii	Encyclopædiæ Mathematicæ
Craig	Religionis Christianæ princip. Mathemat.
Chokieri	Thesaurus Aphorismorum Politicorum
Digby, K.	Treatise of Bodies
Digbei, E.	Theoria Analytica viam ad monarchiam
Dufortii	Gnomologia Homerica
Donelli	in Titulum de Usuris in Pandectis
Everarti	Ephemerides Novæ et Exactæ
	Essays of Natural Experiments made in the Academy del Cimento, translated by Waller
Fuente	Quæstiones Dialecticæ et Physicæ
Florio	First Fruits
Feltham	Resolves
Goodwin	Select Cases of Conscience
Gainsford	Glory of England
Gregorii XIII	Corpus Juris Canonici
Guicciardini	Historia d'Italia
Giles	Hist. Ecclesiastique des Eglises reformées
Godwyn	Jewish and Roman Antiquities
Guevara	Dial of Princes. English'd by North
Guevara	Familiar Epistles
le Grand	Institutio Philosophiæ secundum Principia Renat. des Cartes
Golding	Translation of Ovid's Metamorphoses
Glanvil	Scepsis Scientifica
Galilæi	Dialogus de Systemate Mundi
Goclenii	Apologeticus pro astromantia Discursus
Gadbury	Ephemerides from 1672 to 1681

Hales	Golden Remains
	History of Italy
	History of Life of Philip de Mornay
Hottingeri	Historia Orientalis
Hanmer	View of Antiquity
Hackluit	History of the West Indies
Herodian of Alex.	History of the Roman Caesars
Husband	Exact Collections of Remarkables between the King and Parliament from 1641 to 1643
	History of the Reformation of the Church of Scotland
Hayward	Lives of the 3 Norman Kings of England
Heylin	Little Description of the Great World
Hugenii	Systema Saturnium
Hopton	Geodetical Staffe
Heurnii	Praxis Medicinæ
Hawksbee	Physico-Mechanical Experiments
Harry	Genealogy of K. James I
Jamesii	Catalogus Librorum in Bibliotheca Bodleiana
Lucy	Observations of Notorious Errors in Hobb's Leviatha
Lithgow	Voyages
Lorhardi	Theatrum Philosophicum
Lowthorp	Abridgement of the Philosophical Transactions & Collections to the end of 1700
Liceti	Controversiæ de Cometis
Lansbergii, P.	Commentationes in motum Terræ
Lansbergii, J.	Apologia pro Comment. Philip. Lansberg. in Motum Terræ, adversus Libert.
Leyburn	Geometrical Exercises for young Seamen
Langham	Garden of Health
Luytsii	Introduction ad Geographiam
Luytsii	Introd. ad Astronomiam
H-Mercurio Overo	Historia de' correnti tempi
Miltoni	Defensio pro populo Anglicano cont. Salmasium
Masii	In universam Aristotelis Philosophiam Comment.

M. Meurisse Royen.	Rerum Metaphysicarum
Martialis	Epigrammatum Libri Comment. Remirez de Prædo illustrati
Macchiavel.	Discours de L'Estat de paix et de Guerre
Macchiavel.	Art of War. English'd by P. Withorne
Moore	System of the Mathematicks
Molerii	Accurata descriptio Ecleipsium Solis et Lunæ 1505 & 1607
Moxon	Tutor to Astronomy & Geography
Moxon	Use of the Copernican Sphæres
Markham, G.	Masterpiece
Morisani	Apotelesma in Aristot. Logic. Physi. Ethic.
	Miscellanea Curiosa: sive Ephemeridum Medico-Physicarum Germanicarum, 1670 to 1694, inc., with Index, 1693
	Nomenclator autorum omnium quorum Libri extant in Bibliotheca Academ. Lugd. Batav.
Newton, Isaac	Opticks
Norwoods	Trigonometry
Origani, D.	Ephemerides Brandenburgica, 1595–1655, inc.
Oates, Titus	Picture of K. James
Pitsei, J.	de Rebus Anglicis
Pezelii	Mellificium Historicum
Perrin	History of the Waldenses & Albigenses
	Prelates Tyranny . . . . Prosecution of Prynne, Bastwick and Burton
	Parliaments Diurnal Occurrences, Nov. 1640–Nov. 1641
[Langland]	The Vision of Pierce Plowman, 1650
Platinæ	Historia de Vitis Pontificum
Prideaux	Introduction for Reading Histories
Prynne	Antipathy of Prelacy to Regal Monarchy and Civil Unity
Prynne	Sovereign Power of Parliaments and Kingdoms
Prynne	Histrio-mastix
Prolomæi, A.	Geographia, Interprete Pirckheimherio

	Philosophical Transactions, Savoy. 1665–1678, and Philosophical Collections to No. 7
Primaudaye	French Academy
Polluce	Onomasticon
Petisci	Trigonometria
Palmer	Catholick Planisphaere
	Philai, sive de vero Systemate Mundi
Plateri	Praxeos Medicæ
Phrygii	Comment. in Hist. Epidemicas Hippocratis
Paaw	De Ossibus Human. Corporis primitiæ Anatomicæ
Poeton	Chirurgeon's Closet
Puffendorfii	De Jure Naturæ & Gentium
Pisis	Pantheologiæ
Placæi	Opuscula Nonnulla
Robinson	Essays Moral and Divine
	Of Resisting the Lawful Magistrate
Robinson	Justification of the separation
	Reasons of the Necessity of the Reformation in England
Reineccii	Chronici Hierosolymitani
Ruvii	In 8 Lib. Aristot. de Physico Auditu Comment.
Ruvii	In universam Aristot. Dialectiam Comment.
Regii	Philosophia Naturalis
Raci	Clavis Philosophiæ . . . . seu introductio ad naturæ Contemplationem Aristotelico-Cartesiana
Rami	Arithmet.-Geometr.
Rami	Scholarum Mathemat.
Reinoldi	Prutenicæ Tabulæ cælestium motuum
Rossæi	Commentum de motu Terrae circulari refutatum
Smith	Essex Dove
Swinnock	Of the Dignity & Beauty of Magistracy and the Duty of the Magistrates
Seldeni	De Synedriis & Præfecturis Juridicis Vet. Hebra.

Stow	Annals of England
Simancæ	De Republica Lib. XI.
Soto	Quæst. in 8 Lib. Physicorum Aristot.
Sabatecii	Logica Pet. Rami florens
Scoti, J. Duns	in Isagogen Porphyrii et in Aristot.
Scoti, J. Duns	in 8 Lib. Physicorum Aristotelis
Suarez	Metaphysicarum Disputationum Syllabus
Sophoclis	Tragediæ 7
Sylvayn's	Orator in English
Street	Astronomia Carolina
Schooten	Exercitationes Mathematicæ
Scheineri	Fundamentum Opticum
Sennerti	De febribus
Senguerdii	Philosophia naturalis
Schroderi	Thesaurus Linguæ Aremenicæ
Tarich	Series Regum Persiæ cum Comment.
Toleti	Introductio in Universam Aristot. Logicam Comment. unà cum Quæst. in 3 libros Aristotelis de Animâ
Terrence	Andria Latin & English
Usserii	Veterum Epistolarum Hybernicarum Sylloge
Usserii	Brittanic. Ecclesiarum Antiquitates
Usserii	Quæstionis de Ecclesiarum Successione Historica Explicatio
Ubaldino	Vita de Carlo magno imperadore
Vossii	De Origine & Progressu Idololatriæ
Vossii	De Historicis Græcis
Vossii	De Historicis Latinis
Velagut	Practica Canonica Criminalis secund. Juris Communis ac Doctorum antiquorum et recentium Decreta
Vries	Exercitationes Rationales
Wickliff	Complaint to the King and Parliament
Waseri	De Antiquis numis Hebræorum, Chaldæorum & Syriorum
Wright	Errors in Navigation detected
Wallis	Mechanica, sive de motu Tractat. Geometric
Wing	Ephemerides from 1672 to 1681

Wardi	Idea Trigometriæ
Zanardi	Comment. cum Quæst. in Logicam Aristot.
Zanardi	Disputatio de Universo Elementari
Zanardi	Disputationes de triplici universo

Octavo, Etc.

Appiano	delle guerre Civili de Romani
Adami	Vitæ Germanorum. Theologorum
	Antiquitas Academ. Cantabrigens. & Oxoniens.
	An Abridgement of the Chronicles of Scotland
Angli	Euclides Metaphysicus
Angli	Euclides Physicus
Amama	Dissertationum Marinarum Decas.
Amyraldi	De Libero Arbitrio Disputatio
Alstedii	Logicæ Systema Harmonicum
Aristot.	de Moribus lib. 10
Alciati	Emblemata cum Comment.
Agrippæ, H. C.	De Incertitudine et Vanitate omnium Scientarum Liber
Aviani	Clavis Poeseos Sacræ
Aristot.	Artis Rhetorice
Aesopi	Fabulæ
	Apologies of Justin Martyr, Tertullian & Minutius Foelix, Englished by Reeves
	Ars Sciendi
Alchmariani	Instit. Astronom.
	Annals of King George, Vol. 1.
Boyle, R.	Of the Style of the Scriptures
Boyle, R.	His Seraphic Love
Boyle, R.	Occasional Reflections
Brooke	Of the Nature of Truth
Buchanani	Paraphrasis Poetica Psalmorum
Batei	Elenchi motuum nuperorum in Anglia
Benzonis	Novæ novi orbis Historiæ
Bembo	Letters
Bale, J.	Of Actes or Unchaste Exemples of the Englyshe Votaries

Bedæ	Venerabilis Historia Ecclesiastic. Gentis Anglorum
Baconis	Historia Henrici Septimi
Barclai, J.	Argenis
Boyle, R.	Tracts about Cosmical Qualities
Boyle, R.	New Experiments touching the Relation of Air and Flame
Boyle, R.	Experiments about Colours
Boyle, R.	Cogitationes de Sacræ Scripturæ Stylo
Boyle, R.	Paradoxa Hydrostatica
Boaysteau	Theatrum mundi translated into English
Burgersdicii	Collegium Physicum
Boehmen	Aurora, das ist Morgen Rothe
de Bosnay	Cosmopolite, ou nouvelle Lumiere de la Physique naturale avec une Traicté du Soulphre
Butleri	Rhetoricæ
Burgersdicii	Institutionum Logicarum
Baronii	Metaphysica
Baconis	Historia Ventorum
Baconis	Historia Vitæ & Mortis
Baconis	Essays, 1668
Buscheri	Harmoniæ Logicæ Philipporaneæ
Barclai	Satyricon
Beroaldi	Declamationes
Buchleri	Thesaurus Poeticus
Brown	Description & Use of Triangular Quadrant
Boehmen	Opera nonnulla Teutonic
Boehmen	De Signatura Rerum
Boehmen	Josephus Redivivus
Brodrick	Compleat History of the late War in the Netherlands
Becheri	Supplementum secundum in Physicam Subterraneam
Brome	Travels over England, Scotland, & Wales
	Chroniche Antiche d' Inglilterra
Casaubon	Treatise of Enthusiasm
Casaubon	Diatriba de Verborum Usu
Crantzii	Metropolis, sive Historia Ecclesiast. Saxoniæ

Caesar	Commentarii tradotti [into Italian] per Ortica
Caesarii, Joan	Rhetorica
Camdeni	Annales Rerum . . . . regnante Elizabethâ
	Constitucyons Provincialles; and of Otho & Octobone translated into English
Comine	Ses Memoires
Comitis	Mythologiæ
Casmanni	Marinarum Quæstionum tractatio Philosophica bipartita
Cujacii	Paratila in Libros 50 digestorum seu Pandectarum et in Libros 9. Codicis Justiniani
Comenii	Janua Linguar. Gr. & Lat.
Comenii	Janua Linguar. Trilinguis
Comenii	Janua Linguarum Referata
Camdeni	Institutis Grammatices Græcæ
Ceporini	Compendium Grammaticæ Græcæ
Celestina	Tragicomedia de Calisto y Melibea
Case, M. de la	Le Galateé ou des facons et maniers louables
Causini	Tragediæ Sacræ
Culpeper	English Physician enlarged
Craig	Scotland's Sovereignty asserted
Clarendon	History of the Rebellion
Cross	Taghmical Art
Donne	History of the Septuagint
Delrii	Disquisitionum Magicarum
	Doctrina Antiqua de Natura Animæ
Drax, Tho.	Calliepeia, or Rich store-house of Phrases
Donne	Essayes
Digby	Discours touchant la Guerison par la poudre de sympathie
	Disquisitiones Politicæ
Danaei	Aphorismorum Politicorum Sylva
Donaldsoni	Synopseos Philosoph. Moralis
Derham	Astrotheology
Eitzen	Ethicæ Doctrina
Eberi	Calendarium Historicum
Elenchus	Motuum Nuperorum in Anglia

	Elementa Jurisprudentiæ
Euripidis	Tragædiæ
Erasmi	Moriæ Encomium, cum Ludo Senecæ de Morte Claudii Cœsaris
Freigii	Quæstiones Instinianæ in Institut. Juris Civilis
Fells	Life of Dr. H. Hammond
Fasciculus	Præceptorum Logicorum, unà cum Crackanthorpii Introductione ad Metaphysicam
Fabri	Cursus Physicus et Metaphysicus
Frommen	Exercitationes Metaphysicæ
Fabritii	Poemata
Figon	Discours des Estats & des Offices tant de Gouvernement que de la Justice, & des Finances de France
Fichet	Arcana Studiorum Methodus
Fuchsii	Opera nonulla
Fuchsii	Institutiones Medicinæ
Fuchsii	Historia stirpium
Frambesarii	Scholæ medicæ Examen practicum
Fregii	Pædagogus
Grotii	De jure Belli ac Pacis
Grotii	In Cassandri Consultationem annotata
Grotii	De Imperio summarum Potestatum
Grotii	Apologeticus
Grotii	Votum pro pace Ecclesiast.
Grotii	Defensio fidei Catholicæ
Grotii	Animadversiones in Andr. Riveti
Grotii	Opera nonnulla Argumenti Theolog. Jurid. Politic
Grotii	Et Aliorum Dissertationes
Grotii	Epistolæ ad Gallos
Gaule	Distractions
Gaule	Practique Theories
Gale	Theophilie
Grotest	Tractatus de Cessatione Legalium
Greaves	Pyramidographia
Goodwin	Mystery of Dreams
Gumble	Life of General Monck

Guicciardini	Historiarum sui Temporis
Guicciardini	Fragmentum
Golii	Epitome Doctrinæ moralis ex 10 Lib. Ethic. Aristot.
Galei	Philosophia Generalis
	The Gentleman's Calling
Guillet, Dame du	Rithmes & Poesies
Galilæi	Nuncius Sydereus
Gilfusii	Opusculum Politicum
	Great Treaty of Peace
Hammond	Of Fundamentals in a Notion referring to Practise
Herodoti	Historiæ
Hayward	Life of K. Edw. 6. & Q. Elizabeth
	Historia Ecclesiastica del Scisma del Reyno de Inglaterra
	Historia Persecutionum Ecclesiæ Bohemicæ
Heerebordi	Collegium Ethicum
Harvei	Exercitationes de Generatione Animalium
Hotomani	J. C. Quæstionum illustrium
Hotomani	Partitiones Juris Civilis
Hesselbein	Theoria Logica
Hewis	Survey of English Tongue & Phrases
Horatii Flac.	Poemata
Hieroclis	Philosop. Comment. in Aurea Pythagoreorum Carmina
Holliband	Campo de Fior—flowery Field of four Languages
Herbert	Temple, or Sacred Poems
Jovii	Historiarum sui Temporis
Jure	Life of M. de Reuty Nobleman of France
Jamblicus	de Mysteriis Ægyptiorum
Jacchei	Primæ Philosophiæ Institutiones
Jacobi Regis	Dæmonologia
	Index Expurgatorius
King James	Apology for the Oath of Allegiance
Juvenalis et Persii	Satyræ
Junii	Vindiciæ contra Tyrannos
Johnson	Lexicon Chymicum

Josephus	Works
Johnstoni	Idea Universæ Medicinæ Practicæ
Kempisii	De Imitatione Christi
Keckermanni	Systema Logicæ
Keppleri	Epitomes Astron. Copernicanæ
Lawson	Examination of Hobbs Leviathan
	Lettre Escrite a Monsieur le Coq. Charenton
Lucani	de Bello Civili
Lightfoot	Miscellanies
	Letters between the Ld. George and Sr. Kenelme Digby
Laurentii	Historia Anatomica
Leoni	Ars Medendi
Langii	Elementare Mathematicum
Liddelii	Ars Medica
Lydii	Waldensia
Meisneri	Dissertatio de Legibus
Meisneri	Anthropologiæ Sacræ
Meisneri	Disputationes quinque
More	Chronology
Matchiavelli	Disputat. de Republica
Magiri	Physiologiæ Peripateticæ
Martini	Exercitationum Metaphysic.
Martini	Logicarum Institut.
Martini	Prælectiones extemporaneæ in Systema Logicum Keekermanni
Molinæi	Elementa Logica
Melanchthon	Epitomes Philosoph. moralis
Meurier	Magazin de Planté en Francoises & Flameng.
Moore	Modern Fortification
Mercatoris	Institut. Astronomicarum
Mead	De Imperio Solis ac Lunæ in Corpora humana
Moroni	Directorium medico-practicum
Manuiti	Epistolarum Lib. XII.
Mather, Inc.	Angelographia
Mather, Inc.	Remarkable Providences
Mather, Inc.	Cases of Conscience

Mather, Inc.	[Many more]
Mather, C.	Decennium Luctuosum
Mather, C.	[Many more]
Niem	Historiarum sui Temporis
Neandri	Physice
Neperi	Rabdologia
Nepair	Description of the Table of Logarithms
	Orationes ex historicis Latinis Excerptæ in Usum Scholarum Hollandiæ
Oughtred	Opuscula Mathematica
	Pseaumes mis en Rime Francoise par Marot & Beze
	Psalmi Davidis Hispanicè
Patavini	Defensor Pacis
Pleix	De L'Ethique, ou Philosophie Morale
Pavonii	Summa Ethicæ
Petrarchæ	de remediis utriusque Fortunæ
Petrarcha	nuovamente ridotto alla vera Lettione
Porta	Magia naturalis
Patricii	de Regno & Regis Institutione
Pelegromii	Synonymorum Silva
Politiani	Epistolæ
	Proverbs Espagnols traduit en Francois
Platti	Manuale, seu Flores Petrarchæ
Porphyrii	Philosophi Pythagorici de Abstinentia
Plinii	Secund. Epistolarum Lib. 9
Plauti	Comædiæ
Pisonis	de Cognoscendis & Curandis humani Corporis morbis
	Pharmacopæia Londinens. Colleg.
Phocylidis	Dissertatio Astronomica
Puteani	Statera Belli & Pacis
Purbachii	Dispositiones motuum Caelestium.
Purbachii	Theoriæ novæ Planetarum
Quinti Curtii	Historiarum Libri
Quinti Calabri	Poetæ derelictorum ab Homero
Rutherfoord	Letters
Robinson	Apology for the Brownists
Romani	Commentationes Physicæ & Metaphysicæ

Rami	Scholia in 3 primas liberales Artes
Rami	Schol. in Aristotelis Libros Acroamaticos
Rami	Grammaticæ Lib. 4
Richardson	Logician's School-master
[W. Alabaster]	Roxana Tragædia olim Cantabrig. acta, &c.
Record	Arithmetick
Raii	Catalogus Plantarum Angliæ
Rulandi	Medicinæ Practica
	Remarks on several parts of Italy in 1701, 1702, 1703.
Raleigh	History of the World abrig'd
Sallustii	Opera omnia
Stoughtonii	Fælicitas ultimi seculi
Stafford	Niobe
Stafford	Female Glory
Sulpicii Severi	Opera omnia
Stradæ	de bello Belgico
Selden	de Dis Syriis
Speed	Abridged Description of Britain & Ireland
Sleyden	Key of History
Scaligeri	Exotericarum Exercitationum de Subtilitate
Scaligeri	Poemata
Scaligeri	Epistolæ omnes
Schookii	Collegium Physicum
Sculteti	Ethicorum Libri
Sluteri	Anatomia Logicæ Aristotelicæ
Snellii	In Physicam Corn. Valerii Annotationes
Scheibleri	Metaphysicæ
Senecæ et aliorum	Tragædiae
Senecæ	Tragediae
Senecæ	Epistolæ quæ extant
	Speculum Anglicarum atque Politicarum Observationum
	Schollar's Companion
Smetii	Prosodia
Sennerti	Epitome Institut. Medicinæ
Sylvii	Methodus Medicamenta Componendi
Sutholt	Dissertationes quibus explicatur universum Jus Institutionum

Suetonius	Lives of the 12 Caesars
Shakespear	Plays, 6 vols. London, 1709
Trenchfield	Christian Chymistry
Taciti	Opera
Taciti	Annales
Turselline	Epitome Historiarum
Timpleri	Metaphysicæ Systema Methodicum
Tesmari	Exercitationum Rhetoricarum
Trapezuntii	Rhetoricarum
	A Treatise of Metalica
Trieu	Manuductio ad Logicam
Tullii	De Officio Libri Tres
Turneri	Orationes & Epistolæ
Terentii	Comædiæ Sex
Tacqueti	Arithmeticæ Theoria & Praxis
	Tractatus duo Mathematici; primus de Globis, a Rob. Hues
Timpii	Cynosura Professorum ac Studiosorum Eloquentiæ
Temple, Sir Wm.	Memoirs
Temple, Sir Wm.	Letters
Varenii	Descriptio Regni Japoniæ & Siam
Valerii Max.	De dictis et factis memorabilibus
Velcurionis	Comment. in Aristotel, Physicam Lib. 4
Verronis	Physicorum Libri 10
Valesii	de Sacra Philosophia Liber
Vosii et aliorum	De Studiorum Ratione opuscula
Valerii Ultraj	Grammatic. Institut.
Vallæ	Elegantiæ
Wilkinsoni	Conciones 6 ad Academicos Oxonienses
Walton	Lives
Wotton	Remains
Wendilini	Contemplat. Physicarum
Wallis	Grammatica Linguæ Anglicanæ
Wither	Abuses stript and whipt
Wither	Shepard's Hunting
Wardi	Astronomia Geometrica
Winshemii	Quæstiones Sphæricæ
Witteni	Memoria Jurisconsultorum justa

Witteni	Memoria medicorum semper vivens
Witteni	Memoria Philosophorum sempiterna
Witteni	Memoria Theologorum
Zahn	Ichnographia municipalis
Zuichemi	J. C. Comment. in 10 Titulos Institutionum Juris Civilis

Supplement

Grew	Cosmologia Sacra, or a Discourse of the Universe
Ortelius	Theatre de L'Universe
Milton	Poetical Works, 2 vols. 1720
	Cry from the Desert . . . . things lately come to pass in the Cevennes
Chamberlayne	Present State of Gt. Brittain, 1716
	Lives of the French Philosophers
Langii	Medicina Mentis
Neal	History of New-England
Parecbolæ	Universitatis Oxoniensis
Strada	Histoire de la guerre de Flandre

Selected Titles from the 1725 Supplement to the Catalogue of the Harvard Library.

Folio

Bayle	Dictionaire Historique et Critique
Brandt	History of the Reformation in the Low Countries Englished by John Chamberlayne
Du Pin	New Ecclesiastical History
Grævii	Thesaurus Antiquitatum Romanarum
Hooker	Laws of Ecclesiastical Polity
How, J.	Works
Highmori	Disquisitio Corporis Humani Anatomica

Lightfoot	Works
Lock, J.	Works, 3 vol. 1722
Montfaucon	Antiquity Explained . . . . in Sculptures; Englished by David Humphreys
Ogilby	Translation of Virgil, with Cuts
Robinsoni	Annales Mundi Universales
	Papal Usurpation . . . . with History of the old Waldenses
Sallengre	Novus Thesaurus Antiquitatum Romanarum
Tillotson	Works
Willughby	Ornithology with 3 Discourses of Mr. John Ray

Quarto

Rami	Opticæ Libri quatuor
Speckhan	Quaestionum et Decisionum Juris Caesarii, &c.
Stierii	Præcepta Logicæ, Ethicæ, &c.

Octavo, etc.

Boemi	Enchiridion Precum
Barlow	Exact Survey of the Tide
Burnet, T.	Essay upon Government
Cheselden	On the High Operation for the Stone, 1723
Clerici	Opera Philosophica
	Cromwell's Life, 1724
Cheyne	Essay of the Gout, 1723
Cheyne	Essay of Health & Long Life
	Critical History of England, Ecclesiastical and Civil
Echard	Ecclesiastical History
Fuchsii	Institutiones Medicinæ
Gordon	Geographical Grammar
	History of Virginia, 1722
	Miri-Weys, the Persian Cromwell, 1724
Mather, C.	Life of Increase Mather, London, 1724
Pliny	Panegyrick upon the Emperor Trajan, Englished by Geo. Smith

Potter	Greek Antiquities
Strother	On Sickness and Health, London, 1725
Vareni	Geographia Generalis
Wendelini	Institutiones Politicæ
Whiston	New Theory of Earth, 1722
Watts, I.	Lyrick Poems
Watts, I.	Versions of the Psalms
Watts, I.	Art of Reading & Writing English
Watts, I.	Songs for Children
Watts, I.	Hymns
Watts, I.	Logick

Bibliography.

THE following books have been the chief sources of material for this study. Use has also been made of several manuscripts not included in this list.

ALMANACS, Colonial. All copies from 1657 to 1722 in the possession of the Massachusetts Historical Society, including photostat copies of all in existence which belong to the seventeenth century.

ALMANACS, English. All between 1599 and 1707 in the possession of the Massachusetts Historical Society.

AMERICAN ANTIQUARIAN SOCIETY. Proceedings. Worcester, 1812-1880. New Series, 1881-1914. Continued.

AMERICAN ANTIQUARIAN SOCIETY. Archæologia Americana. Transactions and Collections. Worcester, 1820-1912. Continued.

ANDREWS, CHARLES McLEAN, editor. Narratives of the Insurrections. New York, 1915.

ANDROS TRACTS: being a collection of pamphlets and official papers. William Henry Whitmore, editor. Boston, 1868-1874.

ARBER, EDWARD, editor. The story of the Pilgrim Fathers. Boston, 1897.

BAXTER, RICHARD. Poetical Fragments. London, 1699. 3d Edition.

BEERS, HENRY AUGUSTIN. An Outline Sketch of American Literature. New York, 1887.

BIGELOW, FRANCIS HILL. Historic Silver of the Colonies and its Makers. New York, 1917.

BLACKMORE, SIR RICHARD. Prince Arthur. An Heroick Poem. 2d Edition. London, 1695.

BLAKE, JAMES. Annals of the Town of Dorchester, 1750. Collections of the Dorchester Antiquarian and Historical Society. Boston, 1846.

BRADFORD, WILLIAM. A Dialogue, or the Sum of a Conference between some Young Men born in New England and sundry ancient men that came out of Holland and Old England. Anno Domini 1648. In Young's Chronicles of the Pilgrim Fathers, pp. 414 ff.

———— A Dialogue or 3^d Conference, betweene some yonge-men borne in New-England: and some Ancient-men, which came out of Holand, and Old England concerning the church. Massachusetts Historical Society, Proceedings, 1st Series, Vol. 11, P. 405 ff.

———— History of Plymouth Plantation 1620-1647. Boston, 1912. Massachusetts Historical Society, Collections. 2 vols.

BRADSTREET, ANNE. The Works of Anne Bradstreet in Prose and Verse. Edited by John Harvard Ellis. Charlestown, 1867.

BRODRICK, G. C. A history of the University of Oxford. 2d Edition. London, 1891.

BUCKINGHAM, THOMAS. The Journals of Madam Knight, and Rev. Mr. Buckingham. From the Original Manuscripts, written in 1704 & 1710. New York, Wilder and Campbell, 1825.

BUNYAN, JOHN. The Pilgrim's Progress from this World to that which is to come. Temple Classics. London, 1904.

BURR, GEORGE LINCOLN, editor. Narratives of the Witchcraft Cases, 1648-1706. New York, 1914.

BURTON, ROBERT. The Anatomy of Melancholy. London, 1907.

CALEF, ROBERT. See FOWLER, SAMUEL P.

CALENDAR OF STATE PAPERS, Colonial Series, America and West Indies. 1661-1668. Edited by W. N. Sainsbury. London, 1880.

CAMBRIDGE HISTORY OF AMERICAN LITERATURE, THE. New York, 1917.

CHAPLIN, JEREMIAH. Life of Henry Dunster. Boston, 1872.

CHAUCER, GEOFFREY, The Complete Works of. Edited by Walter W. Skeat. 6 vols. Oxford, 1899.

CLAP, ROGER, Memoirs of. Collections of the Dorchester Antiquarian and Historical Society, Vol. 1. Boston, 1844.

CLAP, THOMAS. The Annals or History of Yale-College. New Haven, 1766.

CLARENDON, EDWARD, Earl of. The History of the Rebellion and Civil Wars in England. Edited by W. Dunn Macray. Oxford, 1888.

COLLIER, JEREMY. The Great Historical, Geographical, Genealogical and Poetical Dictionary.... 2d Edition. London, 1701.

COLONIAL SOCIETY OF MASSACHUSETTS. Publications. Boston, 1895-1915. Continued.

COOK, ELIZABETH CHRISTINE. Literary Influences in Colonial Newspapers, 1704-1750. New York, 1912.

CUNNINGHAM, W. English Influence on the United States. Cambridge, 1916.

DANCKAERTS, JASPER. The Journal of Jasper Danckaerts, 1679-1680. Edited by Bartlett B. James and J. Franklin Jameson. New York, 1913.

DE MONTMORENCY, J. E. G. The Progress of Education in England. London, 1904.

DEXTER, FRANKLIN BOWDITCH. Biographical Sketches of the Graduates of Yale College with Annals of the College History. October, 1701, to May, 1745. New York, 1885.

———— Documentary History of Yale University under the original charter of the Collegiate School of Connecticut, 1701-1745. New Haven, 1916.

———— Estimates of Population in the American Colonies. Worcester, 1887.

DEXTER, HENRY MARTYN and his son, MORTON. The England and Holland of the Pilgrims. Boston, 1905.

DICTIONARY OF NATIONAL BIOGRAPHY. Leslie Stephen, editor. New York, 1885-1900.

DRAKE, SAMUEL GARDNER, editor. Increase Mather's The History of King Philip's War. 1862.

DUNIWAY, CLYDE A. The Development of Freedom of the Press in Massachusetts. New York, 1906.

DUNTON, JOHN. Letters from New-England. Edited by W. H. Whitmore. Boston,1867.

———— The Life and Errors of John Dunton. London, 1705.

EGGLESTON, EDWARD. The Transit of Civilization from England to America in the Seventeenth Century. New York, 1901.

ESSEX COUNTY, MASSACHUSETTS. Records and Files of the Quarterly Courts of Essex County, Massachusetts. 4 vols. Salem, 1911-1914.

ESSEX COUNTY, MASSACHUSETTS, The Probate Records of. Vol. I. Salem, Mass., 1916.

EVANS, CHARLES. American Bibliography. Chicago, 1903.

EVEREST, CHARLES. Poets of Connecticut. Hartford, 1843.

FELT, J. B. Memoir of the Reverend Francis Higginson. Boston, 1852.

FITZ, REGINALD H., M.D. Zabdiel Boylston, Inoculator, and the Epidemic of Smallpox in Boston in 1721. Bulletin of the Johns Hopkins Hospital, xxii. 315.

FORD, WORTHINGTON CHAUNCEY. The Boston Book Market, 1679-1700. Boston, 1917.

FOWLER, SAMUEL P. Salem Witchcraft: comprising More Wonders of the Invisible World, collected by Robert Calef; and Wonders of the Invisible World, by Cotton Mather: together with notes and explanations by S. P. Fowler. Salem, 1861.

FRANKLIN, BENJAMIN. The Autobiography of. New York, no date.

———— Works of. Nurnberg and New York, no date.

FULLER, THOMAS. The Church-History of Britain. London, 1655.

———— The History of the University of Cambridge from the Conquest to the year 1634. Cambridge, 1640.

———— The History of the Worthies of England. Edited by P. A. Nuttall. 2d Edition. 3 vols. London, 1840.

GOOKIN, DANIEL. Historical Collections of the Indians in New England. In Massachusetts Historical Society, Collections, 1st Series, Vol. I, pp. 141-226.

GOOKIN, FREDERICK WILLIAM. Daniel Gookin, 1612-1687....... his Life and Letters and some Account of his Ancestry. Chicago, 1912.

GREEN, SAMUEL ABBOTT. John Foster, the earliest American engraver and the first Boston printer. Boston, 1909.

GREEN, SAMUEL ABBOTT. History of Medicine in Massachusetts. Boston, 1881.

GRISWOLD, RUFUS W. Female Poets of America.

———— Poets and Poetry of America.

HARVARD UNIVERSITY. Library of. Bibliographical Contributions, No. 52. The Librarians of Harvard College, 1667-1877. By A. C. Potter and Charles K. Bolton. Cambridge, 1897.

HARVARD UNIVERSITY. College Books I, III, and IV. Harvard College Records: in manuscript, about to be published and examined in proof sheets.

———— Catalogus Librorum Bibliothecæ Collegij Harvardini Quod est Cantabrigiæ in Nova Anglia. Boston, 1723.

HERBERT, GEORGE. The Temple: Sacred Poems and Private Ejaculations. Fac-simile reprint of first edition of 1633. London, 1882.

HINCKLEY, THOMAS. The Hinckley Papers. Massachusetts Historical Society, Collections, 4th Series, Vol. I.

HULL, JOHN. The Diaries of. In Archæologia Americana: Transactions of the American Antiquarian Society, iii. 109-318.

HUTCHINSON PAPERS. Massachusetts Historical Society, Collections, 3d Series, Vol. I.

JOHNSON, EDWARD. Wonder-Working Providence. Edited by J. Franklin Jameson. New York, 1910.

———— Wonder-Working Providence. Edited by William F. Poole. Andover, 1867.

JOSSELYN, JOHN. An Account of two Voyages to New-England, etc. The Second Addition [sic.] London, 1675. Reprint in Massachusetts Historical Society, Collections, 3rd Series, Vol. 3, p. 211 ff.

———— New-England's Rarities Discovered. With an Introduction and Notes by Edward Tuckerman. In Archæologia Americana, iv. 105-238. Worcester, 1860.

KEEP, AUSTIN BAXTER. History of the New York Society Library with an Introductory Chapter on Libraries in Colonial New York, 1698-1776. New York, 1908.

KETTELL, SAMUEL. Specimens of American Poetry, with Critical and Biographical Notices. 3 vols. Boston, 1829.

KIMBALL, EVERETT. The Public Life of Joseph Dudley. A Study of the Colonial Policy of the Stuarts in New England 1660-1715. New York, 1911.

KNIGHT, SARAH KEMBLE. The Private Journal of. Being the Record of a Journey from Boston to New York in the year 1704. Norwich, Conn., 1901.

LAWSON, DEODAT. Christ's Fidelity the Only Shield against Satan's Malignity. Asserted in a Sermon Deliver'd at Salem-Village the 24th of March, 1692. Boston and London, 1704.

LECHFORD, THOMAS. Note-Book kept by Thomas Lechford, Esq., Lawyer in Boston, Massachusetts Bay, from June 27, 1638, to July 29, 1641. Cambridge, 1885.

LINCOLN, CHARLES H., editor. Narratives of the Indian Wars, 1675-1699. New York, 1913.

LITTLEFIELD, GEORGE EMERY. Early Boston Booksellers, 1642-1711. Boston, 1900.

———— The Early Massachusetts Press, 1638-1711. Boston, 1907.

———— Early Schools and School Books of New England. Boston, 1904.

MAINE HISTORICAL SOCIETY. Collections and Proceedings. Portland, 1890-1906.

MARVELL, ANDREW. Poems of. Muses Library. London, no date.

MASSACHUSETTS BAY. Records of the Governor and Company of the Massachusetts Bay in New England. Boston, 1854.

MASSACHUSETTS HISTORICAL SOCIETY. Collections. Boston or Cambridge, 1792-1914. Continued.

———— Lectures delivered in a course before the Lowell Institute, in Boston, by members of the Massachusetts Historical Society on subjects relating to the Early History of Massachusetts. Boston, 1869.

———— Proceedings. Boston, 1879-1916. Continued.

MASSON, DAVID. The Life of John Milton. 7 vols. London, 1881.

MATHER, COTTON. The Accomplished Singer. Boston, 1721.

———— A Brand Pluck'd out of the Burning. In G. L. Burr's Narratives of the Witchcraft Cases, pp. 259-286.

———— Diary. Massachusetts Historical Society, Collections, 7th Series, Vols. 7 and 8.

———— Magnalia Christi Americana; or the Ecclesiastical History of New-England. Edited by Thomas Robbins. 2 vols. Hartford, 1855.

MATHER, COTTON. Memorable Providences, Relating to Witch-
crafts and Possessions. In G. L. Burr's Narratives of the
Witchcraft Cases, pp. 93-144.
————— A New Year Well Begun. New London, 1719.
————— Psalterium Americanum. The Book of Psalms. Boston,
1718.
————— Repeated Warnings. Another Essay, to warn young
people. Page headings use title of *Children of Disobedience*.
Boston, 1712.
————— The Right Way to Shake off a Viper. Boston, 1720.
————— Speedy Repentance Urged. Boston, 1690.
————— The Wonders of the Invisible World. To which is
added A Farther Account of the Tryals of the New-England
Witches by Increase Mather, D.D. London, 1862.
————— The World Alarm'd. Boston, 1721.
MATHER, INCREASE. Diary. Massachusetts Historical Society,
Proceedings, 2d Series, Vol. 13, p. 339 ff.
————— Early History of New England. Together with an
Historical Discourse concerning the Prevalency of Prayer.
Boston, 1677.
————— A Farther Account of the Tryals of the New-England
Witches. Published with Cotton Mather's The Wonders of
the Invisible World. London, 1862.
————— Life and Death of that Reverend Man of God Mr.
Richard Mather. Cambridge, 1670.
————— Remarkable Providences Illustrative of the Earlier
Days of American Colonisation. Edited by George Offor.
London, 1890.
MATHER, RICHARD, Journal of. 1635. His Life and Death, 1670.
Collections of the Dorchester Antiquarian and Historical
Society. Both in one volume, paged consecutively. Boston,
1850.
MATHER PAPERS, THE. Massachusetts Historical Society, Col-
lections, 4th Series, Vol. 8. Boston, 1868.
MAYFLOWER DESCENDANT, THE. A Quarterly Magazine of Pil-
grim Genealogy and History. Boston, 1899-1916. Con-
tinued.
MILTON, JOHN, The Poetical Works of. Edited by David Masson.
London and New York, 1903.

MILTON, JOHN. A Selection from the English Prose Works of.
    Boston, 1826.

MORTON, NATHANIEL. New England's Memorial. Boston, 1855.

MORTON, THOMAS. The New English Canaan. Edited by Charles
    Francis Adams, Jr., Boston, 1883.

MULLINGER, JAMES BASS. Cambridge Characteristics in the Seven-
    teenth Century. London, 1867.

————A History of the University of Cambridge. London,
    1888.

————The University of Cambridge. Vol. 3. Cambridge,
    1911.

NEAL, DANIEL. The History of New England. 2d Edition. 2
    vols. London, 1747.

NEW ENGLAND HISTORICAL AND GENEALOGICAL REGISTER, THE.
    Boston, 1847-1916. Continued.

NEW HAMPSHIRE HISTORICAL SOCIETY. Collections. Concord,
    1824-1915. Continued.

NEW HAVEN COLONY HISTORICAL SOCIETY. Papers. New Haven,
    1865-1914. Continued.

NORTH AMERICAN REVIEW. Vol. 107.

ONDERDONK, J. L. History of American Verse. 1610-1897. Chi-
    cago, 1901.

OTIS, WILLIAM BRADLEY. American Verse 1625-1807. A History.
    New York, 1909.

OVIATT, EDWIN. The Beginnings of Yale 1701-1726. New Haven,
    1916.

PALFREY, JOHN GORHAM. History of New England during the
    Stuart Dynasty. 5 vols. Boston, 1858.

PATTERSON, S. W. The Spirit of the American Revolution as re-
    vealed in the poetry of the period. Boston, 1915.

PENHALLOW, SAMUEL. The History of the Wars of New-England
    with the Eastern Indians . . . Collections of the New
    Hampshire Historical Society for the Year 1824. Vol. 1 of
    the series.

PLYMOUTH COLONY, Records of. Wills. In manuscript.

PRIOR, MATTHEW, Selected Poems of. Edited by Austin Dobson.
    London, 1889.

QUINCY, JOSIAH. The History of Harvard University. 2 vols.
    Cambridge, 1840.

RICHARDSON, C. F. American Literature. 2 vols. New York, 1887, 1889.

RODEN, ROBERT F. The Cambridge Press 1638-1692. New York, 1905.

ROSSITER, WILLIAM S., editor. Days and Ways in Old Boston. Boston, 1915.

ROYAL SOCIETY. Philosophical Transactions. London, 1666-1916. Continued.

SANDYS, GEORGE. Ovid's Metamorphosis Englished, mythologiz'd and represented in figures. London, 1640.

SEWALL, SAMUEL. Diary of, 1674-1729. 3 vols. Massachusetts Historical Society, Collections, 5th Series, Vols. 5-7. Boston, 1878.

————Letter-Book of. 2 vols. Massachusetts Historical Society, Collections, 6th Series, Vols. 1-2. Boston, 1886.

————The Selling of Joseph. In George H. Moore's Notes on the History of Slavery in Massachusetts, pp. 83-87. New York, 1866.

SHEPARD, THOMAS. Autobiography. Manuscript volume in the Harvard Library.

SIBLEY, JOHN LANGDON. Biographical Sketches of Graduates of Harvard University. 3 vols. Cambridge, 1873.

SMALL, WALTER HERBERT. Early New England Schools. Boston, 1914.

STEINER, BERNARD C. A History of the Plantation of Menunkatuck . . . . comprising the present towns of Guilford and Madison. Baltimore, 1897.

THOMAS, ISAIAH. The History of Printing in America. 2d Edition. Transactions and Collections of the American Antiquarian Society, Vols. 5-6. Albany, 1874.

THOMPSON, E. N. S. Essays on Milton. New Haven, 1914.

TRUEBNER's Bibliographical Guide to American Literature. London, 1855.

TURELL, EBENEZER. The Life and Character of the Reverend Benjamin Colman, D.D. Boston, 1749.

TUTTLE, JULIUS H. The Mather Libraries. American Antiquarian Society, Proceedings, New Series, Vol. 20, pp. 269-356.

TYLER, MOSES COIT. A History of American Literature, 1607-1765. 2 vols. New York, 1879.

VERSTEGAN, RICHARD. The Restitution of Decayed Intelligence in Antiquities, concerning the most Noble and Renowned English Nation. London, 1673.

WATERS, THOMAS FRANKLIN. Ipswich in the Massachusetts Bay Colony. Ipswich, 1905.

WEEDEN, WILLIAM B. Economic and Social History of New England, 1620-1789. 2 vols. Boston, 1890.

WEGELIN, OSCAR. Early American Poetry. A Compilation of the Titles of Volumes of Verse and Broadsides, Written by Writers Born or Residing in North America, and Issued during the Seventeenth and Eighteenth Centuries. New York, 1903.

———— Early American Poetry 1800–1820 with an Appendix containing the Titles of Volumes and Broadsides issued during the Seventeenth and Eighteenth Centuries which were omitted in the Volume containing the years 1650–1799. New York, 1907.

WENDELL, BARRETT. Cotton Mather, the Puritan Priest. New York, no date [1891].

———— A Literary History of America. New York, 1900.

WHEELWRIGHT, JOHN, Memoir of. Boston, 1876.

WIGGLESWORTH, MICHAEL. The Day of Doom . . . . . with other Poems. New York, 1867.

WILLIAMS, ROGER. The Bloudy Tenet of Persecution for Cause of Conscience discussed. Edited by E. B. Underhill, London, 1848.

WINSLOW, EDWARD. Good News from New England. Massachusetts Historical Society, Collections, 1st Series, Vol. 8, pp. 239–276.

———— New-England's Salamander, Discovered . . . . Massachusetts Historical Society, Collections, 3d Series, Vol. 2, pp. 110 ff.

WINSOR, JUSTIN, editor. The Memorial History of Boston, 1630–1880. 4 vols. Boston, 1880.

WINTHROP, JOHN, Journal of. [History of New England, 1630–1649.] Edited by James Kendall Hosmer. 2 vols. New York, 1908.

WINTHROP, ROBERT C. Life and Letters of John Winthrop. Boston, 1869.

WINTHROP PAPERS, THE. Massachusetts Historical Society, Collections, 3d Series, Vols. 9–10.

WOLCOTT, SAMUEL. Memorial of Henry Wolcott. New, York 1881.

Index.

THE *following Index includes names of individuals mentioned in the main text, authors of books listed or referred to, titles of unidentified books and of periodicals published before 1720. The Appendix has not been included. The editor is indexing the entire volume, including the Appendix, and will deposit the complete Index with Mr. Wright's manuscript in the Yale University Library.*

Quotations and book lists have been taken without change from the sources quoted, variations or errors in spelling having been retained. The Index, however, lists the name of each individual under one spelling only.

Index.

Errata and Notes.

Page 128, l. 12: For "augment [atione]" read "augment [is]."
Page 131, l. 6: For "State of E [urope]" read "State of E [ngland]."
Page 150, ls. 4 and 5: Hornius' "Carthaginian Dream" is a reference to page
129 of Lib. II of "De Originibus Americanis."
Page 185, l. 3: For "Huylin" read "Heylyn."
Page 197, l. 17: For "Edward Calamy" read "Edmund Calamy."